I0754900

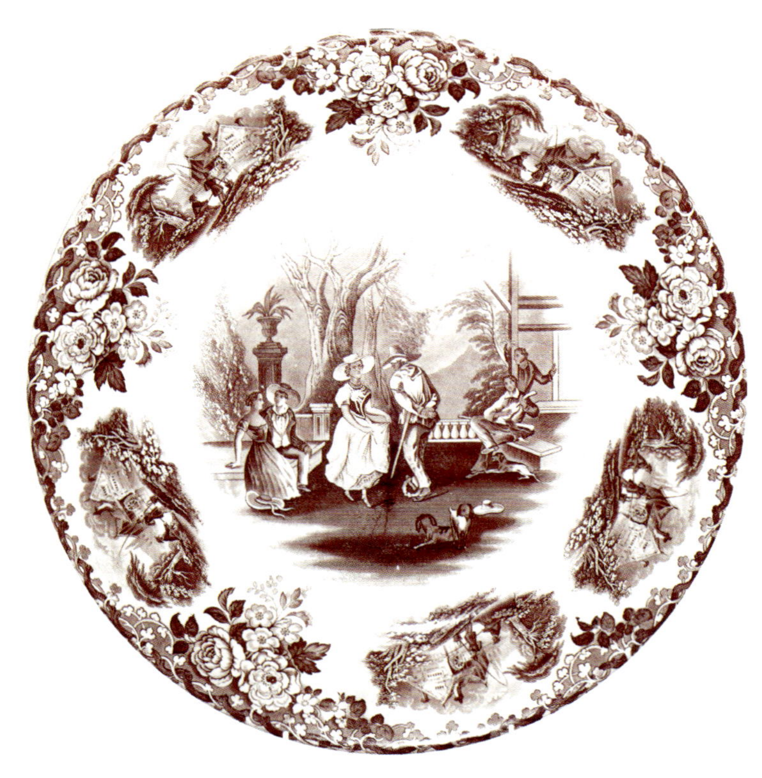

Inspired by CUBA!

A survey of Cuba-themed ceramics

Inspired by CUBA!

A survey of Cuba-themed ceramics

EMILIO CUETO / JULIO LARRAMENDI

LibraryPress@UF
GAINESVILLE, FLORIDA 2018

Inspired by Cuba! A survey of Cuba-themed ceramics

DESIGN
Yamilet Moya Silva
Frank E. Cala

DIGITAL PROCESSING
Yamilet Moya Silva
Frank E. Cala

ISBN: 978-1-944455-08-8

Printed in Canada

Library of Congress Cataloging-in-Publication Data
Cueto, Emilio.
Inspired by Cuba! : a survey of Cuba-themed ceramics / Emilio Cueto, Julio Larramendi.
p. 160; color illustrations; 21 cm.
Gainesville, FL : LibraryPress@UF, 2018
Summary: This book explores the many ways in which the island of Cuba has been immortalized in ceramic pieces. While the works of several Cuban ceramists are present in these pages, this is not a book about Cuban ceramics featuring Cuban artists working in that medium. The protagonist of this book is Cuba itself, seen through the eyes of Ceramists — native and foreign.
ISBN: 978-1-944455-08-8
1. LCSH: Cuba--In art. 2. Ceramics--Cuba. 3. Pottery--Cuba.
NK4051 .C84 2018

To the memory of the anonymous artisans from *Argentina, Austria, Belgium, Brazil, China, Cuba, the Czech Republic, Denmark, Dominican Republic, France, Germany, Holland, Hungary, Ireland, Italy, Japan, Mexico, Norway, Portugal, the Soviet Union, Spain, Sweden, the United Kingdom and the U.S.* who immortalized the name and image of Cuba in ceramic pieces for all to use and admire.

With great thanks to my friends *Julio Larramendi* for his countless hours of expert photography; *Yamilet Moya* and *Frank E Cala*, superb designers; *Judith Russell*, guiding light of this project; and the wonderful people at the University of Florida in Gainsville, Florida.

¡GRACIAS!

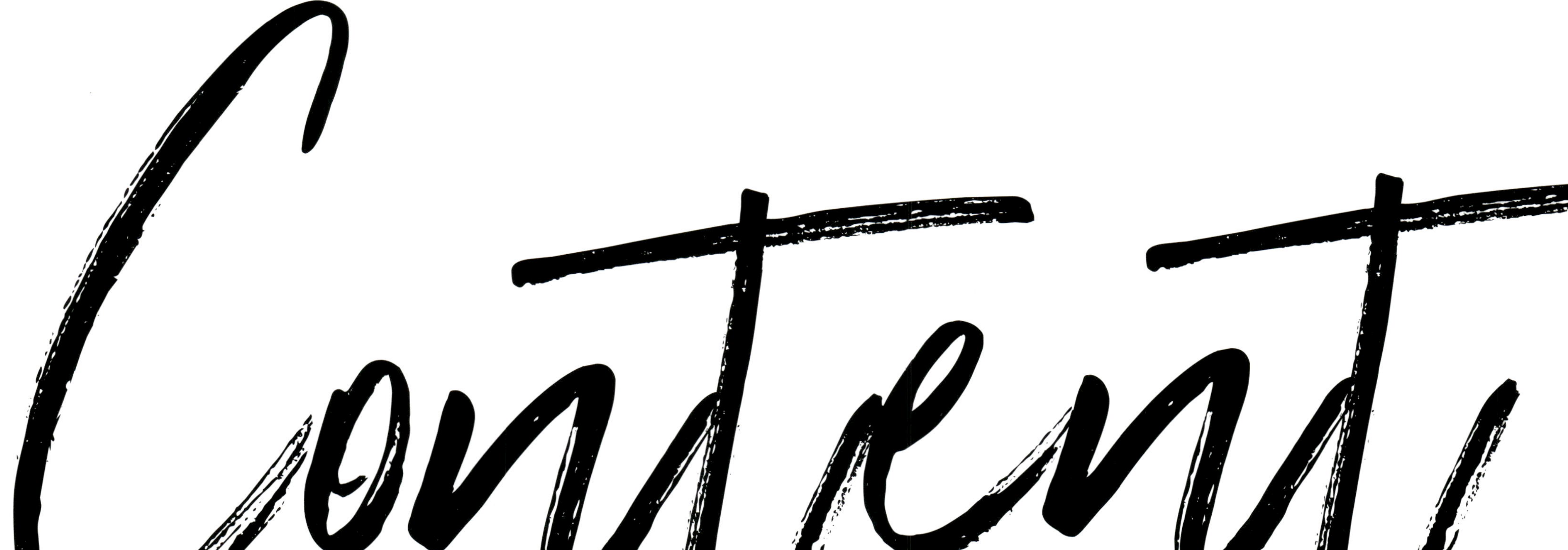

Earth

INTRODUCTION

Earth. It is so familiar to us that such is the name we have given to our planet... even though there is far more water on it. We live on it. We live off it. Earth is our most trusted friend and ally. It is Home.

Humans eventually found out that, properly baked, earth would harden and turn into bricks, clay pots and other utilitarian pieces, figurines, and ornaments. Ceramics was born. It has been with us for thousands of years.

This book explores the many ways in which the island of Cuba has been immortalized in ceramic pieces. While the works of several Cuban ceramists are present in these pages, this is not a book about Cuban ceramics featuring Cuban artists working in that medium.[1] The protagonist of this book is Cuba itself, seen through the eyes of ceramists –native and foreign.

In this essay I am using the word "ceramics" in its widest sense. According to one standard definition, it refers to "objects produced by shaping pieces of clay that are then hardened by baking".[2] The reader should be aware that this is a comprehensive term and includes many variations within a broad spectrum, ranging from a simple piece of pottery to more elaborate objects with varying chemical and physical properties, as exemplified by the terms bone china, earthenware, ironstone, majolica, porcelain, royal vitrified, semi-porcelain, *azulejos, gres, loza, porcelana, terracota, vidriado,* etc.[3]

Similarly, the techniques of displaying an image onto the ceramic surface are manifold. Some pieces are hand-painted, before or after the clay has been fired. A good number result from transfer printing, a decorative technique invented in England in the mid-1750s, similar to the process used for engraving views on paper.[4] This method offered a much cheaper alternative than hand painting each item individually. This, in turn, allowed many middle-class families to acquire beautifully decorated plates (which, before, only the very rich could afford) and ensure a large international market for these wares.

I have been collecting and studying Cuba-related pieces for several decades and, for purposes of this essay, I propose a two-fold classification. First, those pieces illustrated with images and symbols of the island or its people, or with references to name places, official institutions or commercial establishments inside, and even outside, the island (Section "Cuba Illustrated"). Next, those items which use the name of Cuba (and variations thereof) or Havana, as a catchy, attractive brand, even though the patterns displayed therein have no real reference to Cuba (Section "Cuba sells"). Cuba sells indeed. We can trace this phenomenon to the 19th century, and manufacturers of all kinds of items have ever since been exploiting the consumer's fascination and desire for all things Cuban.

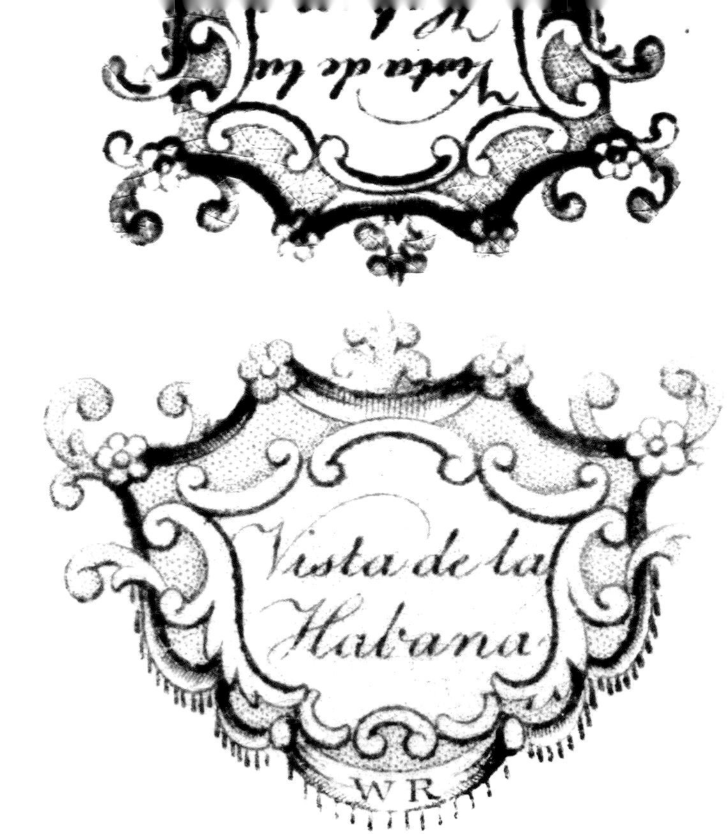

1. Readers interested in that subject may consult Teresita Gómez Vallejo, *Acercamiento a la cerámica artística cubana. La Habana*, Editorial Científico-Técnica, 2010, María Elena Jubrías, *La cerámica cubana entre el moderno y posmoderno.* Habana, ediciones Boloña, 2017 and *Retrospectiva de la cerámica cubana: exposición*. Habana, Museo de Artes Decorativas, 1978. Among the Cuban artists who have excelled in this medium, we can name Marta Arjona (1923), Miami-based twins Nelson and Ronald Currás (1939); Grupo Terracota 4 (1985), Wifredo Lam (1902-1982), Laura Luna (1958), Amelia Peláez (1896-1968), José Antonio Rodríguez Fuster (1946) and Alfredo Sosabravo (1930). Cubana de Aviación issued (1980s?) a set of 8 postcards, "Cuba Cerámica", featuring the pottery from the Isle of Youth. The Cuban ceramics museum is located on Mercaderes Street in Old Havana.

2. *Cambridge Academic Content Dictionary*. Cambridge University Press. Consulted online.

3. The bibliography of the ceramic world is truly voluminous. Here I will refer the reader only to the useful primers by Louise Ade Boger and Emmanuel Cooper, fully cited in the Bibliography.

4. The Victoria and Albert Museum in London displays a set of instruments and parts involved in the process. A very informative video by Paul Holdway, former engraver at the English Spode factory, can be enjoyed on Youtube.

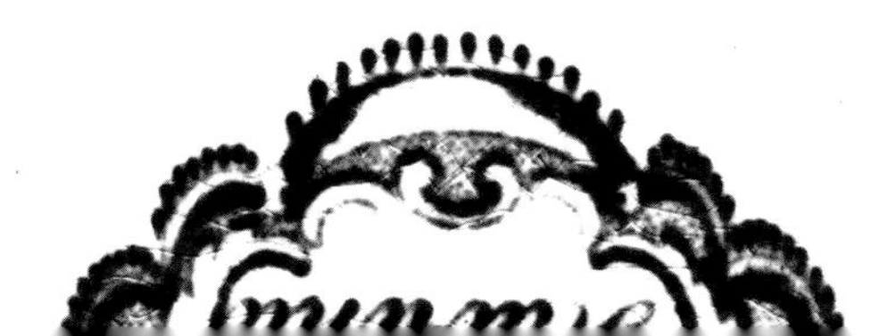

Because images are central to the understanding of our topic, we have attempted to make as ample a selection of pieces as possible. In order for the reader to better appreciate such images and place them in their appropriate context(s), the captions thereunder contain the relevant information in the following sequence: Artist. "Pattern" and/ or image. Factory (City, country) and date. Whenever such data is available, of course.

The pieces analyzed herein range from the mid-18th century (tobacco Delft jars, Figs. 116, 118) to very recent items (Tabletops Unlimited casual dinnerware, Fig. 238).

Dating individual pieces is always a challenge, but the British Patent Office did devise a very clever dating system for the 1842-1867 and 1868-1883 periods, using a diamond-shape mark with letters and numbers (Fig. 1-2). When such information appears stamped on the back of a dish, then the task becomes much easier, as we can pinpoint with confidence the day, month and year that the item was registered! Thus, an "I" would indicate it was patented in the month of July, and a "K" that it was in November. For identifying the years, an "A" would be 1845, "B", 1858, "C", 1844, "Y", 1853 and so on.[5]

Unfortunately, most pieces discussed in this book are undated and each item must be researched individually, quite often with no luck. As a result, in some cases all I can provide is a guestimate. I apologize in advance to the reader if I have inadvertently assigned the wrong date to any item.

One final note. The vast majority of the Cuban-themed pieces produced remained unsigned. And thus, with few exceptions (less than thirty, according to the Index of Artists at the end), they are the magnificent work of anonymous artisans whose talent we can admire but whose names we will not be able to remember.

5. For an explanation of how this system works see "Table of Registration Marks 1843-1883", in Geoffrey A. Godden, *A Handbook of British Pottery and Porcelain marks*. London, Barrie & Kenkins, 1982, pp. 109-111. The subject is also clearly explained online at the site thepotteries.org/mark/reg.htm. Please note that this system refers to registration, not production, dates.

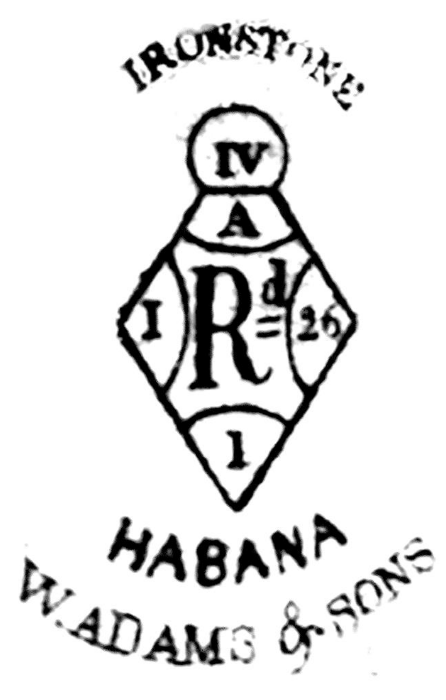

1.

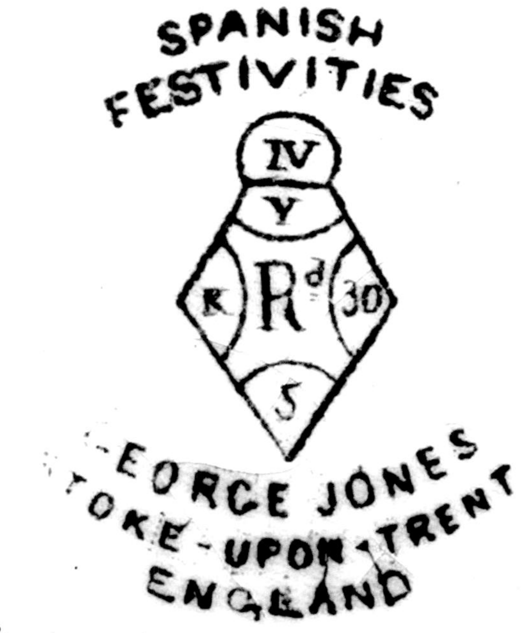

2.

· 1

Registration date stamp:

July 26, 1845 (I 26 A).

· 2

Registration date stamp:

November 30, 1853 (K 30 Y).

The Island

THE ISLAND ILLUSTRATED

A large number of the pieces examined here display views of the island of Cuba, mostly places within its capital city. As in other areas of our culture and history, Havana overshadows the countryside. Cuban ceramics is mostly a Havana affair. Nonetheless, views of other sections of Cuba do exist, and, to date, I can report the following items, under each of the Cuban Provinces as they were named before the 1974 reorganization:

Pinar del Río. Its coat of arms has been reproduced in ceramic plates, and a view of Viñales valley shows up in a 20th century Brazilian dinnerware set made for a wealthy family.

Matanzas. The Carnicería Bridge, originally painted by French artist Frédéric Mialhe (1810-1881),[6] was transferred to porcelain in the 19th century both in England and Spain (Fig. 59). A view of the main building of the 1881 Exhibition Fair in Matanzas also ended up in a British (?) dish.[7] During the early 20th century, a view of *Libertad* Park in downtown Matanzas found its way into fancy dishes from the Hotel Inglaterra in Havana (Fig. 79). The coat of arms of the province has been reproduced in ceramic plates. And I have seen a pitcher illustrating the Tinguaro sugar mill, located in Perico, made in Santiago de Las Vegas.

Las Villas. An ancient bridge in Sancti Spíritus is also present in the already mentioned Brazilian dinnerware set (Fig. 75). The Trinidad hills are depicted in a beautiful hand-painted vase (Fig. 177), and nearby Topes de Collantes hospital appears on a Batista propaganda ashtray of the 1950s (Fig. 135).

A Miami dish illustrates a crab from Caibarién (Fig. 188), while the 25th anniversary of the Battle of Santa Clara organized by Che Guevara has been celebrated in an East German plate (Fig. 191). For Cienfuegos I can report three references: a Punta Gorda souvenir plate and two patriotic pieces (a pitcher and a plate) made during the Spanish American War depicting the USS *Nashville* (Fig. 110), which was involved with the cable-cutting operation in the waters around that city in 1898. The Province's coat of arms has also been reproduced in ceramic plates.

Camagüey.[8] Like all the other provinces, its coat of arms has been reproduced in ceramic plates. I am the fortunate owner of a 1949 souvenir *tinajón* (water jar) embellished with a local landscape by Pedro Castillo (Fig. 178). Also in my collection, a small ashtray advertising the Casas jewelry establishment, a gift from my friend Julio Hernández Figueredo; another gift: a delicate saxophone depicting the tower of the city's cathedral by Jaime A. López García (Fig. 215). In 2014, I was presented with a beautiful ceramic reproduction of the façade of the 1847 Teatro Principal. As a gift to Pope John Paul II during his 1988 visit to Cuba, local artist Maydelina Pérez offered him a *tinajón* with a panoramic view of the city.

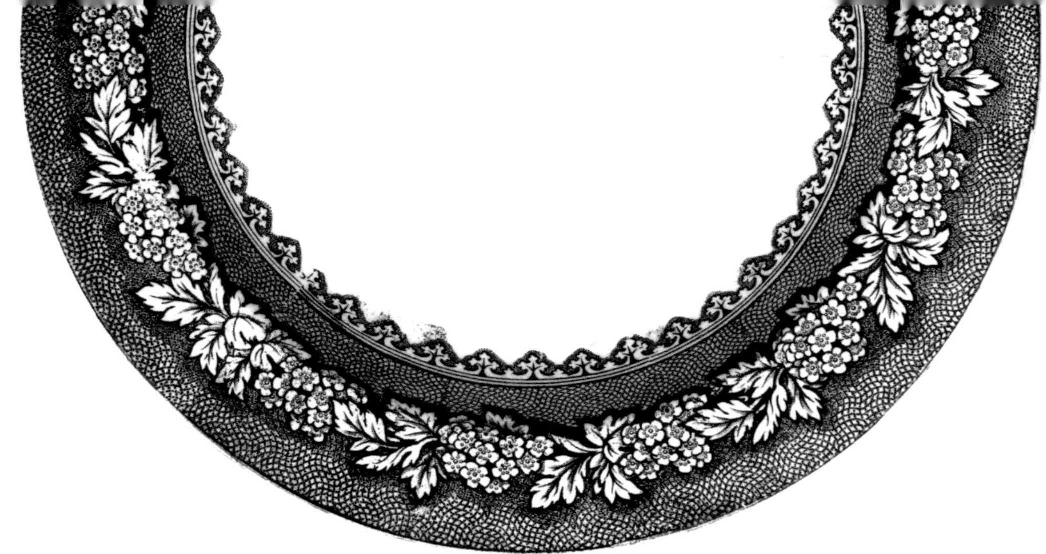

[6] On this artist, see Emilio Cueto, *Mialhe's colonial Cuba*. Miami, The Historical Association of Southern Florida, 1994 and Emilio Cueto, *La Cuba pintoresca de Frédéric Mialhe.* La Habana, Biblioteca Nacional de Cuba José Martí, 2010.

[7] Reproduced in Miguel Bretos, *Matanzas, The Cuba Nobody knows.* Gainesville, University of Florida Press, 2010, p. 115.

[8] See Yaxely González Carmenates, “Caracterización de la cerámica arquitectónica camagüeyana”. *Antenas* (Camagüey), sept-dic, 2004, pp. 48-52.

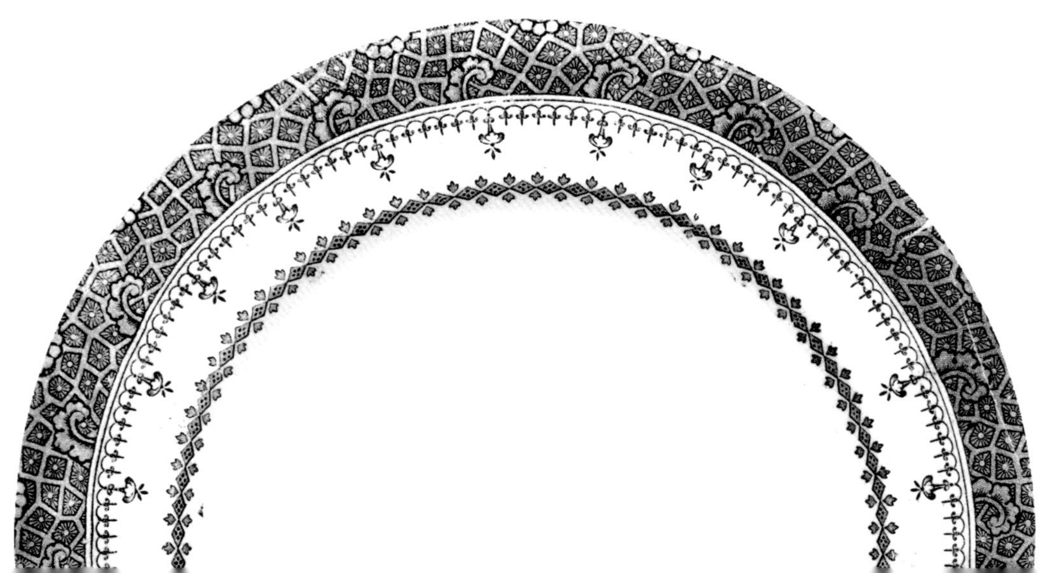

Oriente. During the Spanish American War of 1898 a few plates showed references to the San Juan Hill episode led by "Teddy" Roosevelt (Figs. 106, 107), and to the naval battle around Santiago de Cuba (Figs. 108, 109). On a quite different note, the Archdiocesan Museum in Santiago displays a ceramic piece with the arms of Bishop Felice Ambrogio Guerra Fezza (1866-1957), made in 1916 in Talavera de la Reina, Spain.

Later on, Santiago's Morro Castle (Fig. 71) and El Cobre Shrine to Our Lady of Charity, nearby (Fig. 74) showed up in the Brazilian dinnerware set mentioned earlier. The city name has also appeared in recent house ornaments in the shape of tobacco humidors from Casa Cristina by CBK. The quaint Padre Pico street peeks out of a *Miami Herald* plate illustrated with Cuban photographs (Fig. 199); and, as usual, the provincial coat of arms shows up in ceramic pieces.

In December 2008 I saw an old French demitasse cup displayed at the Bacardí Museum in Santiago with a shield similar to the design of Oriente's arms (three mountains and a shining star). In recent times, plates with Santiago decorations are produced in Cuba for the advantage of tourists, and in the US to meet the needs of the Cuban American market.

Finally, I will mention that I once had a German dish with a small 19th century view of the North Coast of the Eastern province, but it broke into pieces several years ago in my home. Which explains why, generally speaking, we have relatively few ceramic pieces.

Unlike furniture, silverware, metal and plastic ornaments, textiles, books, oil paintings and music CDs, the potter's work is quite fragile and breaks very easily. It also explains why cups have a low surviving rate: handles cannot usually handle too much stress.

Official use: Dinnerware with Cuban logos

The oldest relevant pieces I have been able to locate within this category are a plate and a covered dish (most probably belonging to a larger matching set) with the Havana coat of arms, the "*Siempre fiel*"/"Always faithful" legend (bestowed upon the city around 1818), and an "F-7" notation within a star (Figs. 3-4).

From the presence of the Havana arms I have concluded it belonged to the Municipality or other official Havana body. The "F-7" suggests to me that these two important pieces date from the second reign of Spanish King Ferdinand VII (1813-1833). Quite old for Cuba.

They were manufactured by the Ridgway factory (one of my pieces is so marked), located in the area of Staffordshire in West-central England, U.K. In time, this section of the English countryside became the center of the English ceramics trade, with dozens of factories, including Ridgway Potteries, which was founded in the 1790s in Stoke-on-Trent.

Unfortunately, I have not been able to ascertain the origins of the relationship between the Cuban authorities and the Ridgway group or why would a Spanish possession reach out to a foreign English company for its official china.

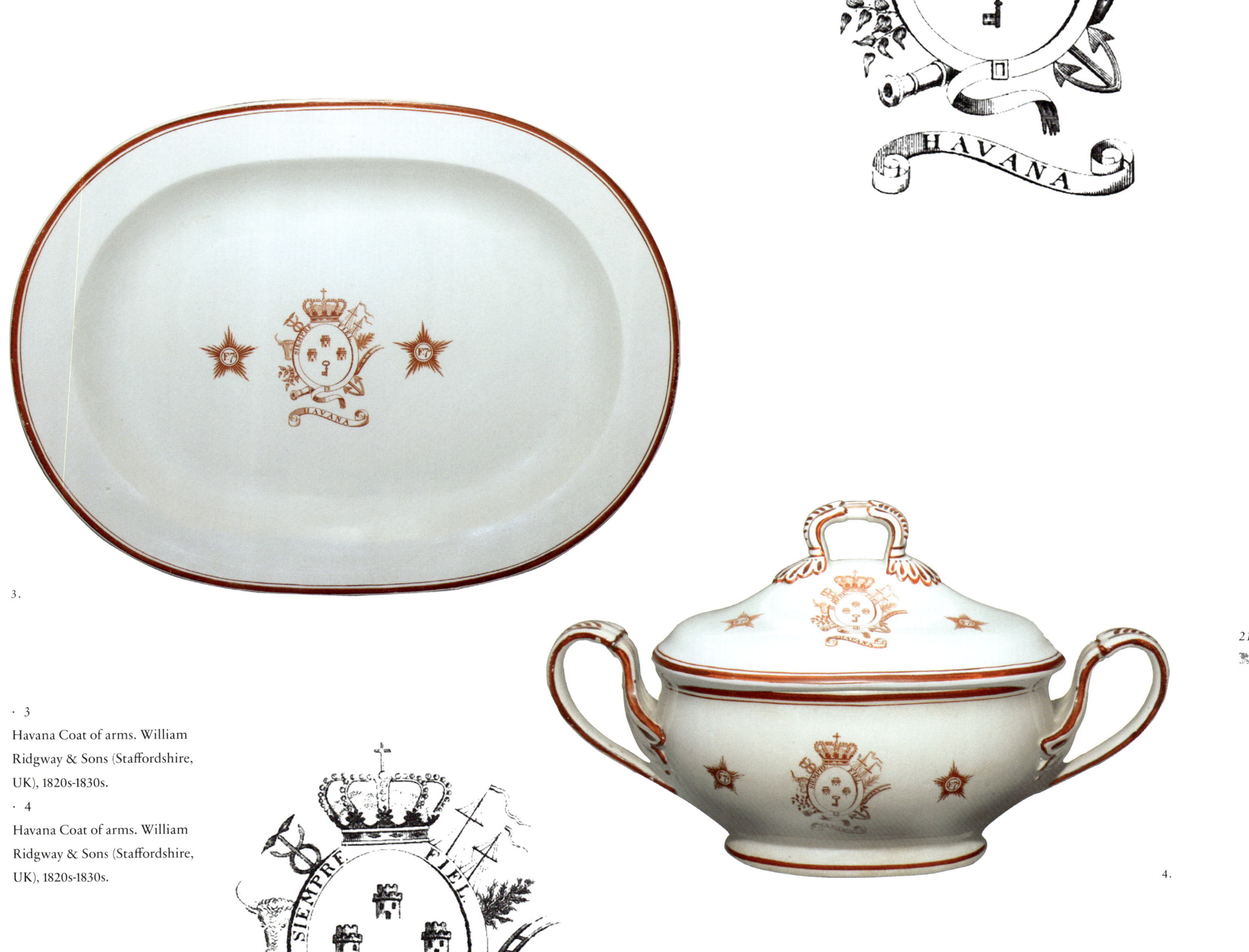

3.

4.

· 3
Havana Coat of arms. William Ridgway & Sons (Staffordshire, UK), 1820s-1830s.

· 4
Havana Coat of arms. William Ridgway & Sons (Staffordshire, UK), 1820s-1830s.

Throughout the XIX century, the Captain General of Cuba had the island's coat of arms engraved in the official dinnerware, manufactured, as would have been expected, in Spain, probably at the Buen Retiro ("B") Royal Factory ("F.R."), in the outskirts of Madrid (Fig. 5).[9] Perhaps other potteries were also used for those kinds of dishes.

This tradition of displaying the country's arms in official dinnerware was carried into the 20th century. And so, Cuban Presidents ordered their china services with the Cuban Republic Coat of Arms engraved therein. This time, however, they would not turn to the former Metropolis, but, instead, to the United States. Twice.

The 1920s model closely followed the pattern then used by the White House, which should not be surprising once we learn that it was designed by the Washington firm of Dulin & Martin, which also designed china during the presidency of Woodrow Wilson (1913 to 1921). And like Wilson's, Cuba's china would also be manufactured by Lenox, in Newark, New Jersey (Fig. 6). Lenox was also summoned to produce the new set of presidential dishes in the 1950s (Fig. 7). On both occasions our coat of arms was prominently displayed.

For its part, the Cuban Congress had its plates made (in the 1940s?) by Bauscher, a factory founded in 1881 in Weiden, Bavaria, Germany (Figs. 8).

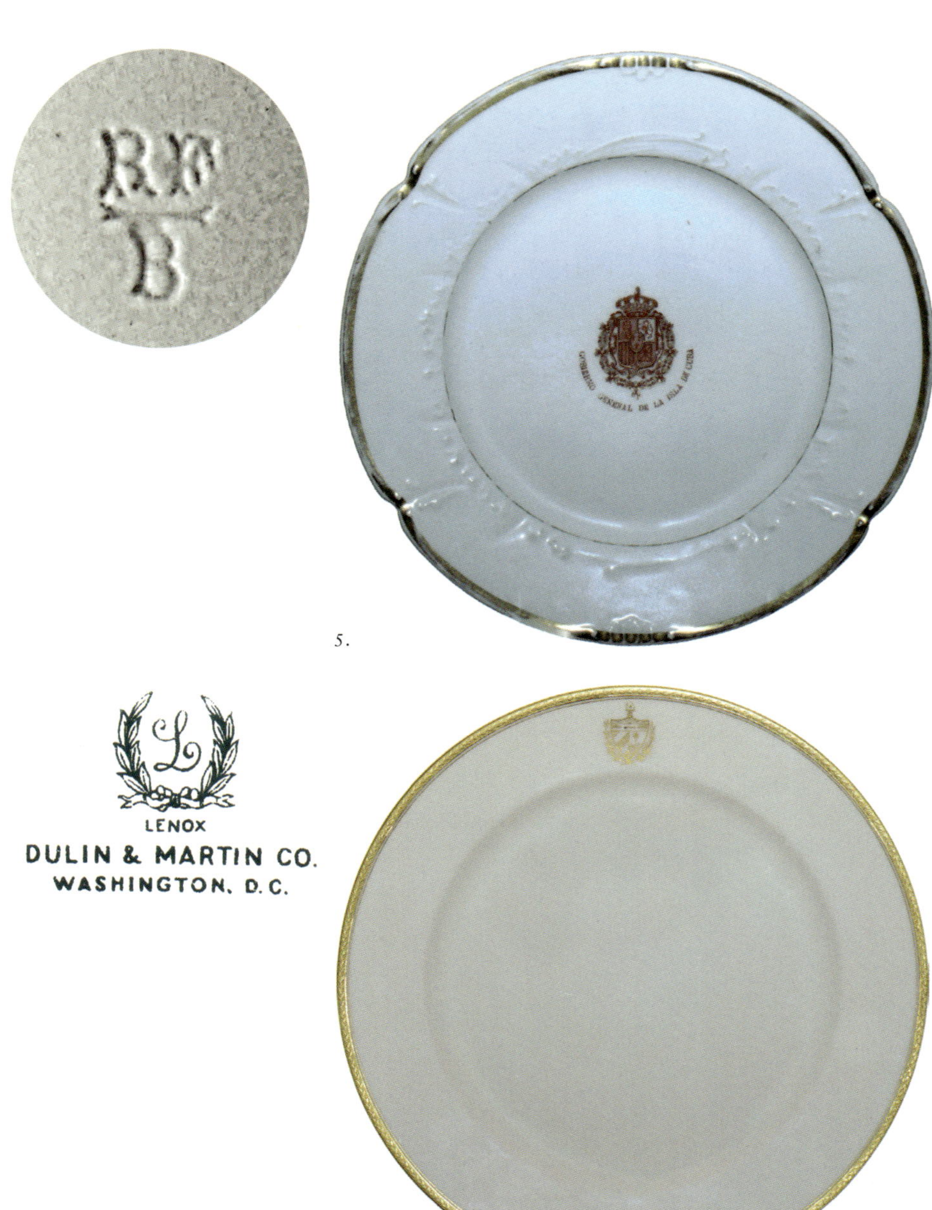

5.

6.

[9] Many such pieces are on display in Havana at the Palacio Lombillo, on Cathedral Square.

The pieces I know also bear the mark of J. F. [John Frederick] Berndes & Co., an English company incorporated in 1887 with Havana offices. I do not know their role in this process (perhaps as brokers between purchaser and factory).

Other governmental entities may also have had their own official dinnerware sets, but I have not been able to locate any porcelain pieces used by the Cuban Judiciary or by Cuban Embassies abroad. Nor have I seen the china which the current Executive Branch of Cuba uses in its official events. Further research is required.

· 5
Colonial Coat of arms. Buen Retiro (Madrid, Spain), 1870s.

· 6
Cuban Coat of arms. Lenox (New Jersey, US), 1920s.

· 7
Cuban Coat of arms. Lenox (New Jersey, US), 1950s.

· 8
Cuban Republic initials. Bauscher (Weiden, Germany), 1940s?

LENOX

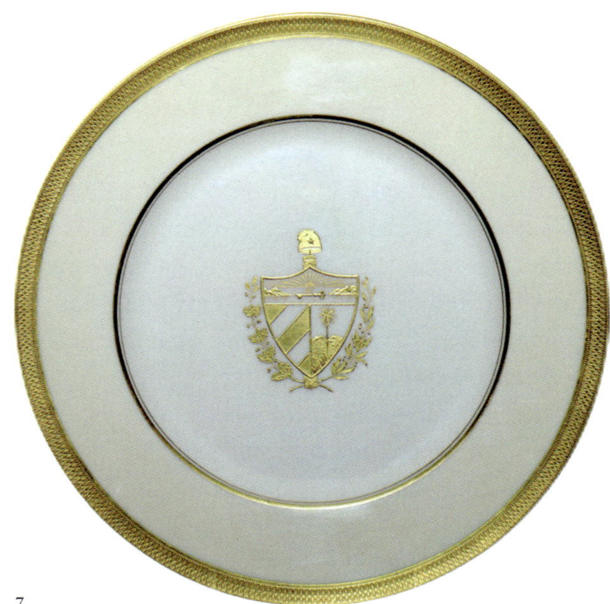

7.

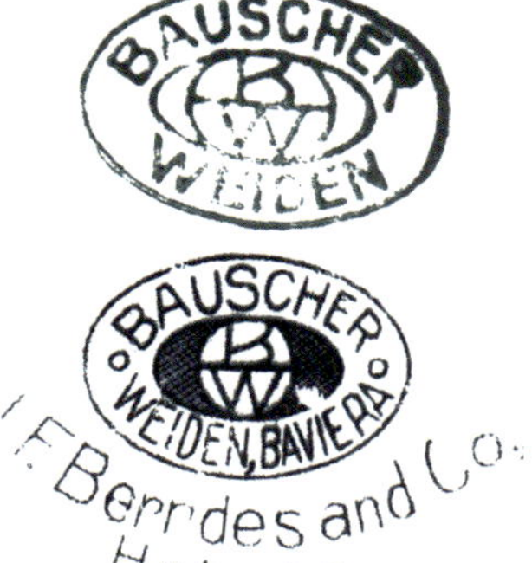

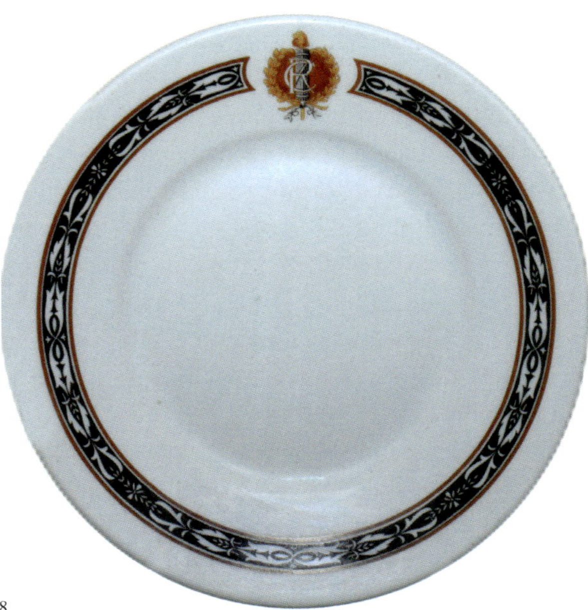

8.

Home use: Dinnerware, Toiletry and Desktop items with Cuban images, symbols or names

I will first discuss the commercial ceramics made in large quantities and offered for sale by the manufacturers to the public-at-large. Second, I will turn my attention to the special-order items of wealthy patrons who requested a unique set of wares for their own personal use. These they shared only with family and friends, some of whom may have surreptitiously taken them as souvenirs since, from time to time, some pieces appear for sale on antique markets. With friends like that…

Commercial ceramics

To the best of my knowledge, only three countries included Cuban views in their commercial ware for home use: The United Kingdom, Spain and Holland. At first, the pieces were made exclusively in traditional blue and white, using cobalt as the coloring ingredient. Later on, other pigments and shades were employed, giving the sets a growing and glowing array of colors. With respect to the Cuban views under study, I have seen that English potters used blue, red, black, light and dark purple and lilac, and, on one occasion, a moss green. Bright green, however, was used more frequently by the Spaniards (who also used blue, black and a reddish brown, but no red, purple or lilac), and also by the Dutch (who also used two shades of blue, red, black and lilac, but no brown). A feast in technicolor indeed.

United Kingdom[10]

Ridgway. England led the way. At some point in the early 1830s the Ridgway factory made a dining set with various Havana views ("Vista de La Habana" pattern). The Ridgway family has been extensively involved in the pottery business at various places and dates and under different commercial names. In November 1830, brothers John and William Ridgway went their separate ways and William's views were stamped "W.R.", which is the mark we find in our Habana pieces.

These Habana plates are undated, but the same delicate border was used in the Ridgway "Italian" set ("Rome", "A view in Venice"), produced in 1832-1834, and so our plates should follow closely those dates.[11]

I know of five different ceramic images copied from four printed views (although further research may lead to additional items) (Figs. 9-14).

---

10. On British ceramics, particularly Staffordshire, see Paul Atterbury, Ada Walker Camehl, Robert Cluett, Arthur Wilfred Coysh. John P. Cushion, Mary J. Finegan, David A. Furniss, Mary Frank Gaston, Geoffrey A. Godden, Rosemary Halliday, Richard K. Henrywood, Bob Page, Arnold A. Kowalsky, W. L. Little, Kathryn McNerney, Gillian Neale, Jeffrey B. Snyder and Cyril Williams-Wood, all cited in full in the Bibliography.

11. See Jeffrey B. Snyder, *Romantic Staffordshire ceramics*. Atglen, Pa., Schiffer Pub., 1997, p. 5 and Petra Williams, *et. al. Staffordshire II, romantic transfer patterns*. Jeffersontown, Ky., Fountain House East, 1986.

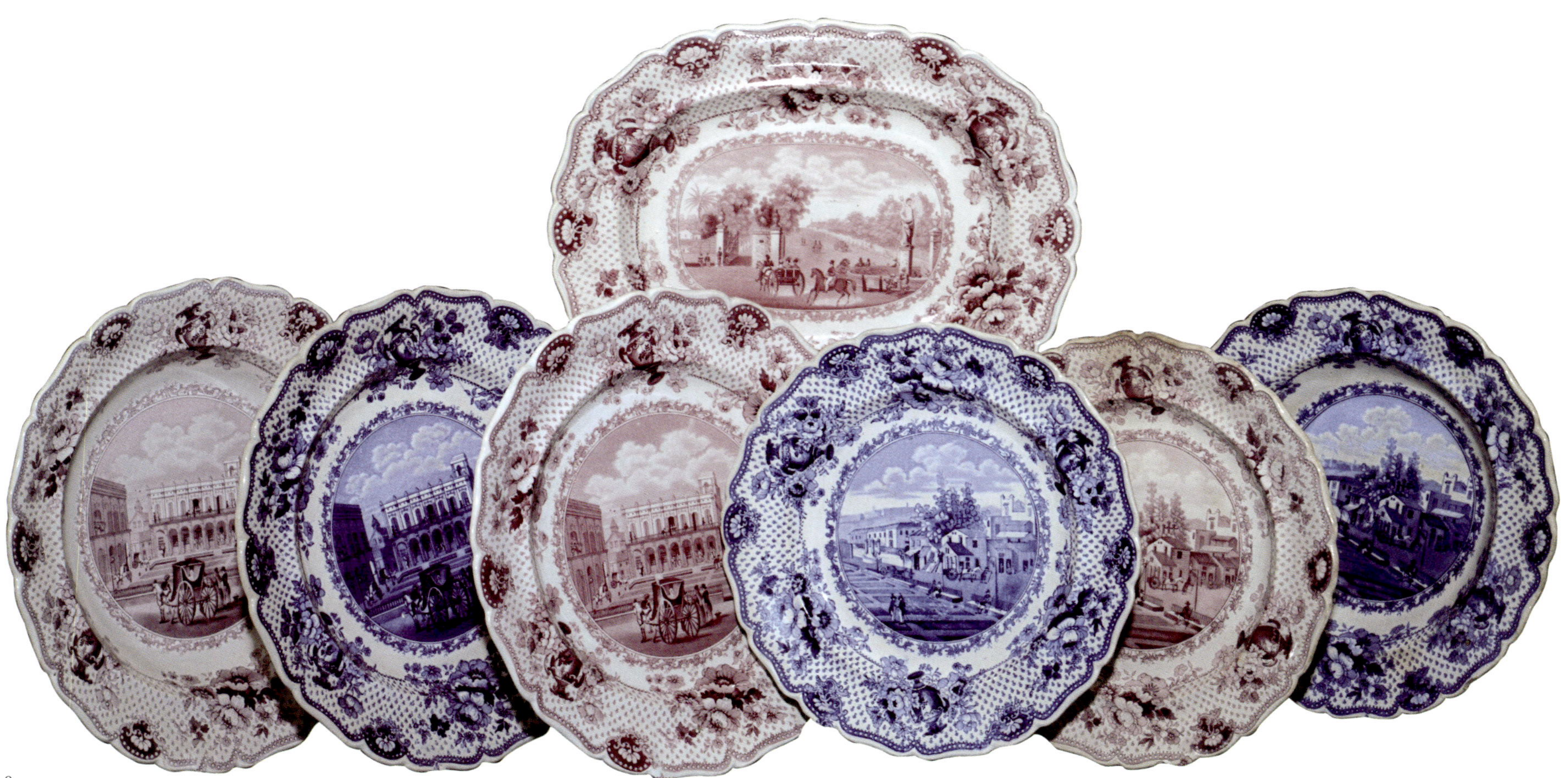

9.

· 9
Hyppolite Garneray.
“Vista de La Habana”.
W. R. Ridgway
(Staffordshire, UK), 1830s.

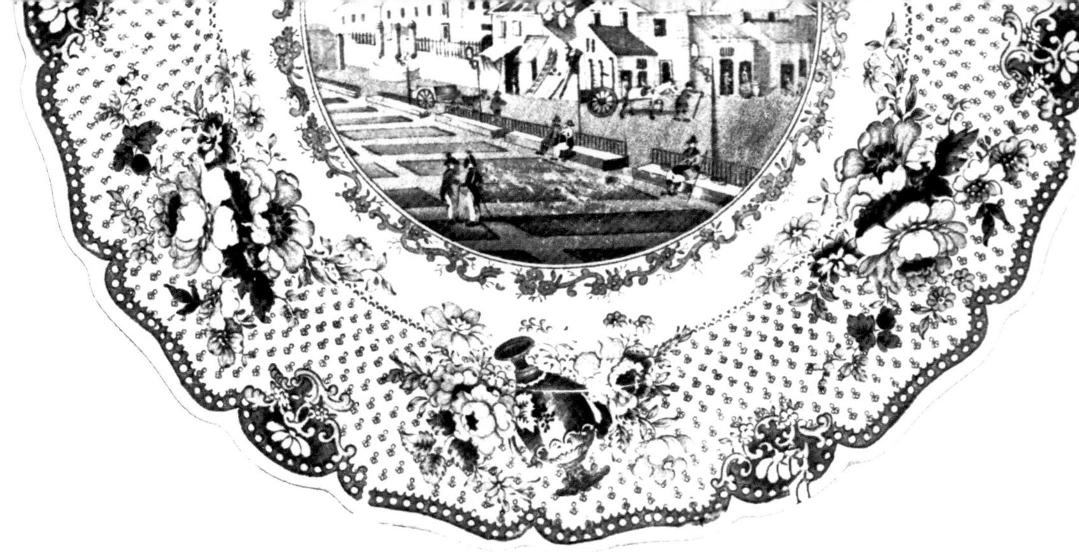

The four views used by Ridgway were taken from aquatint engravings printed in Paris around 1830 (other sources say 1825), after water colors by Frenchman Hyppolite Garneray/ Garnerey (1787–1858) around 1822-1824.[12] The titles on the prints (but not on the dishes) are:

1. *Vista de la Plaza de Armas de La Habana* This view was split into two separate images, each becoming the design of an individual porcelain dish (Figs. 10-12).
2. *Vista de la Plaza Vieja o mercado principal de La Habana*[13]
3. *Vista de la Alameda de Paula en La Habana*[14]
4. *Vista del Paseo Extramuros de La Habana* (Fig. 9, 13-14).

I do not know the context in which the porcelain factory undertook this assignment, but it is important to note that the images had been printed in Paris and would have been readily available in London. Moreover, it was Ridgway which had provided the Havana Municipality with its official set of dishes in the early 1830s, so perhaps it was on that occasion that Ridgway management decided it would be profitable to produce their Habana porcelain set.

A few of those plates did find their way to Havana. I have seen one pink platter on the wall of one of the rooms at Havana's Colonial Museum. Another large platter displaying the Paula Promenade was a gift from Cajón y Hermanos to the Havana Museum of Fine Arts when it opened in 1912 (I saw it on display a century later and was told it is now kept at the Museum of Decorative Arts in the Vedado section of Havana).

We will encounter other Ridgway potters in the 20th century, to be discussed later on so as not to interrupt the chronological flow.

---

12. See Zoila Lapique, *Música colonial cubana en las publicaciones periódicas: (1812-1902)*. La Habana, Letras Cubanas, 1979, p. 97. In 1979, one of the Garneray's original watercolors on 1822 Whatman paper surfaced in an antique gallery in London. Other sources have mentioned a Garneray presence in Havana around 1807, but I believe such a view is unsubstantiated.

13. The ceramic plate is Illustrated in Antonio Núñez Jiménez, *Cuba: La Naturaleza y el Hombre / Geopoética*. La Habana, 1983, p. 46.

14. The ceramic plate, originally owned by the Count of Pinofiel, is Illustrated in Eugenio Sánchez de Fuentes y Peláez, *Cuba monumental, estatuaria y epigráfica*. La Habana, Academia Nacional de Artes y Letras de La Habana, 1917, p. 213.

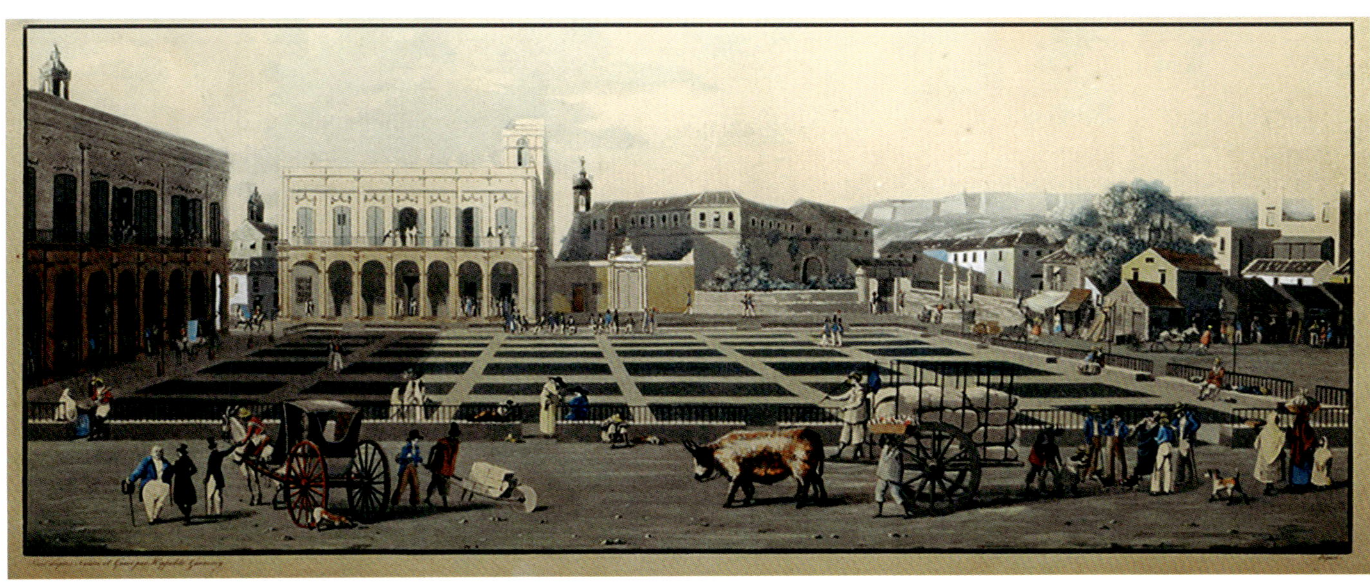

10 .

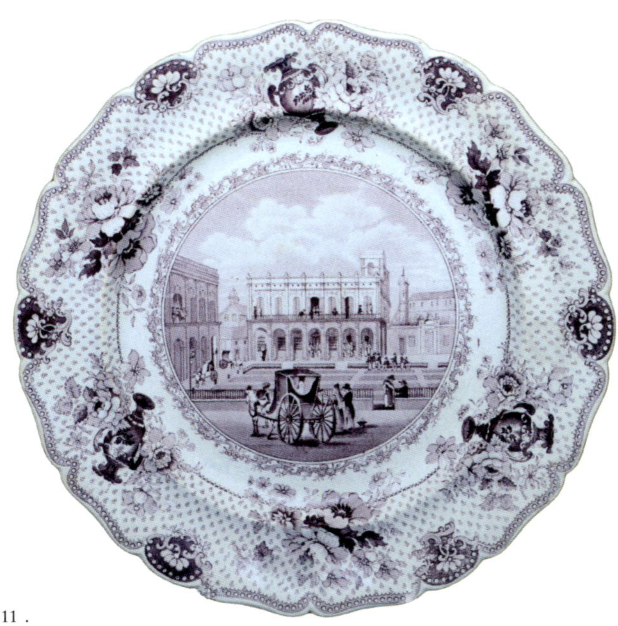

11 .

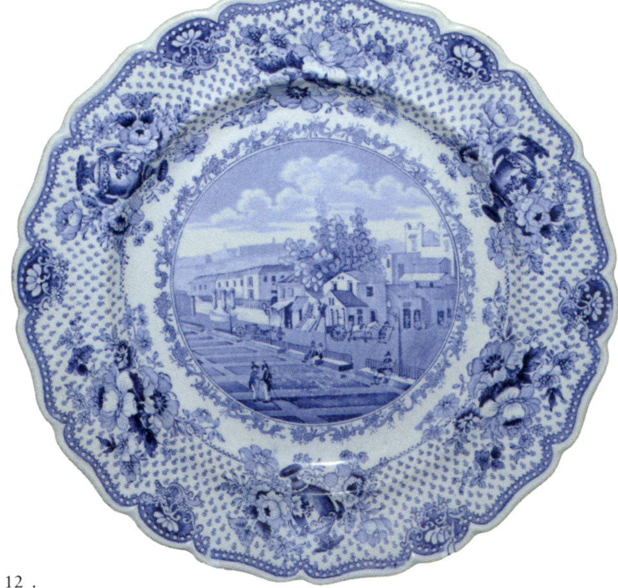

12 .

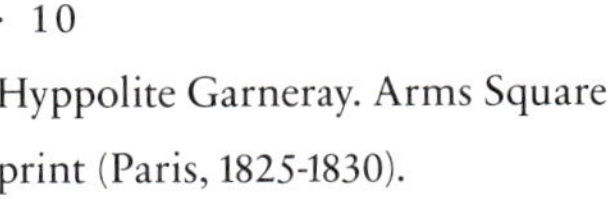

· 10
Hyppolite Garneray. Arms Square print (Paris, 1825-1830).
· 11
Hyppolite Garneray. Arms Square, detail I. “Vista de La Habana”. W. R. Ridgway (Staffordshire, UK), 1830s.
· 12
Hyppolite Garneray. Arms Square, detail II. “Vista de La Habana”. W. R. Ridgway (Staffordshire, UK), 1830s.

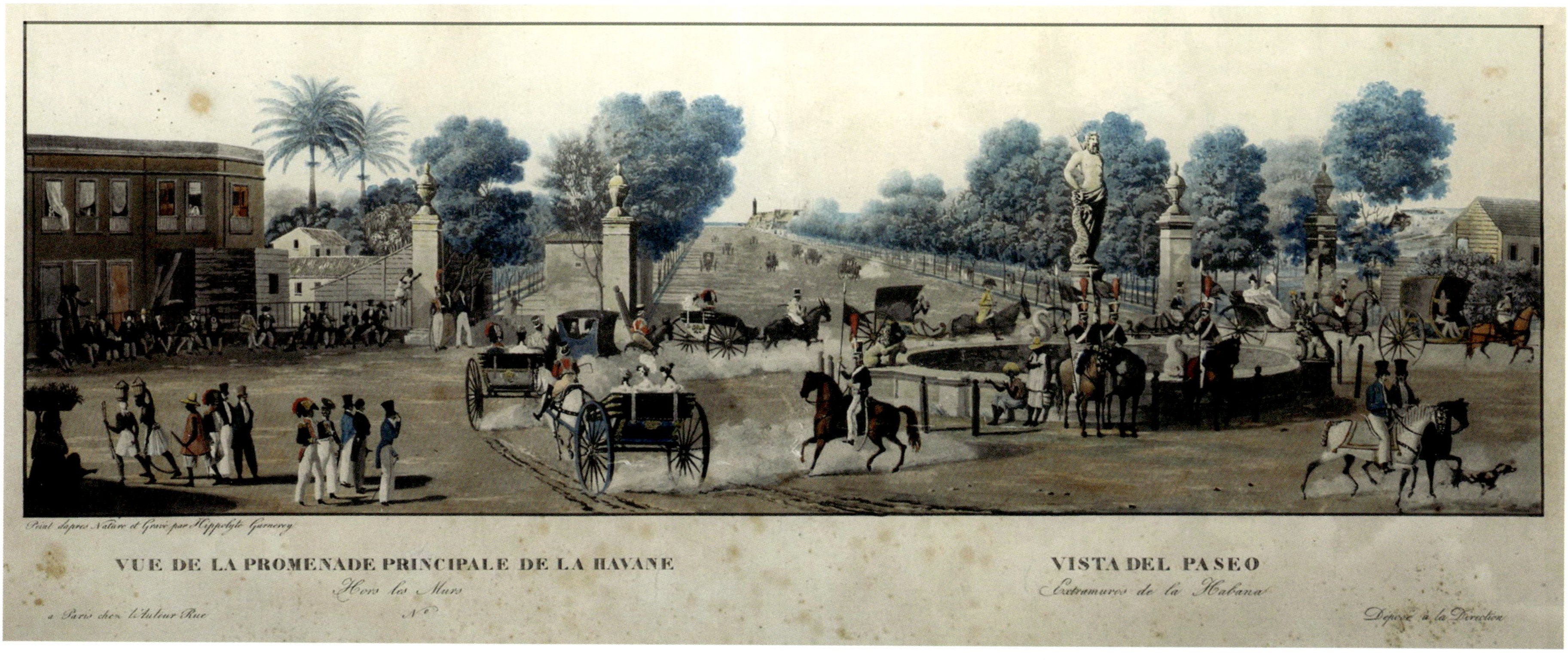

13 .

· 13

Hyppolite Garneray. Paseo print (Paris), 1825-1830.

· 14

Hyppolite Garneray. Paseo. "Vista de La Habana". W. R. Ridgway (Staffordshire, UK), 1830s.

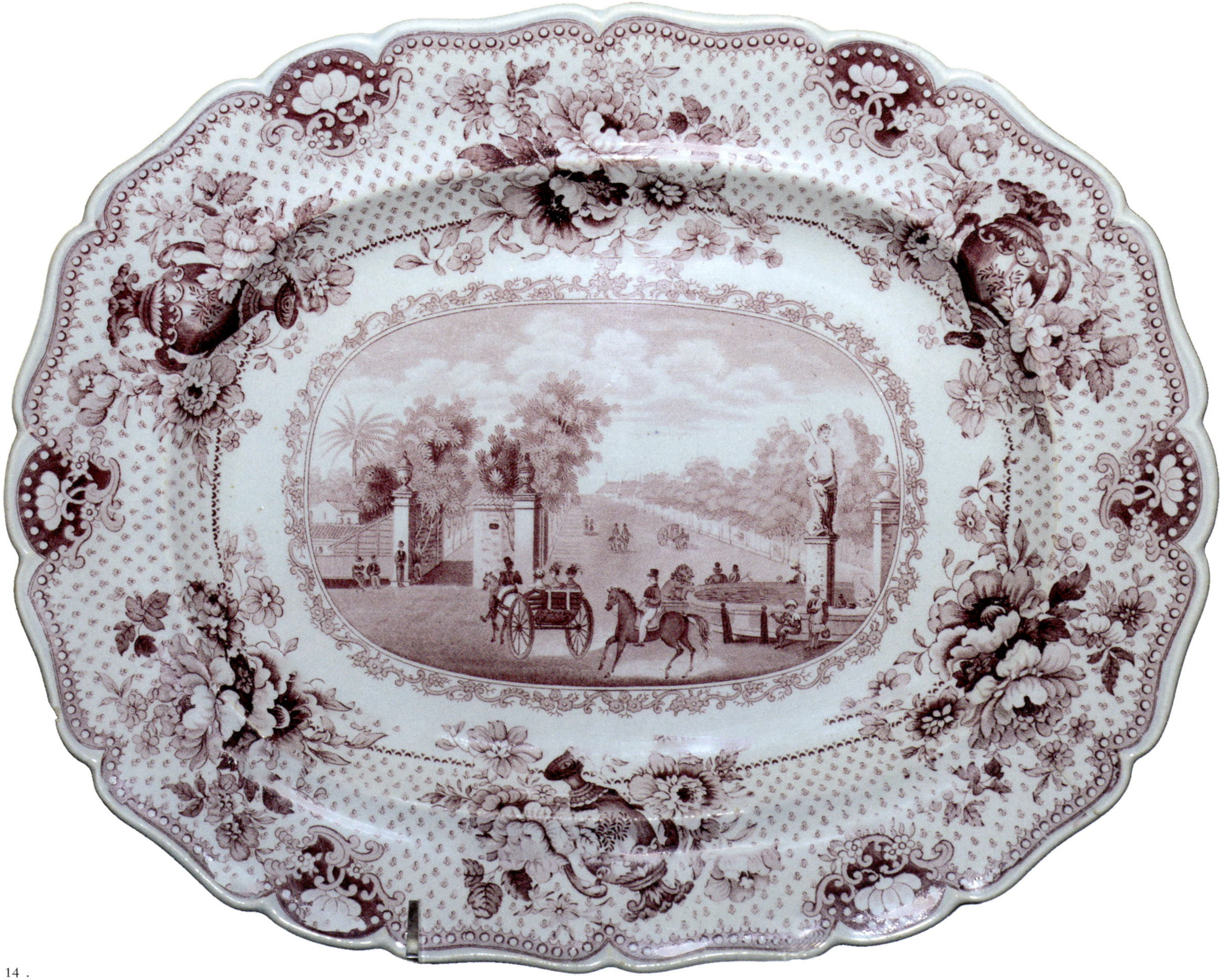

14 .

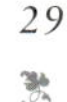

Enoch Wood. Also in the 1840s (my best guess), two views from Frédéric Mialhe's first set of Cuban images (*Isla de Cuba Pintoresca* album, 1839-1841) were transferred onto ceramic platters in England by Enoch Wood.

One view depicts the Tacón theater and I have seen two different pieces with the same image. The first, an octogonal «pearl china» platter, is marked «E & .E. W» (which stands for Enoch and Edward Wood). It is also marked «Chusan border», which could be a reference to the border pattern used therein (Fig. 15). The second ovoid platter is marked «Dresden ironstone china» (Fig. 16). This Dresden mark here bears no relationship to Dresden Germany, and it was used by several English potters. While there are no Enoch Wood[15] stamps on this item, it is clear to me that it came from the same factory.

The second view depicts the Carnicería Bridge in Matanzas (Fig. 17). While it is also unmarked, the plate's border, however, tells its own story. It was used by Enoch Wood in his "Belzoni" pattern, and this, in my opinion, strongly indicates that we should trace the authorship of this Cuban item also to Wood. Besides, it makes perfect sense that both Mialhe views would have been used by the same ceramics factory which, somehow, managed to acquire them at the same time.

[15]. See Arthur Wilfred Coysh, *The dictionary of blue and white pottery, 1780-1880*. Woodbridge, Suffolk, Antique Collector's Club, 1989, Volume I, p. 171.

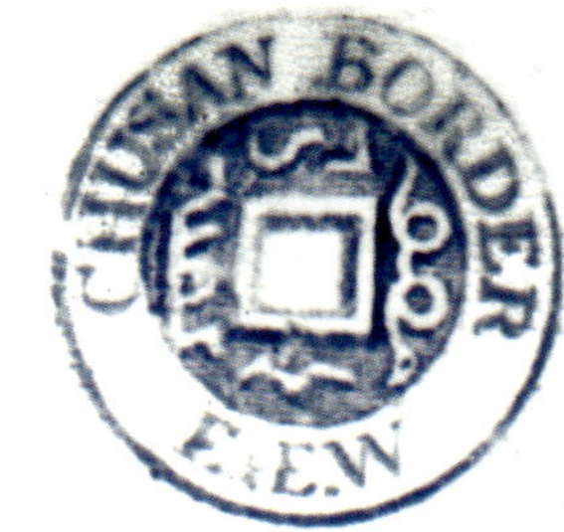

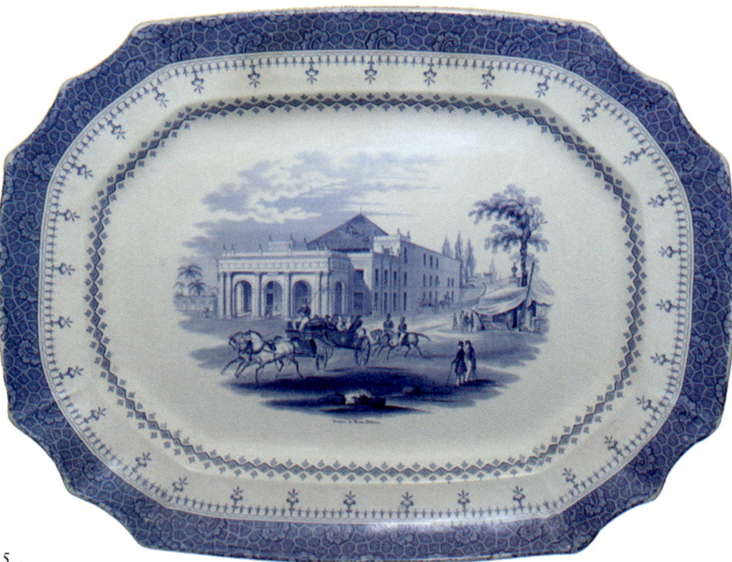

15 .

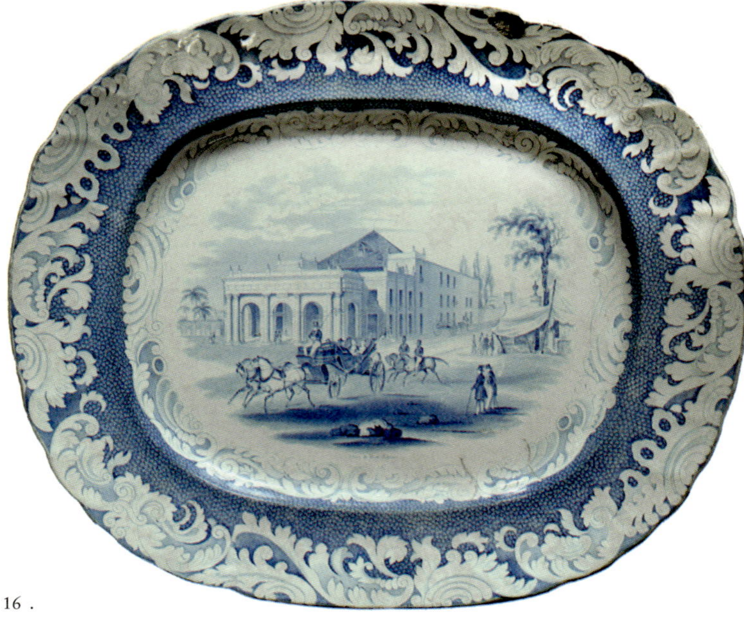

16 .

· 15
Frédéric Mialhe. Tacón Theater.
Enoch Wood (Staffordshire, UK),
1840s.

· 16
Frédéric Mialhe. Tacón Theater.
Enoch Wood (Staffordshire, UK),
1840s.

· 17
Frédéric Mialhe. Carnicería Bridge.
Enoch Wood (Staffordshire, UK),
1840s.

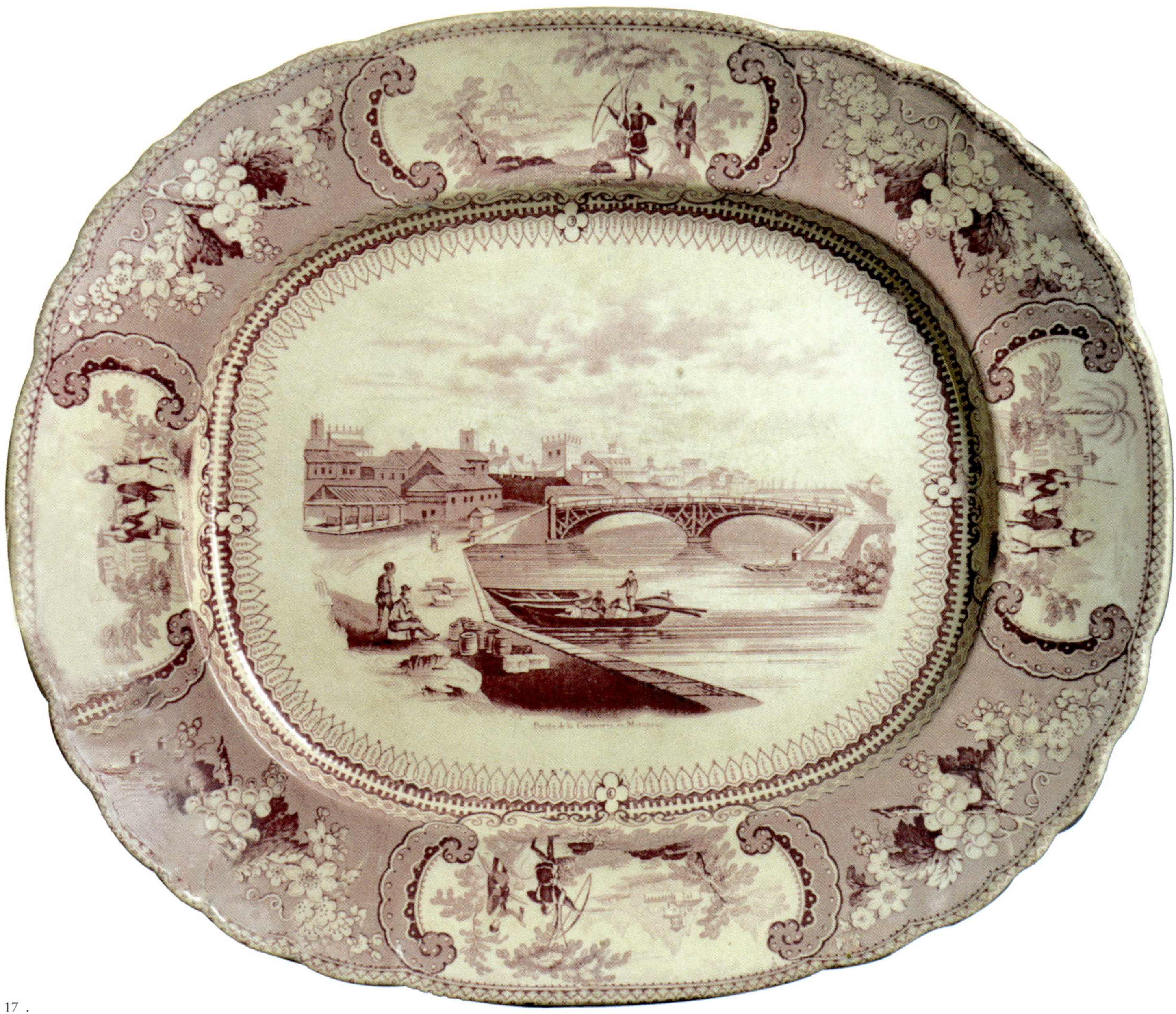

17 .

Unfortunately, I have been unable to ascertain how these Mialhe images printed in Havana in 1839-1841 made their way to England so quickly. We do know, however, that British potters were always on the lookout for foreign, exotic scenes to add to their inventories.

Adams. The Adams family of potters intersect with Cuba-themed ceramics at several times, and, most particularly, around 1840, 1845, 1853, 1861 and 1898.

1840. In his comprehensive work on the Adams group, David A. Furniss has documented two rare Cuba-related views ca. 1840 by the William Adams factory, located in Stoke-on-Trent, also in Staffordshire county. They are "El amparo de Cuba" depicting a mother and three children, and "La Sierra de Guanalay" (which I presume is Guanajay, a city in today's Artemisa province). Furniss believes there may be more related pieces in the set and that they were made for the Cuban market.[16]

1845. On July 26, 1845, the Adams potters registered their «Habana» trade name, although they also meant tc include views from Madrid and Seville in their wares (after all, the three cities were part of the same Spanish nation).[17] The unusual border for this pattern featured 3 different medallions: The legendary Spanish Catholic Kings, Ferdinand and Isabella (center top and bottom), the current young queen, Isabella II (top right and bottom left) and the Queen Regnant, María Cristina (top left and bottom right). It is quite possible that they saw a market in Spain for this set (Fig. 18).

The individual Havana views known to me (the Spanish ones are not under consideration in this book) are six, although in the future others may surface. They depict the following Havana scenes:

1. *The Paula Promenade* (Fig. 20)
2. *The Indian Fountain statue* (Fig. 23)
3. *The Arms Square on an outdoor concert night* (retreta) (Fig. 21)
4. *The Tacón theater and surrounding park.*[18]
5. *Railroad scene No. 1* (Fig. 19)
6. *Railroad scene No. 2* (Fig. 22)

16. David A. Furniss, *op. cit.*, pp. 66 and 86.

17. We can calculate the exact date thanks to the diamond-shape British dating system, mentioned earlier.

18. Illustrated in the cover of *Social* (La Habana), January 1937, and in Antonio Núñez Jiménez, *Cuba: La Naturaleza y el Hombre / Geopoética.* La Habana, 1983, p. 46.

· 18
"Habana". William Adams,
(Staffordshire, UK), 1845.

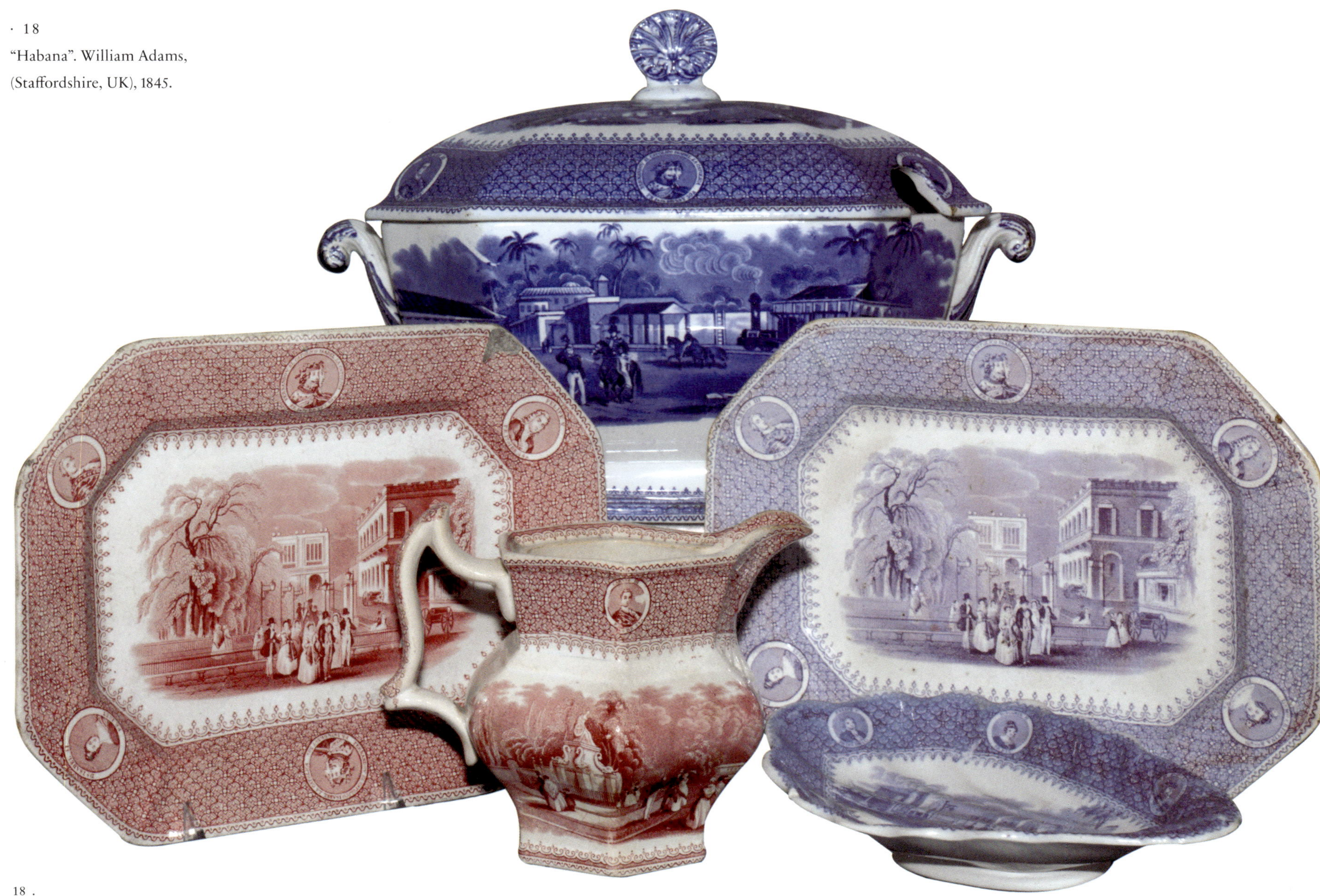

18 .

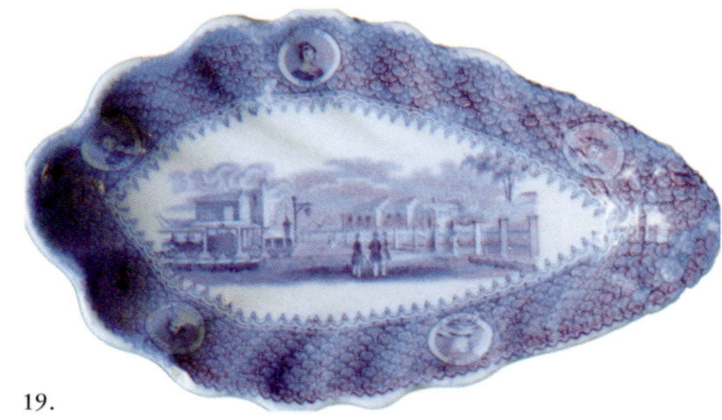
19.

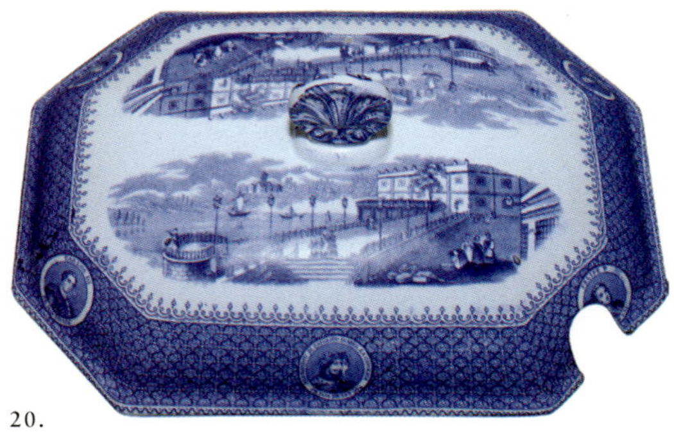
20.

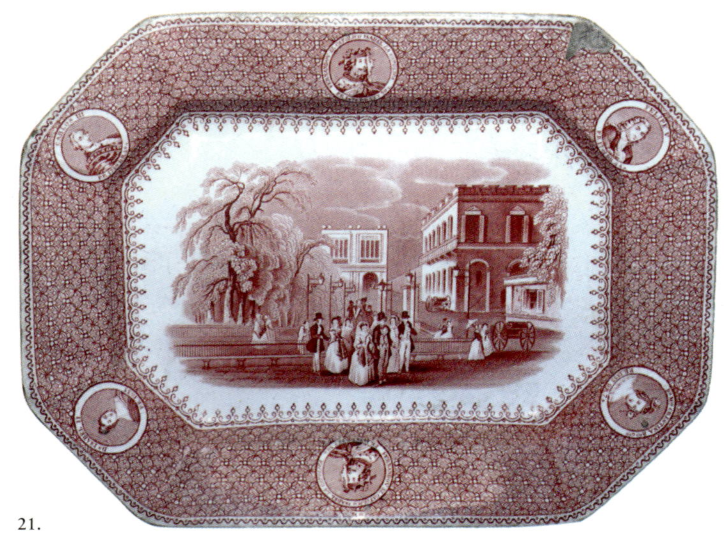
21.

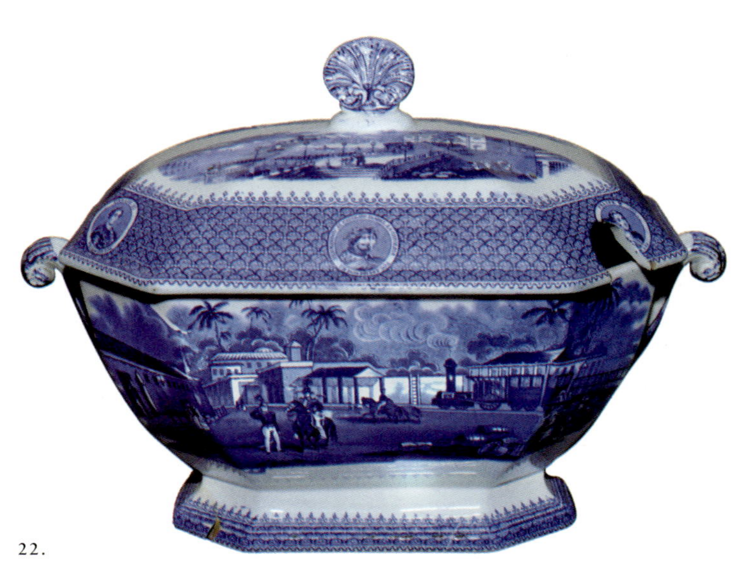
22.

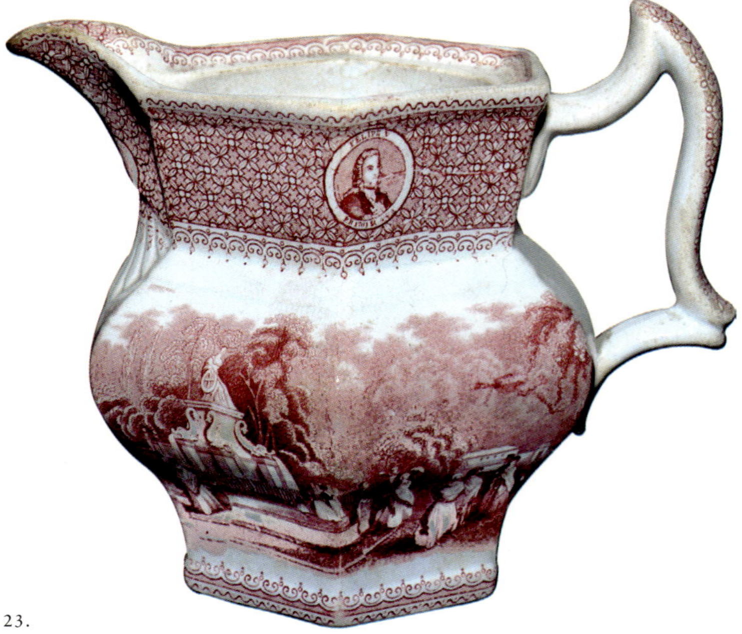
23.

The Paula view was taken from the *Paseo Pintoresco de la Isla de Cuba* printed in Havana in 1841-42 by the Spanish lithographers Fernando Costa and Laureano Cuevas (*Alameda de Paula. Habana,* facing p. 256, Fig. 24).[19] The Indian Fountain view comes from the same source (*Fuente de la India en el Paseo Nuevo,* facing p. 139).

And the Arms Square image bears great resemblance to the *Plaza de Armas en noche de retreta* print in that album (facing, p. 120, Fig. 25). For the remaining three views I have yet to find their printed counterparts. Perhaps they were specially commissioned to complete the set.

19. *Paseo pintoresco por la Isla de Cuba*. Habana, Imprenta de Soler y Comp., 1841; Miami, Fla., Ediciones Universal, 1999.

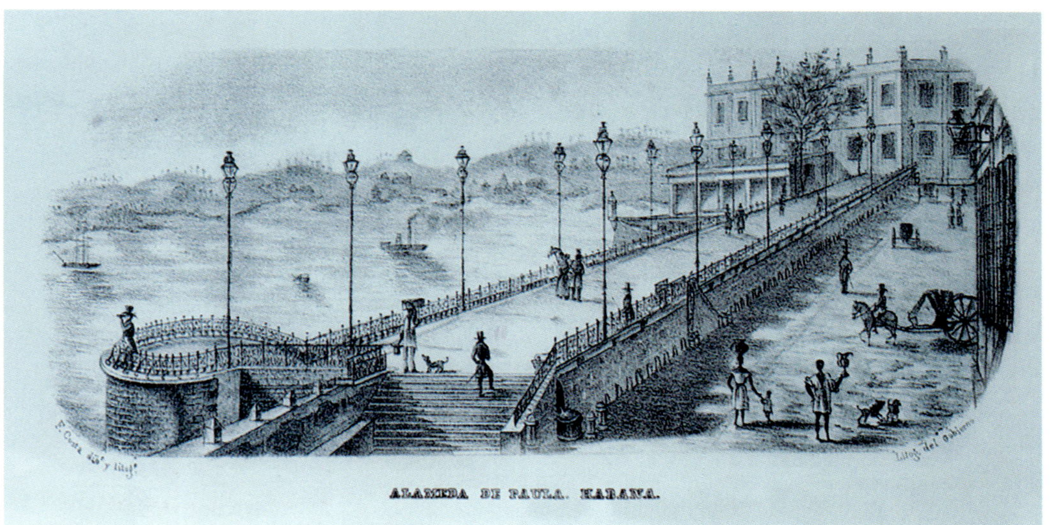

24.

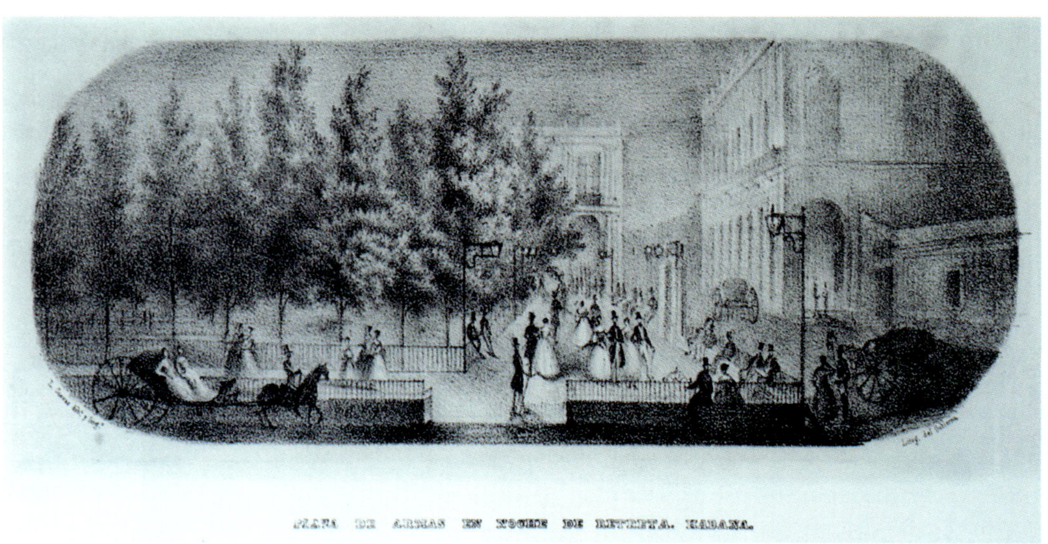

25.

· 19
Anonymous. Railroad scene No. 1. "Habana". William Adams (Staffordshire, UK), 1845.

· 20
Fernando Costa. Paula Promenade. "Habana". William Adams (Staffordshire, UK), 1845.

· 21
After Fernando Costa. Arms square. "Habana". William Adams (Staffordshire, UK), 1845.

· 22
Anonymous. Railroad scene No. 2. "Habana". William Adams (Staffordshire, UK), 1845.

· 23
After Fernando Costa. Indian Fountain statue. "Habana". William Adams (Staffordshire, UK), 1845.

· 24,25
Fernando Costa. Lithographs, *Paseo Pintoresco*, Havana, 1841-1842.

1853. The Adams factory also reproduced some Cuban genre views after the 1848 lithographs in Frédéric Mialhe's second album (*Viaje Pintoresco al-rededor de la Isla de Cuba*), under the pattern name "Spanish Festivities". That name was registered on November 30 1853, according to the stamps marked on the back of the pieces I know. To date, I have found five such views: The Cock fight, on a purple platter (Fig. 26); the *Zapateado* peasant dance, which showed up in in regular dishes (blue and red), and also in a rare barber's plate (Fig. 27); the *Sabaneros* (cow boys) in a pink pitcher;[20] the poultry seller (*El casero*); and the bread and fodder sellers (*El panadero y el malojero*).

These last two appear decorating a soup tureen, which can be admired in internet, courtesy of Getty pictures (which, most unfortunately, does not divulge its provenance). They also appear in pieces actually made a decade later, although these are not stamped by William Adams (who by then had died) but by George Jones, whom we will meet shortly.

I also own a lilac zapateado dance platter which is unmarked, but could come from William Adams (similar border, similar view). Surprisingly, that pattern does not include the two dogs which usually appear in the picture (Compare Fig. 28 and Figs. 32-33). Further research needs to be done on this variant pattern.

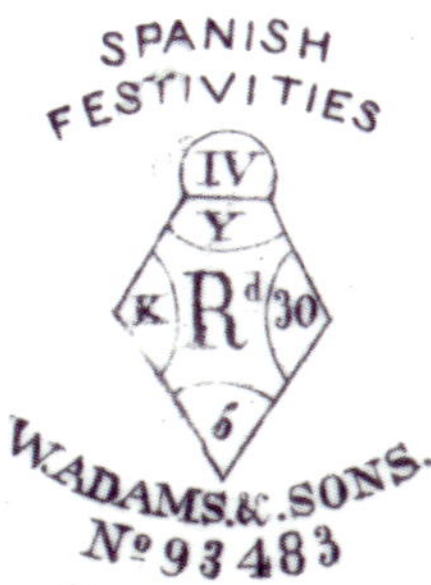

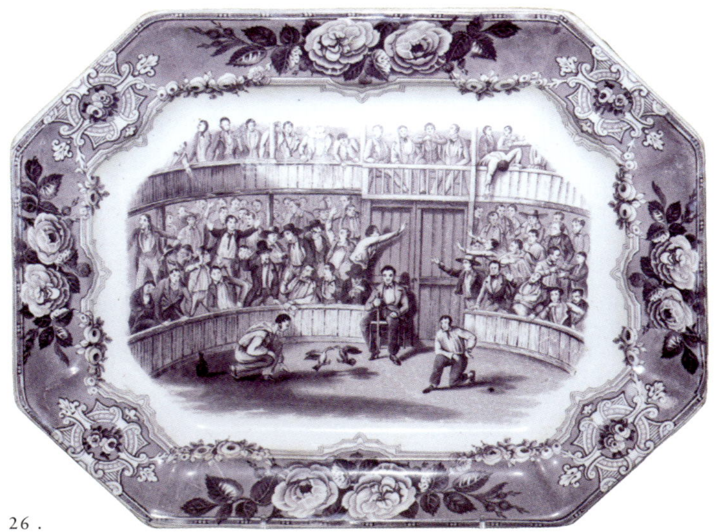

26.

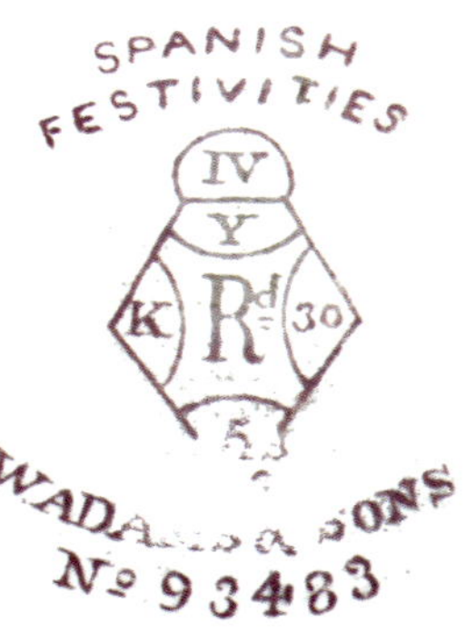

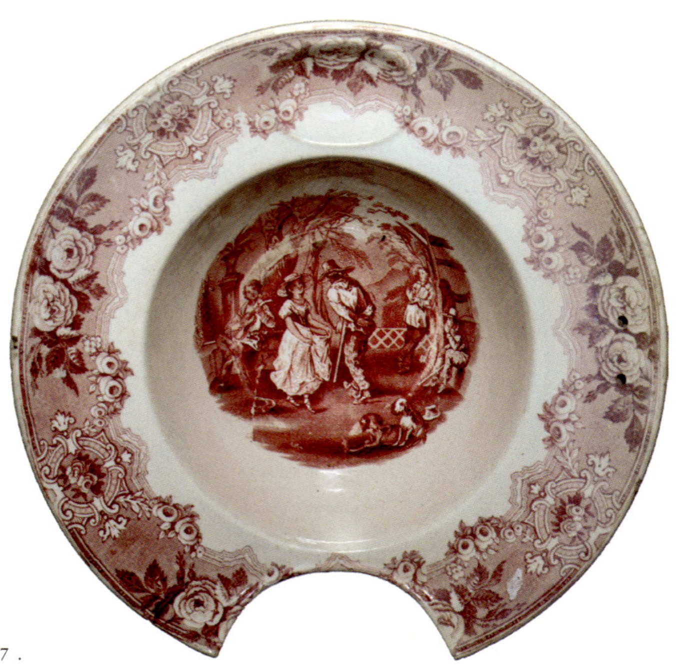

27.

---

20. Both the ceramic pitcher (at Havana's Colonial Museum) and the original print are Illustrated in Emilio Cueto, *La Cuba pintoresca de Frédéric Mialhe*. La Habana, Biblioteca Nacional de Cuba José Martí, 2010, p.212.

· 26
Frédéric Mialhe. Cock Fight.
"Spanish Festivities".
William Adams (Staffordshire, UK),
1853-1861.
· 27
Frédéric Mialhe. Zapateado dance.
"Spanish Festivities".
William Adams (Staffordshire, UK),
1853-1861.
· 28
Frédéric Mialhe. Zapateado dance.
Unmarked, but possibly from
William Adams (Staffordshire, UK),
1853-1861.

28 .

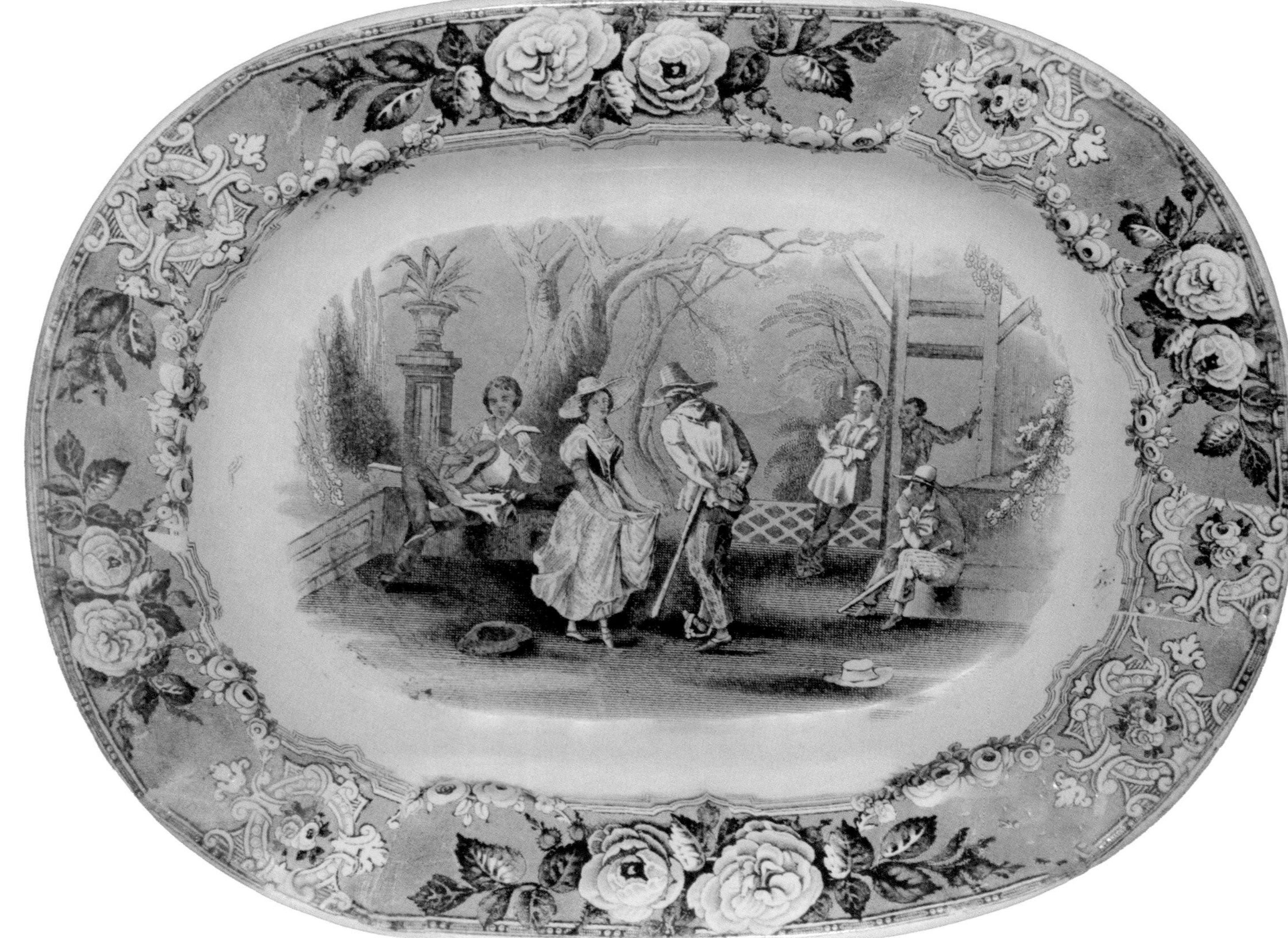

The date 1853 is important. That year, the Mialhe views printed in Havana in 1848 were plagiarized by Bernardo May & Co., who printed a new set —*Album pintoresco de la isla de Cuba*— in Germany (probably Hamburg). The circulation of this bogus set in the European market may have made the Adams family aware of the existence of the Mialhe prints. Or perhaps the views came directly from Havana, where they had been printed only seven years before.

1861. Shortly before the death of William Adams (1798-1865), the factory was sold at auction to George Jones (April 8-10 1861), and two of Adams sons, William and Percy, moved to nearby Tunstall where they began conducting business as Wm. Adams & Co. Having sold the title to the "Spanish Festivities" name and the related plates, they could no longer produce such wares. But, apparently, they conceived the idea of making a new composition with a collage of two of the Mialhe views, artfully combining the poultry seller and the bread seller in one sweeping panorama. They thought perhaps they could get away with it. And they did.

And so, at some point during the 1860s or 1870s, they registered this new, composite view under the trade name "Lasso".[21] Only one of the pieces known to me has that Lasso mark but, since all of them display the exact same image, I see no reason not to assign them to the same pattern and the same potter (the platter in the set bears the name of F [Fedele] Primavesi, a pottery dealer in Cardiff, United Kingdom) (Fig. 29). But there is another twist: according to Furniss, between 1917 and 1965 this image was issued by Adams under the name "Amazon".[22] Confusing… and fascinating.

1898. The Adams pieces for those years will be discussed under the section dealing with the Cuban War of Independence.

[21] Not to be confused with at least three other "Lasso" patterns depicting a farm hand attempting to catch running horses. One such image was made by William Adams (ca. 1829), another by W. Barker & Co. (ca. 1860), and another is attributed both to William Bourne and to T. Goodwin and he Seacombe Pottery (ca. 1882).

[22] David A. Furniss, *op. cit.*, pp. 152-153.

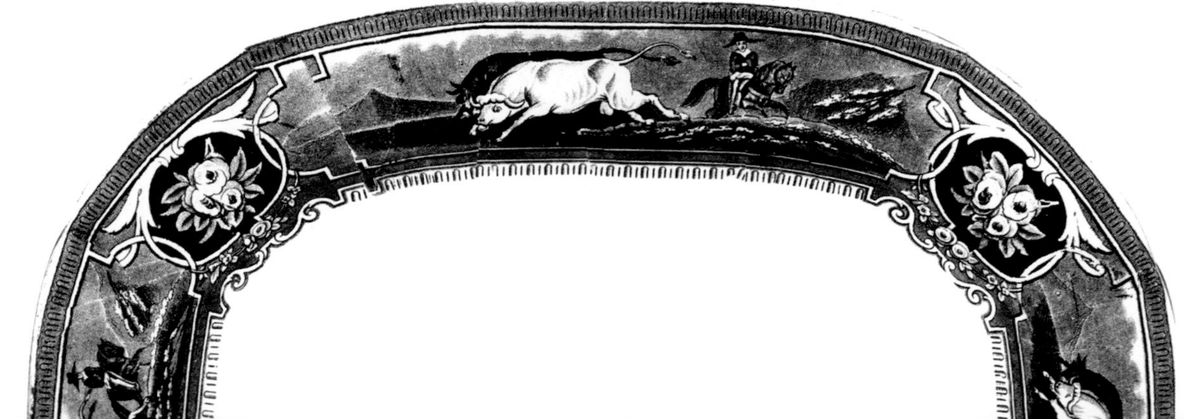

· 29

Frédéric Mialhe. The poultry, bread and fodder sellers. "Lasso". William Adams & Co. (Staffordshire, UK), 1861. Large platter bears mark F. Primavesi.

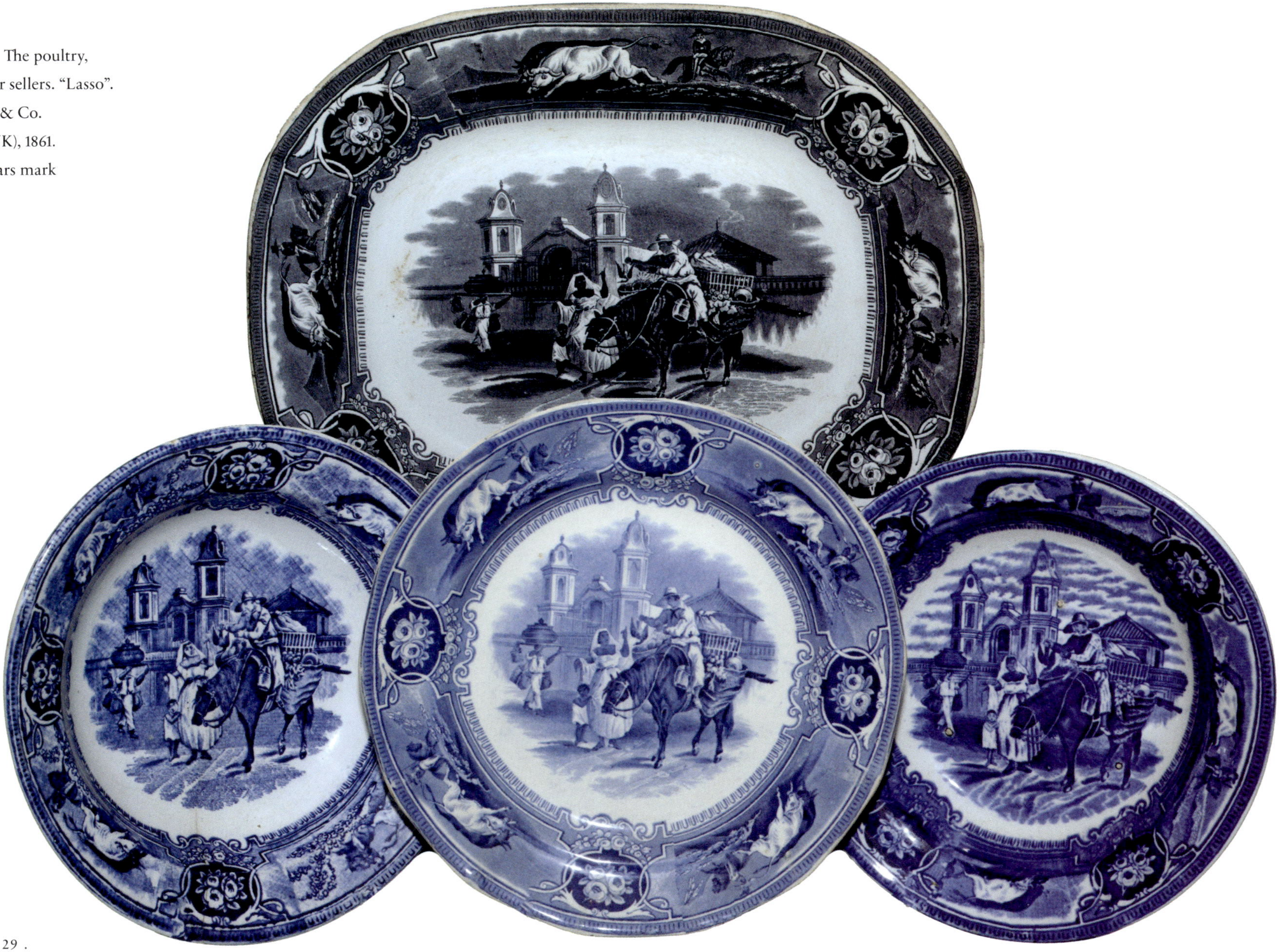

29 .

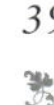

George Jones. As we saw, the assets and original patterns of William Adams the father were purchased in 1861 by George Jones, who remained in Stoke-on-Trent and soon began reproducing the Mialhe genre views under the same generic name of "Spanish Festivities". He reissued the poultry seller (Fig. 30), and the bread and fodder sellers (Fig. 31), some bearing the diamond shape mark showing the original registration date. Jones also reissued two earlier Mialhe/Adams views: the cock fight (Fig. 34) and the Zapateado dance (Figs. 32-33). Perhaps he also reproduced the cowboy image, but I have never seen that view with a Jones mark.

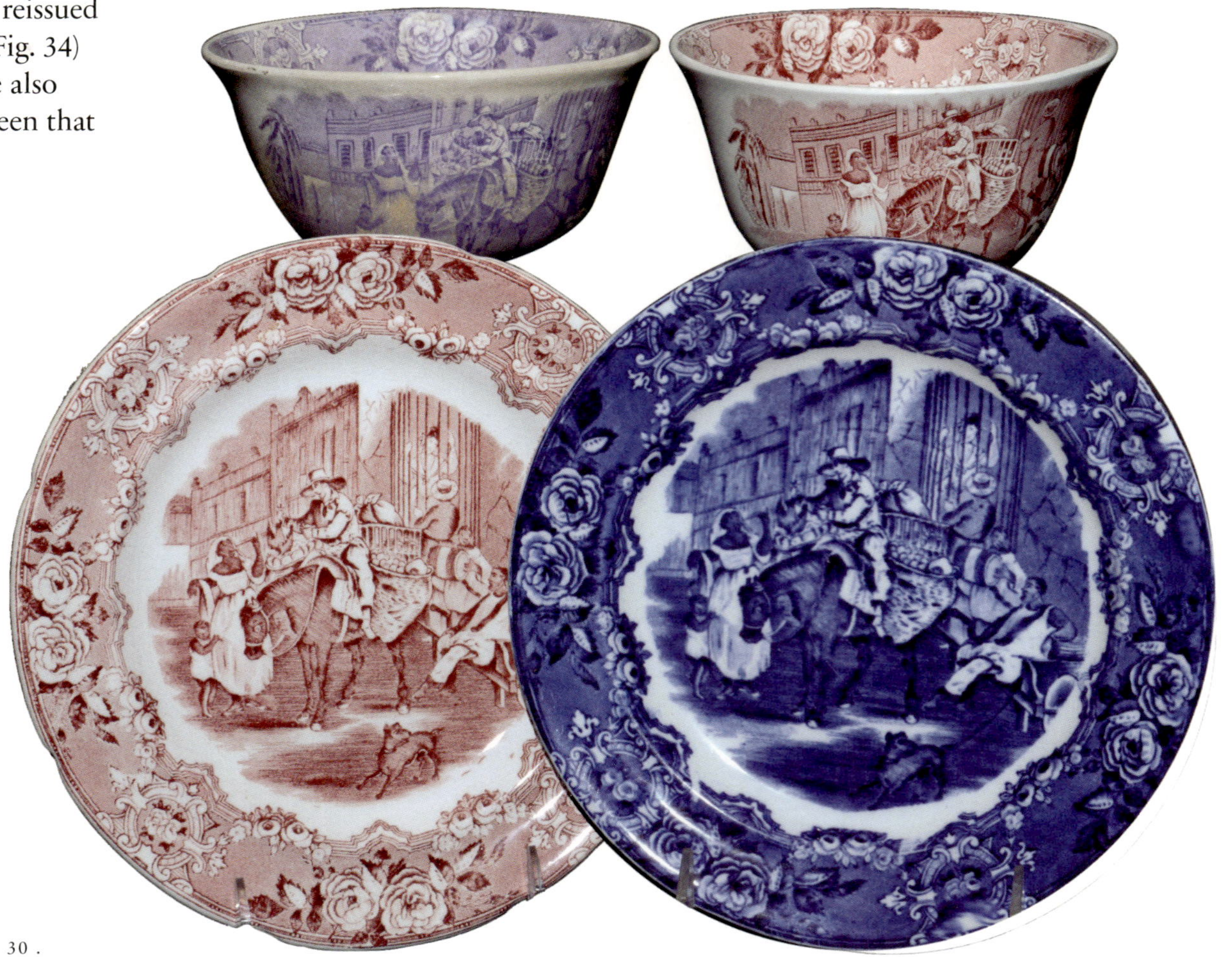

30 .

· 30

Frédéric Mialhe. The poultry seller. "Spanish Festivities". George Jones (Staffordshire, UK), 1861-.

· 31

Frédéric Mialhe. The bread and fodder sellers. "Spanish Festivities". George Jones (Staffordshire, UK), 1861-.

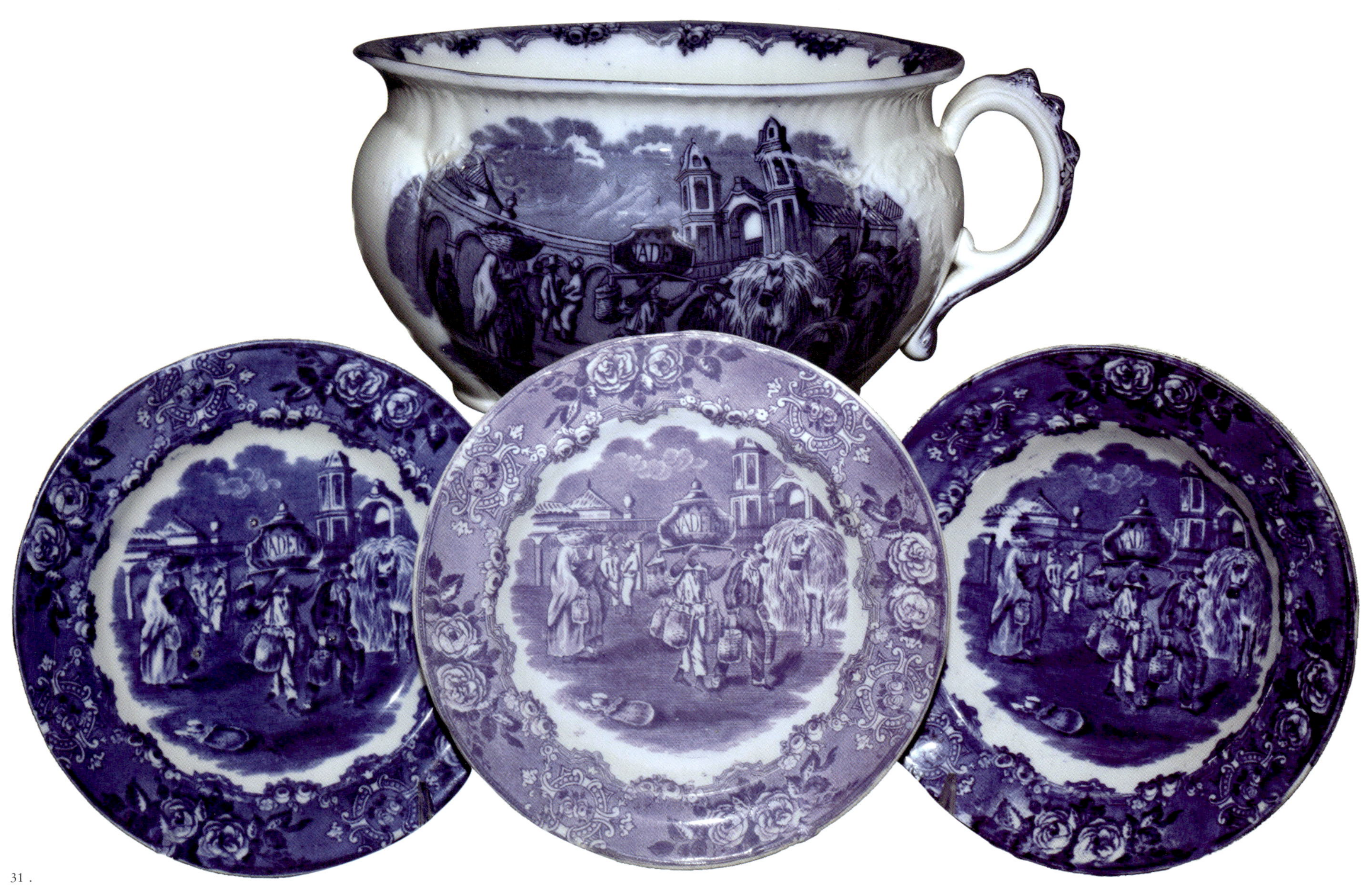

31 .

32 .

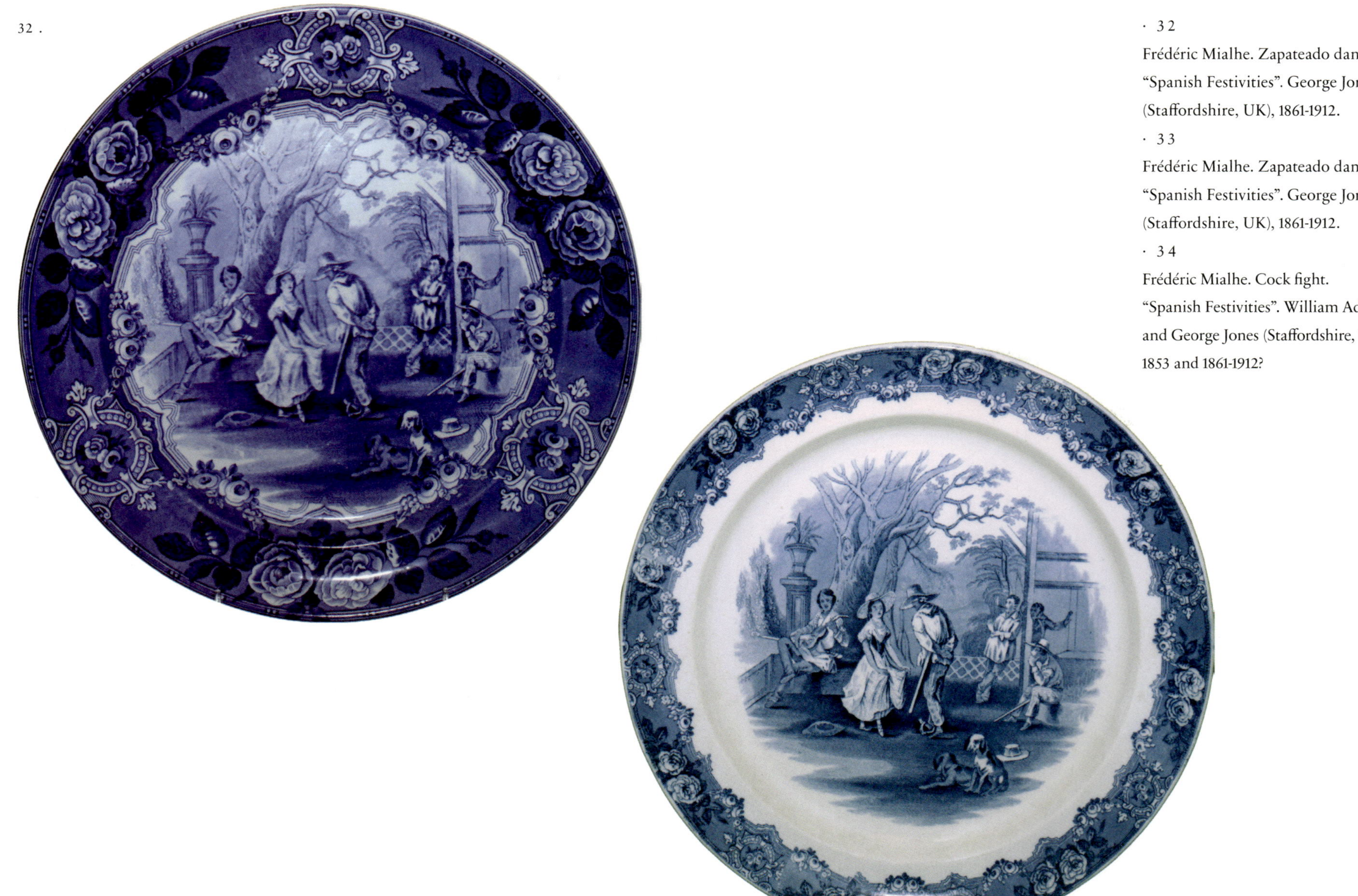

33 .

· 32

Frédéric Mialhe. Zapateado dance. "Spanish Festivities". George Jones (Staffordshire, UK), 1861-1912.

· 33

Frédéric Mialhe. Zapateado dance. "Spanish Festivities". George Jones (Staffordshire, UK), 1861-1912.

· 34

Frédéric Mialhe. Cock fight. "Spanish Festivities". William Adams and George Jones (Staffordshire, UK), 1853 and 1861-1912?

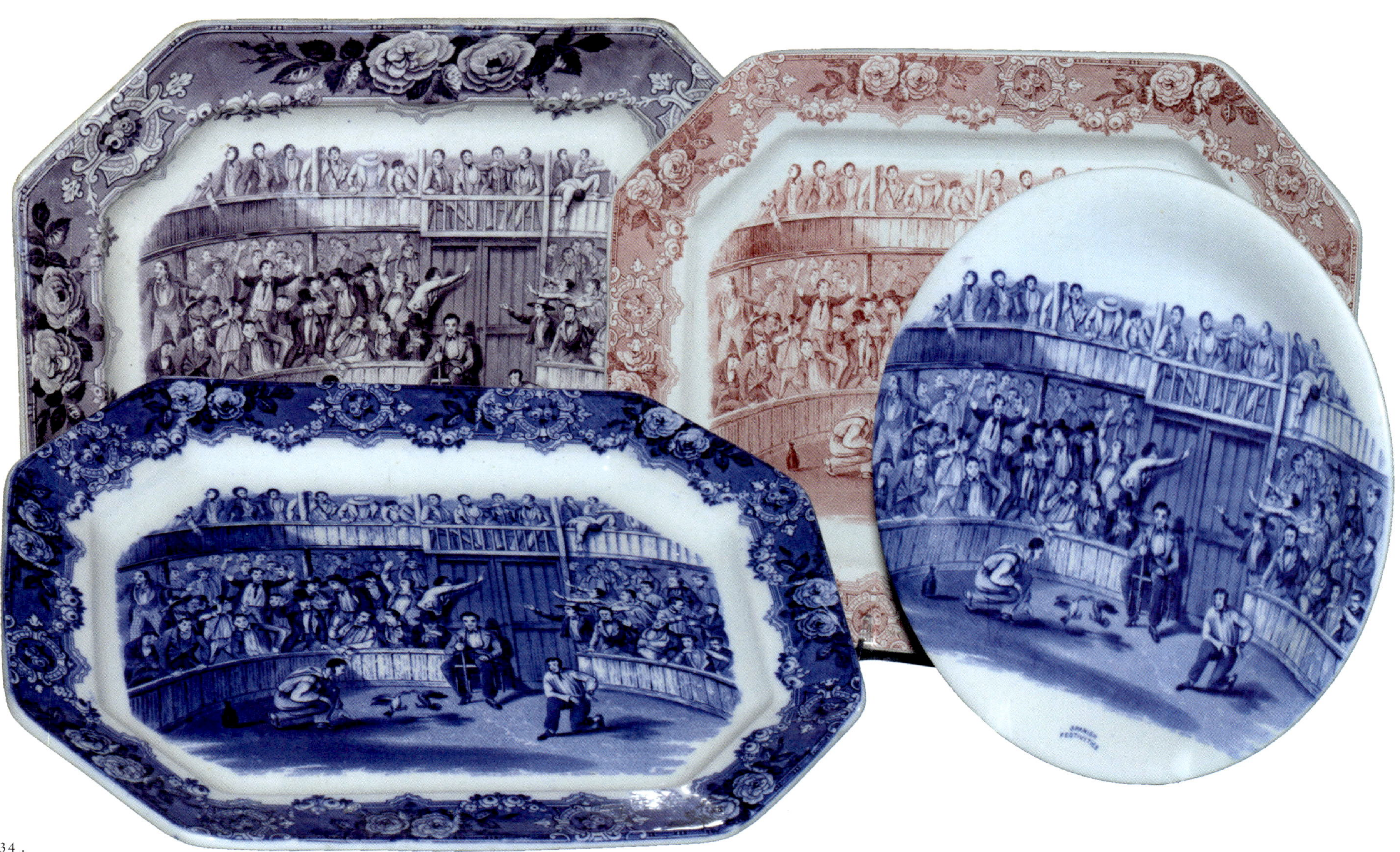

34.

George Jones went on to produce two additional Mialhe images: the iconic *Quitrín* open carriage (issued in four colors, blue, black, red and lilac / purple) (Figs. 35-37) and the King's Day celebration by slaves (Fig. 38).

Altogether, I have so far documented seven views from Mialhe's second 1848 album transferred by George Jones. It would make perfect sense if all seven were originally registered by Adams in 1853, but the Quitrín and King's Day views known to me have appeared only in Jones, not Adams, ware and without the diamond mark dating them in 1853. This is a task which requires further research (and luck) and perhaps these two views bearing the Adams mark will surface some day.

Production continued for the most part of the second half of the 19th century, although the *Zapateado* charger plate is often dated as late as the 1920s and I have been told that the Quitrín model was produced as late as 1905, and other sources say even into the 1950s. I have noticed that, of all of the Cuban views by Jones, it is the Quitrín the one most often found in the United States. Thus, I have assumed it was deliberately sent from England into the US market.

· 35
Frédéric Mialhe. Quitrín carriage. “Spanish Festivities”. George Jones (Staffordshire, UK), 1861-.

· 36
Frédéric Mialhe. Quitrín carriage. “Spanish Festivities”. George Jones (Staffordshire, UK), 1861-.

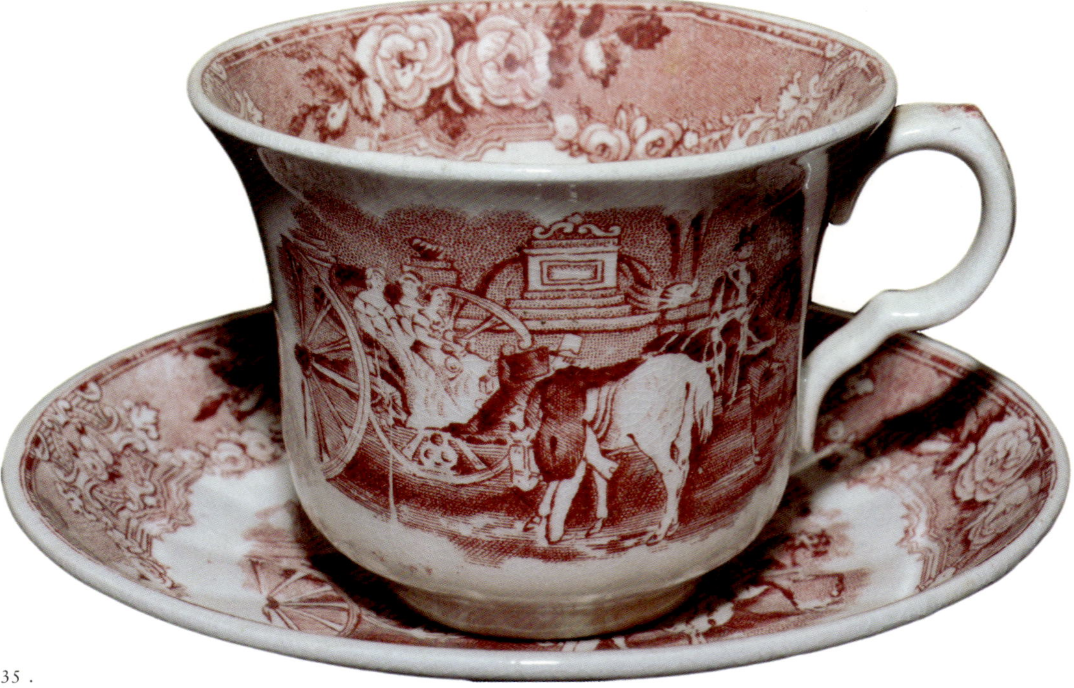

35 .

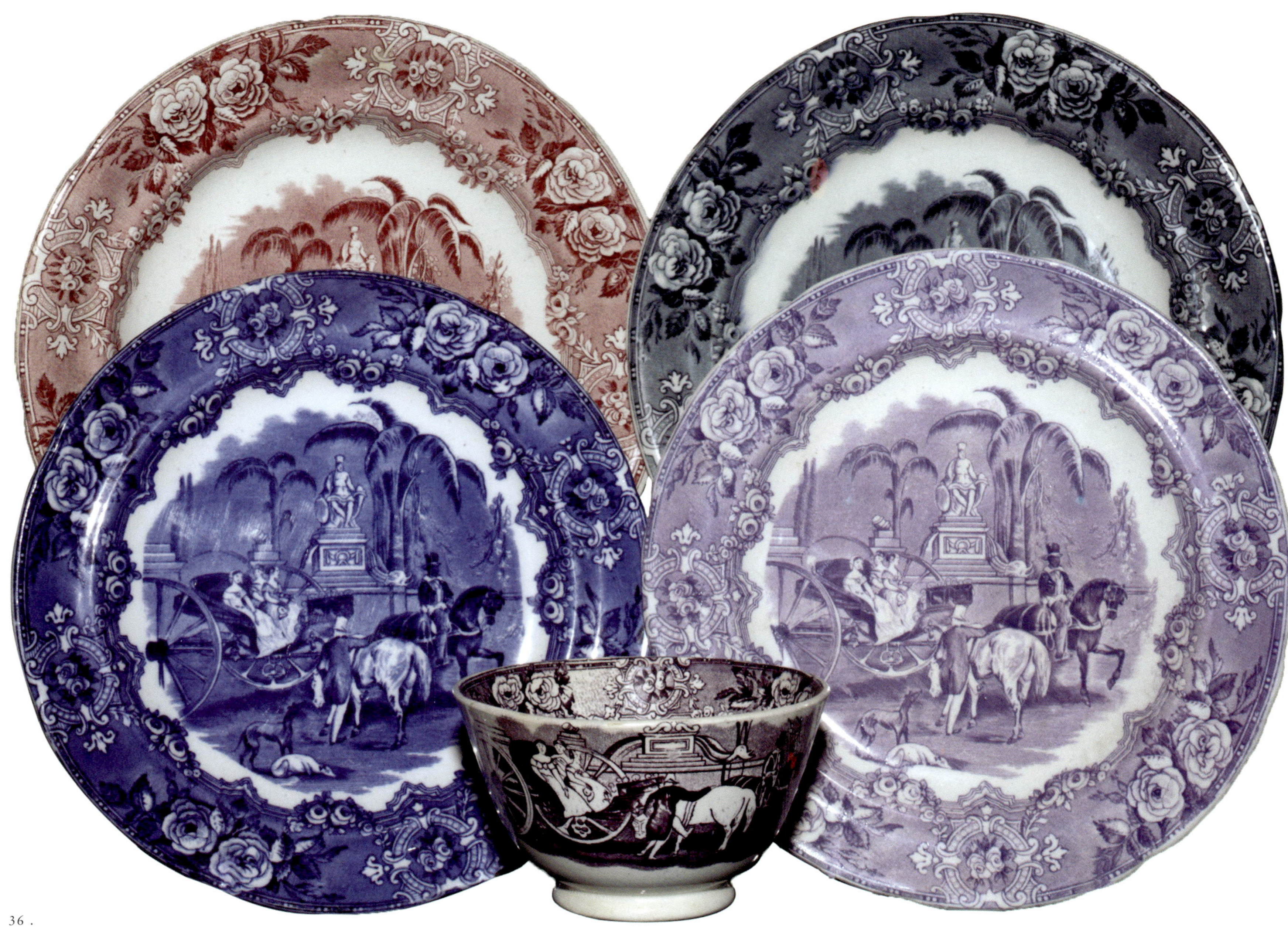

36 .

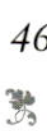

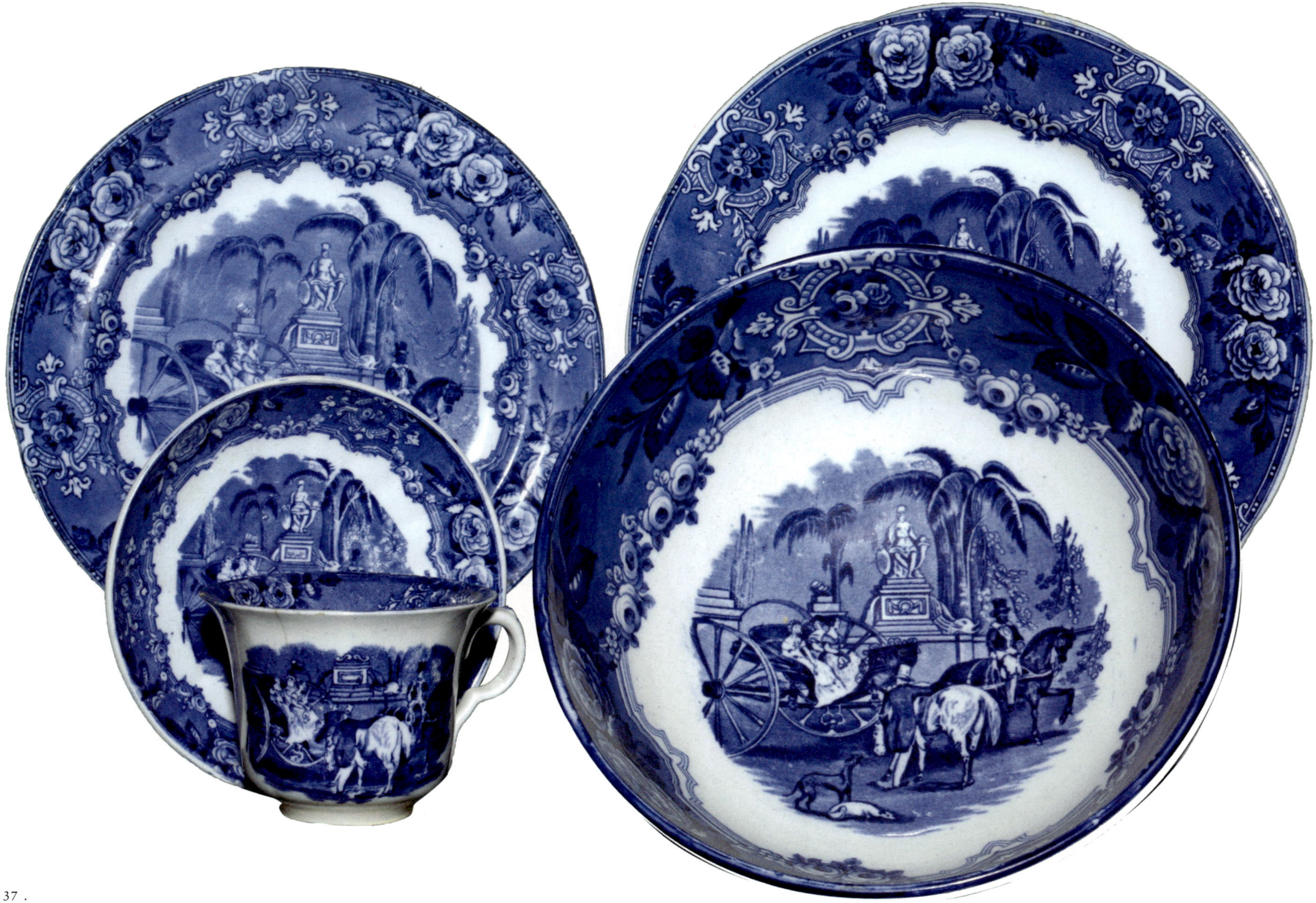

37 .

· 37

Frédéric Mialhe. Quitrín carriage. "Spanish Festivities". George Jones (Staffordshire, UK), 1861-1950?

· 38

Frédéric Mialhe. King's Day feast. "Spanish Festivities". George Jones (Staffordshire, UK), 1861-1912?

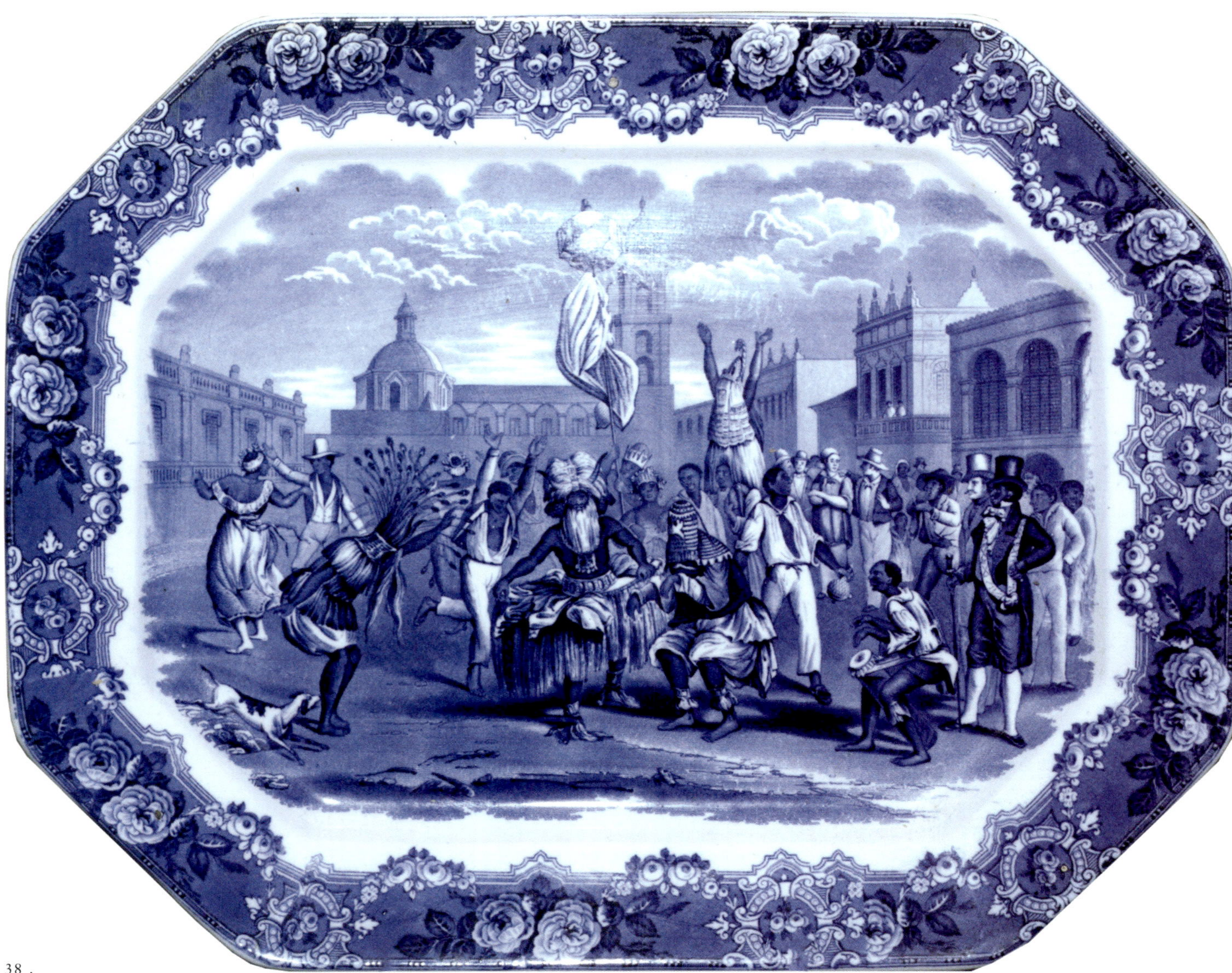

38 .

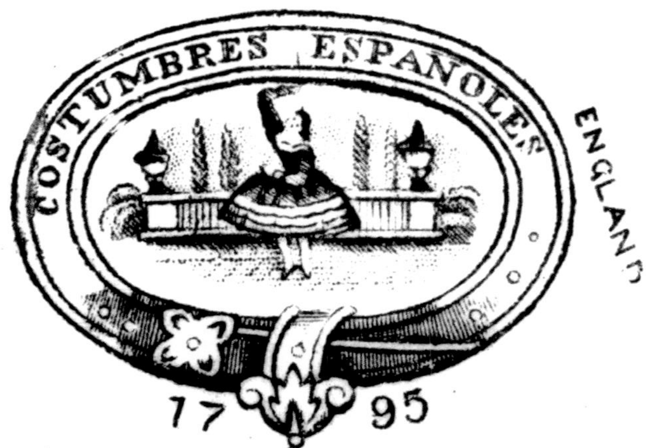

· 39
Frédéric Mialhe. The Quitrín carriage. "Costumbres españoles". George Jones (Staffordshire, UK) 1890-1912.

· 40
Frédéric Mialhe. The zapateado dance. "Costumbres españoles". George Jones (Staffordshire, UK) 1890-1912.

For reasons I cannot explain, between 1891 and the 1910s, George Jones marketed at least a couple of Mialhe genre views (any others?), notably the *Quitrín* (Fig. 39) and the *zapateado* (Fig. 40) under the trade name "costumbres españoles" ("Spanish customs", misspelled), close enough, but not quite the original "Spanish Festivities". Jones also added a new, quite different border. What prompted the Jones factory to switch trade names while continuing to produce the same views under the original name? Did they intend to sell these wares in the Spanish market? (a different image forming part of the same pattern shows a bull fight, a scene not taken from any Cuban print I have seen).

Another puzzle which remains in the agenda for further research is the Jones "Indian Traffic" pattern. Cluett's scholarly book on Jones ceramics, presents this pattern, dated ca. 1912, depicting Mialhe's poultry seller surrounded by a new, different border. Considering that pattern names must remain constant in order for customers to order replacements when the pieces break or are lost, why would Jones have produced this new set?[23]

After much thought, I am inclined to consider the possibility that it was a mistake by the author of the book. Both A. Coyish[24] and Petra Williams[25] have indicated that Dutch Regout views (to be discussed later) bear such resemblance to British wares that they are often confused with them. Indeed, there is a Dutch "Indian Trafic" (only one f) pattern with Mialhe's poultry seller and it is fairly easy to confuse the Dutch for the English model. I should add that, other than in the Cluett book, I have never seen a reference to an English "Indian Traffic" pattern nor have I ever seen an example thereof.

---

23. Robert Cluett, *George Jones ceramics*. Atglen, Pa., Schiffer Publishing, 1998, Fig. 222, p. 95.

24. Coyish, *op, cit.*, p. 298.

25. Petra Williams, *op. cit.*, pp. 486-505.

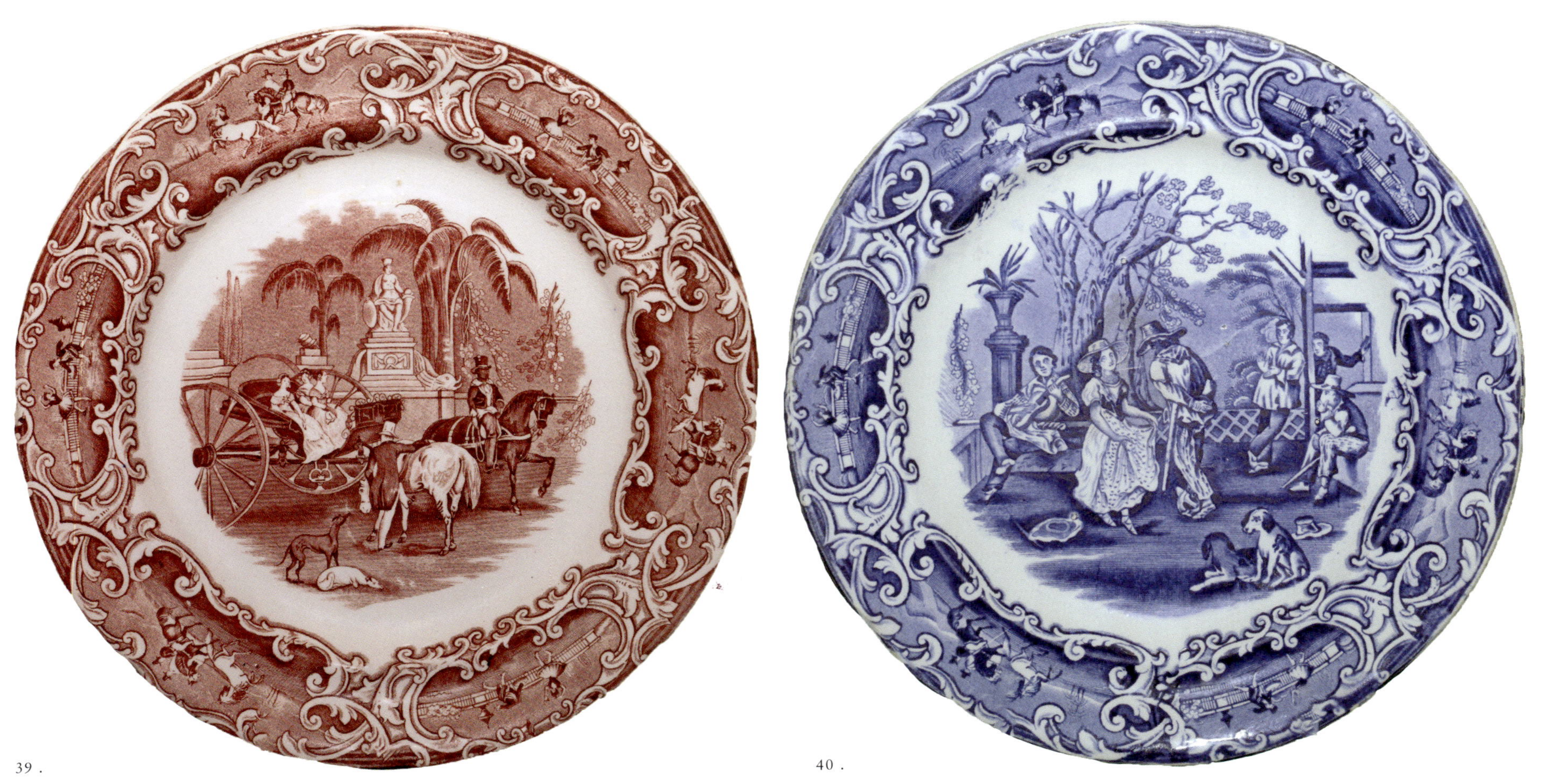

39.

40.

It should also be pointed out that, while most of these Jones pieces belong on top of the dining table at meal time, a few items are a bit more unusual. Mialhe's *zapateado* dance pattern, for example, showed up in also in soap holders (Fig. 41-43). Furthermore, his view of the bread seller in front of Christ Church in Havana ended up in a chamber pot. I had to travel all the way to a small English town to pick it up (the seller was afraid it would break and would not ship), but it certainly was worth it.

One final word on George Jones. On October 18, 1873 he registered a "Cuba" mark, but not with a Cuban view but with a very intricate, irregular design very much in line with the tenets of the so-called Aesthetic Movement.[26] Because this pattern does not display an image of Cuba, but merely its name, it will be discussed in the Section "Cuba sells", below (Fig. 260).

41.

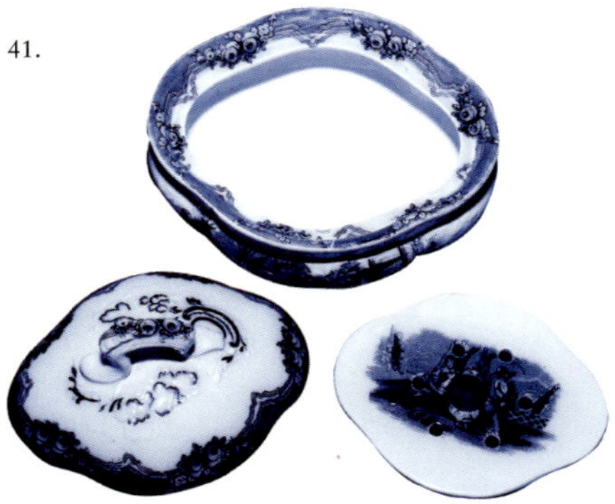

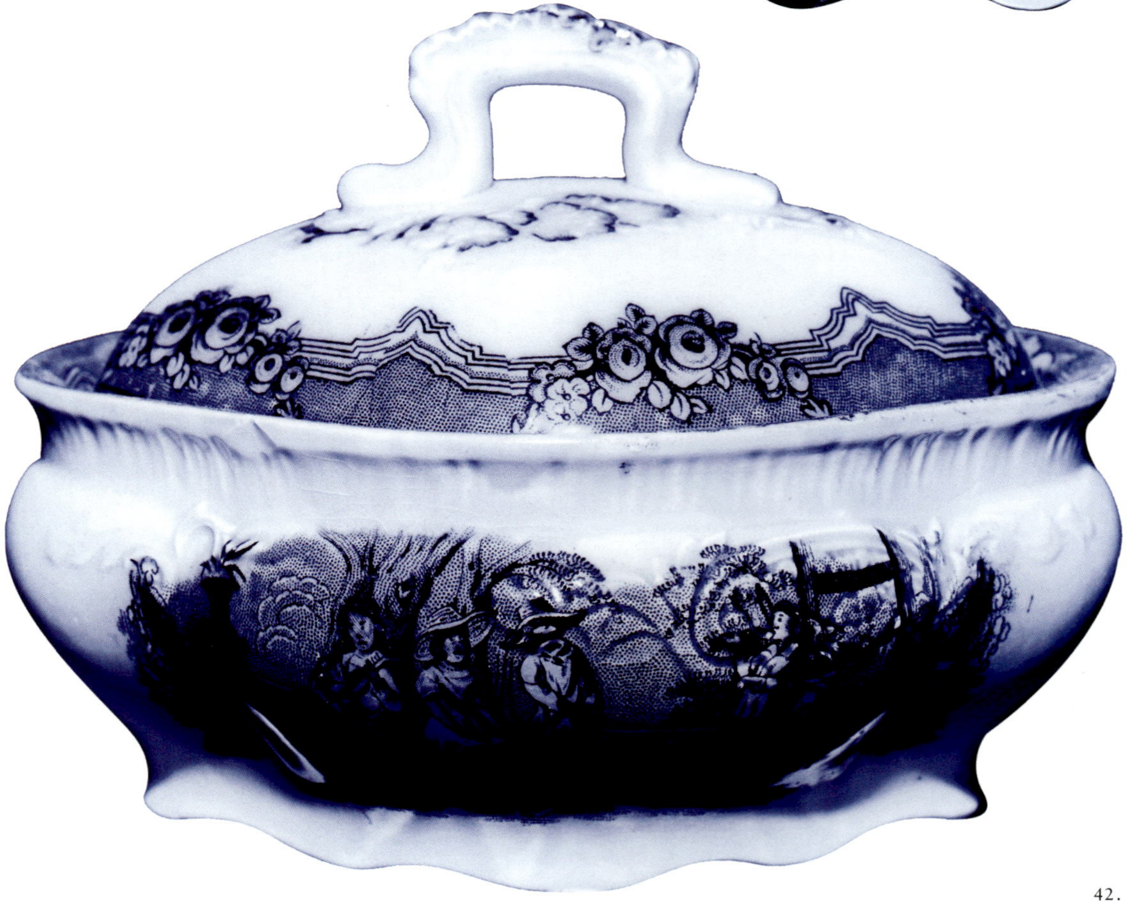

42.

26. See Eric Bradley, "Ceramic decorative art of the Aesthetic Movement". *Antique Trader*, January 19, 2012. Viewed online.

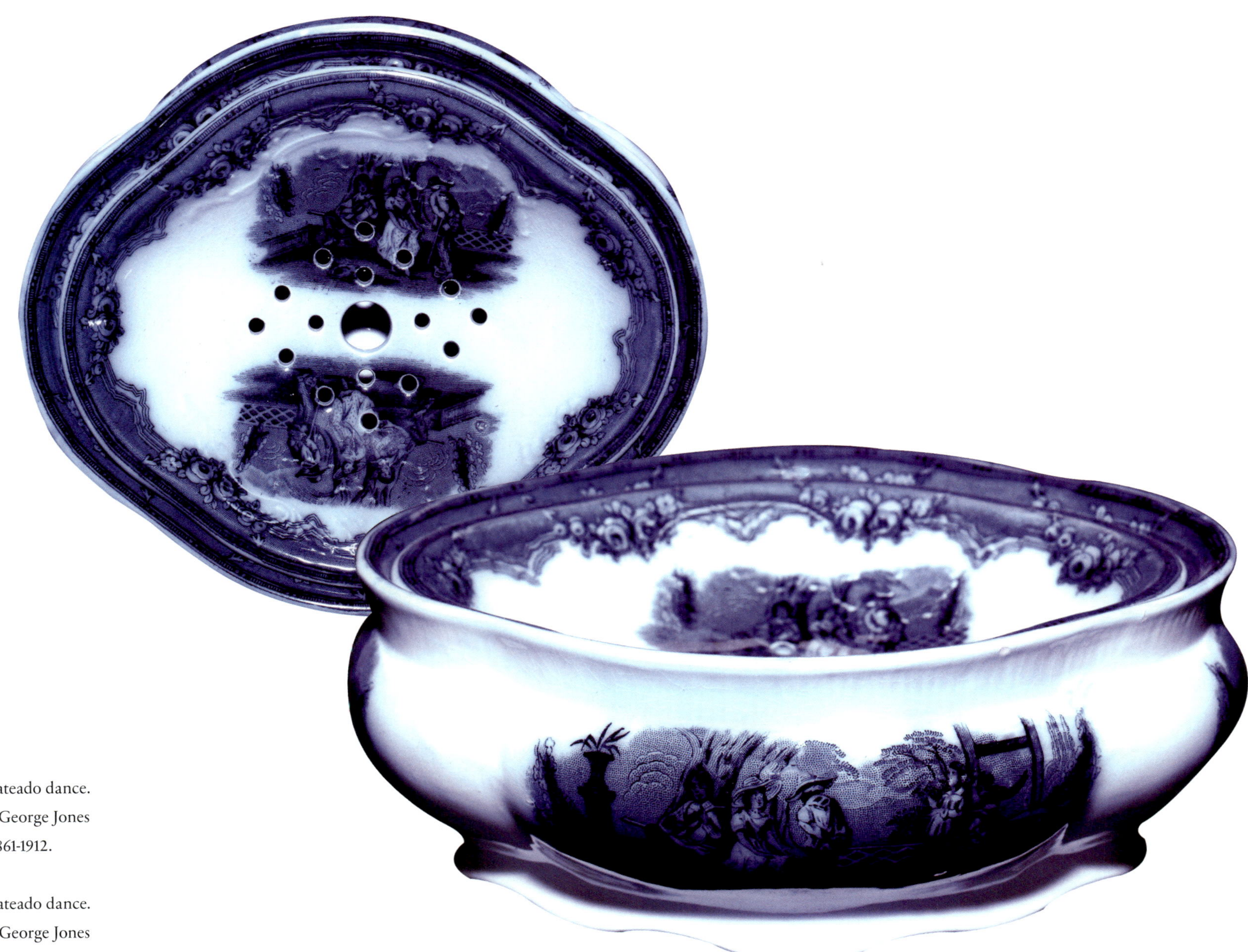

· 41-42
Frédéric Mialhe. Zapateado dance. "Spanish Festivities". George Jones (Staffordshire, UK), 1861-1912.

· 43
Frédéric Mialhe. Zapateado dance. "Spanish Festivities". George Jones (Staffordshire, UK), 1861-1912.

43.

Ridgway, part II. During the early part of the 20th century another English Ridgway factory (the stamped mark looks like a torch or a bird) produced a very different set of Cuban views (Cathedral, Morro Castle, palm trees) for a tea set. They were made in three attractive and unusual, metallic colors: amber (Fig. 44), yellowish green (Fig. 45) and faded white and green.

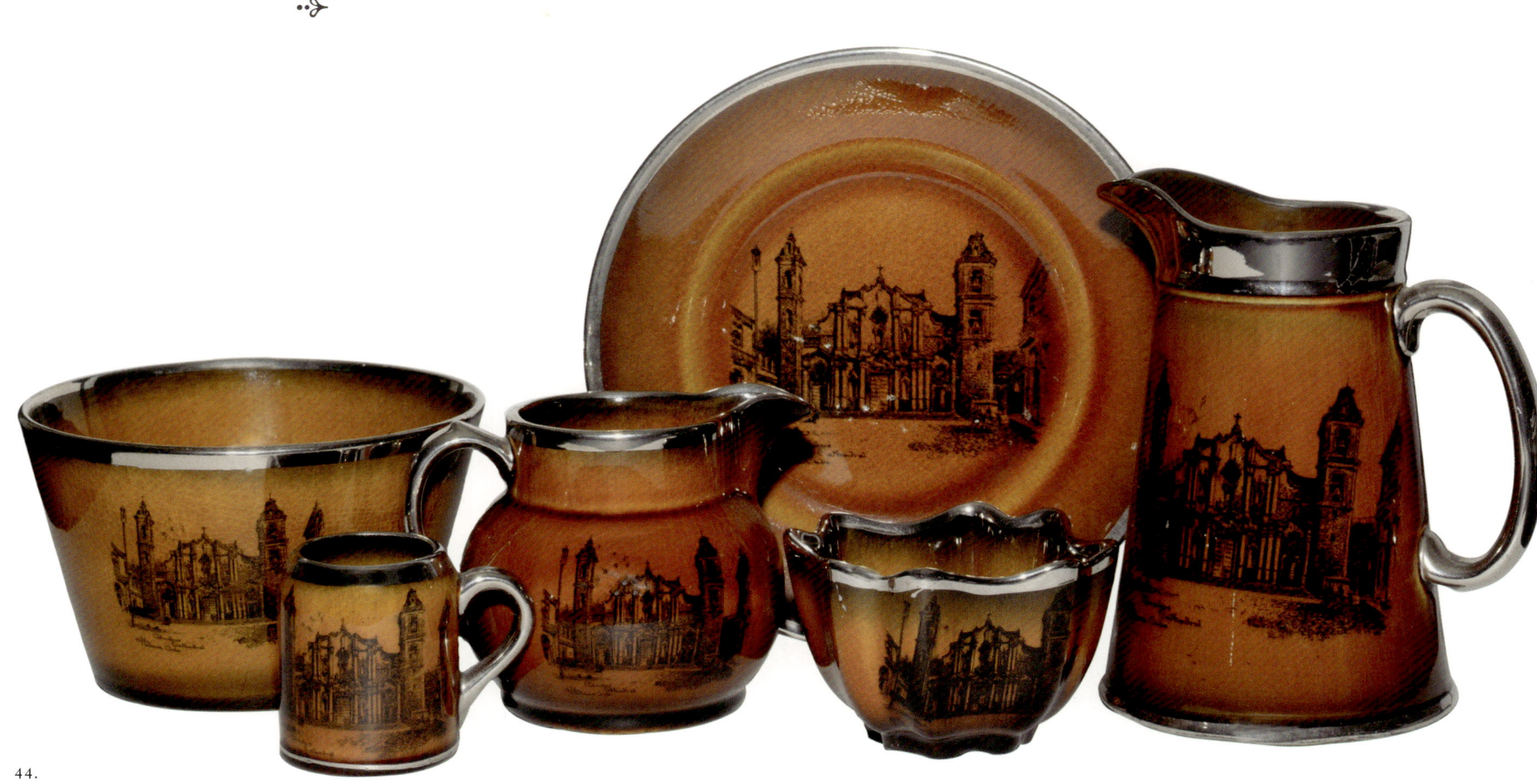

44.

· 44
Morro Castle, Havana Cathedral, palm trees. Ridgway (Staffordshire, UK), 1920s.

· 45
Morro Castle, Havana Cathedral, palm trees. Ridgway (Staffordshire, UK), 1920s.

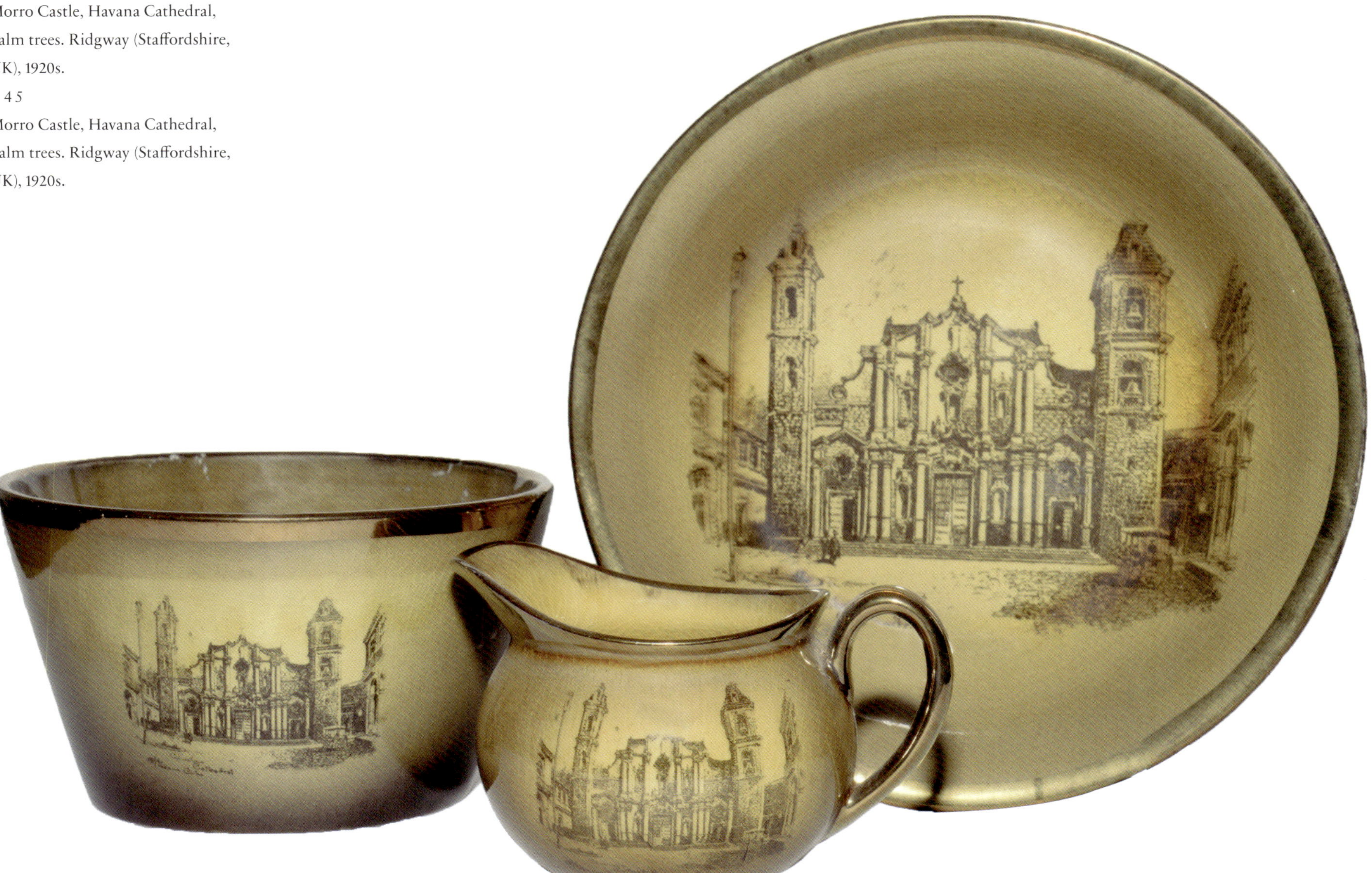

45.

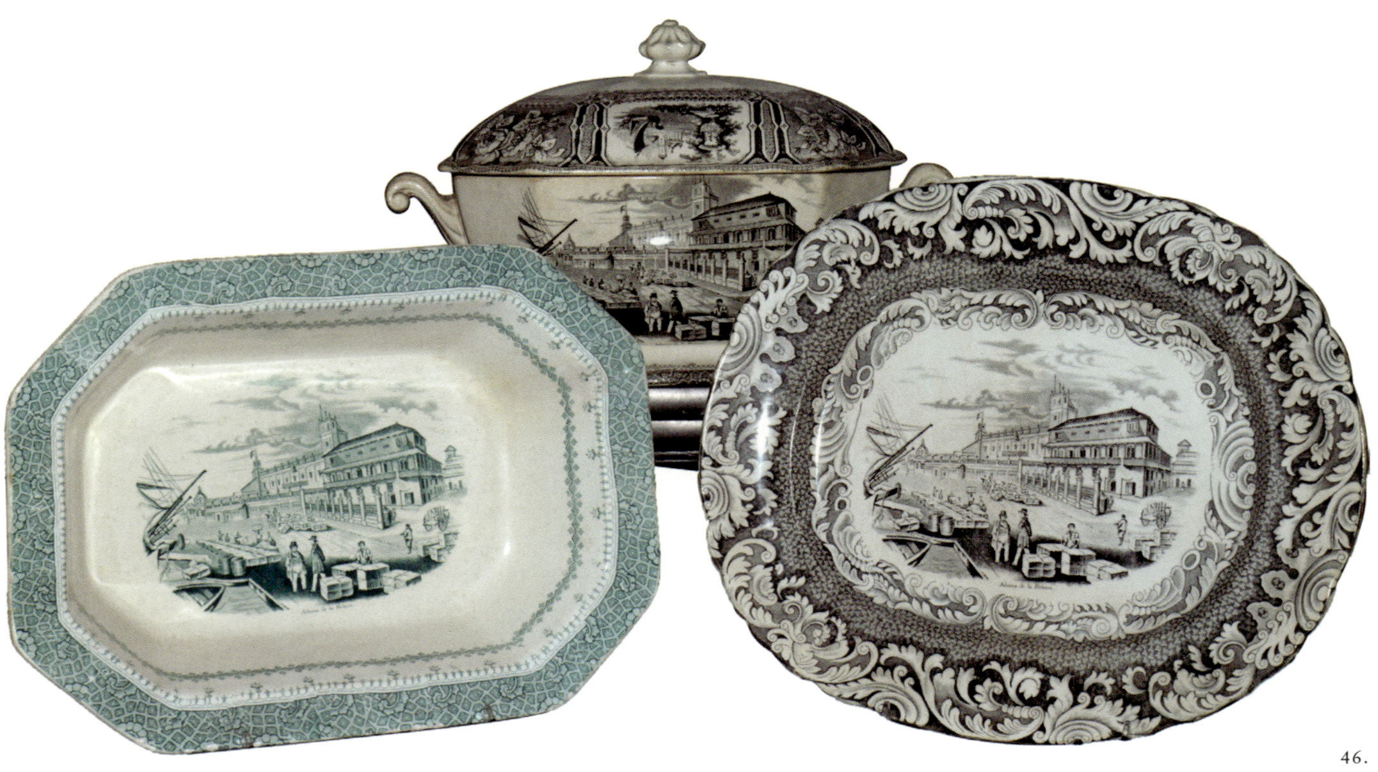

46.

· 46
Frédéric Mialhe. Custom House. Sargadelos (Galicia, Spain), 1845-1862.

· 47
Frédéric Mialhe. Indian Fountain. Sargadelos (Galicia, Spain), 1845-1862.

Spain[27]

During the 1840s, in the region of Sargadelos, Galicia, in the Northern part of Spain, the second Marquis of Sargadelos also made the decision to transfer Cuban views into ceramics.[28] The first piece I ever saw, a desktop ink and pen set, was in a Madrid museum several decades ago. As I began to research the subject, I made trips to various cities in Spain, where I could admire the collections in the Museums of Lugo and Oviedo, among other institutions. I have also had many conversations with Spanish antique dealers and curators throughout the last thirty five years.

In order to produce better quality wares, the Marquis of Sargadelos requested technical assistance from more advanced English potters and, during the period 1845-1862 (the so-called "third period" of the factory), they turned out twelve Cuban views from thirteen original prints (one ceramic piece combined two separate images). Four of them were copied from Mialhe's first set of views (*Isla de Cuba Pintoresca* album) printed during 1839-1841: The Custom House (Fig. 46), Indian fountain statue (Fig. 47), Carnicería bridge (Fig. 48), and Tacón theater (Fig. 49).

47.

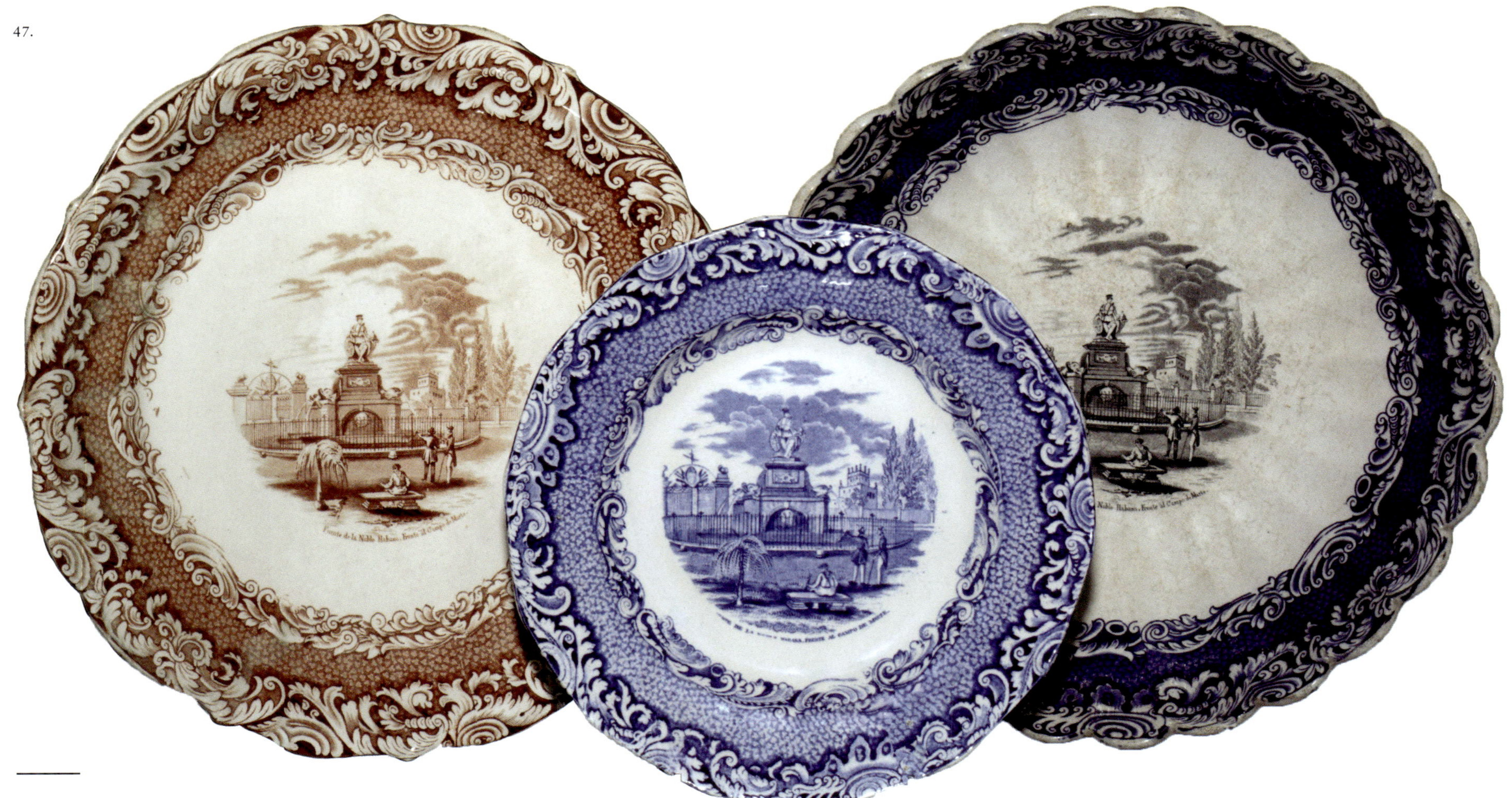

---

[27] On Sargadelos ceramics, see Felipe Bello Piñeiro, José Filgueira Valverde, Antonio Meijide Pardo, Juan Olives Orrit, María Quiroga Figueroa, Gaye Blake Roberts, F. J. Sánchez Cantón, Roberto Suárez Menéndez and Eloísa Vilar Checa; On Pickman ware, see *La historia hecha cerámica,* all cited in full in the Bibliography.

[28] The pottery factory had originally been set up by his father, Antonio Raimundo Ibáñez (1749-1809).

· 48

Frédéric Mialhe.

Carnicería Bridge in Matanzas.

Sargadelos (Galicia, Spain), 1845-1862.

· 49

Frédéric Mialhe. Tacón Theater.

Sargadelos (Galicia, Spain), 1845-1862.

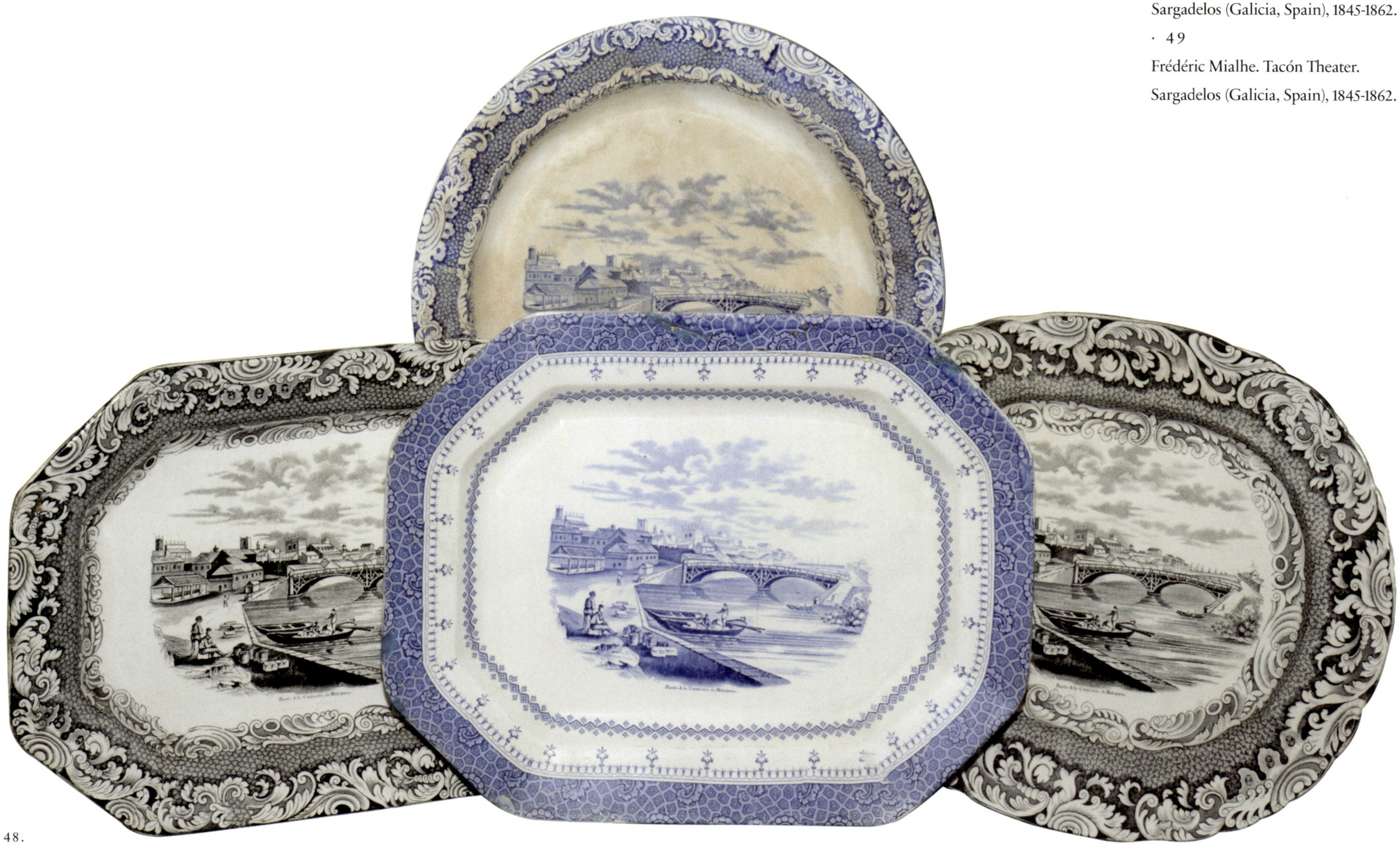

48.

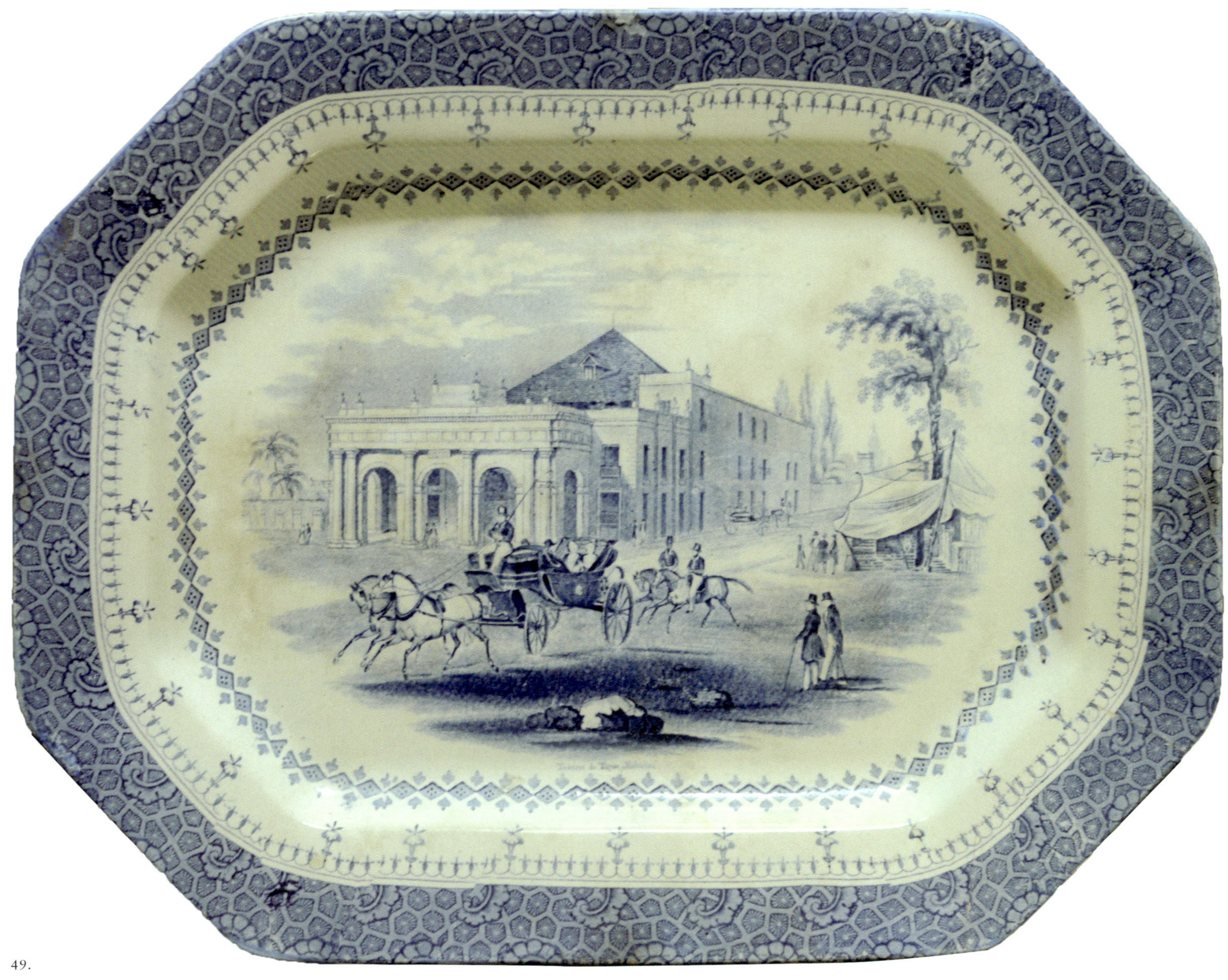

49.

The remaining nine views came from the *Paseo Pintoresco de la Isla de Cuba*, printed in Havana in 1841-42 by the Spanish lithographers Fernando Costa and Laureano Cuevas.[29] The list of these *Paseo* views follow:

1. *Casa de parada en el sitio de los almacenes del camino de hierro*, facing p. 12 (Fig. 50).
2. *Castillo del Morro de la Habana*, facing p. 2 and *Entrada del Vapor Almendares en el muelle de La Habana*, facing p. 42, combining two separate views into one composite image (Fig. 51).
3. *Comandancia General de Marina de La Habana*, facing p. 219 (Fig. 52).
4. *Camino de Hierro en la Aguada del Cura*, facing p. 55 (Fig. 53).
5. *Cementerio General. Habana*, facing p. 99 (Fig. 54).
6. *El Tivoli. Habana*, facing p. 49 (Fig. 55).
7. *Iglesia y Hospital de San Francisco de Paula. Habana*, facing p. 6 (Fig. 56).
8. *Fuente de la India en el Paseo Nuevo*, facing p. 139 (Fig. 57).

---

[29] See Emilio Cueto, "Las láminas del Paseo Pintoresco por la Isla de Cuba". *Paseo pintoresco por la Isla de Cuba*. Miami, Fla., Ediciones Universal, 1999, pp. XIII-XLII.

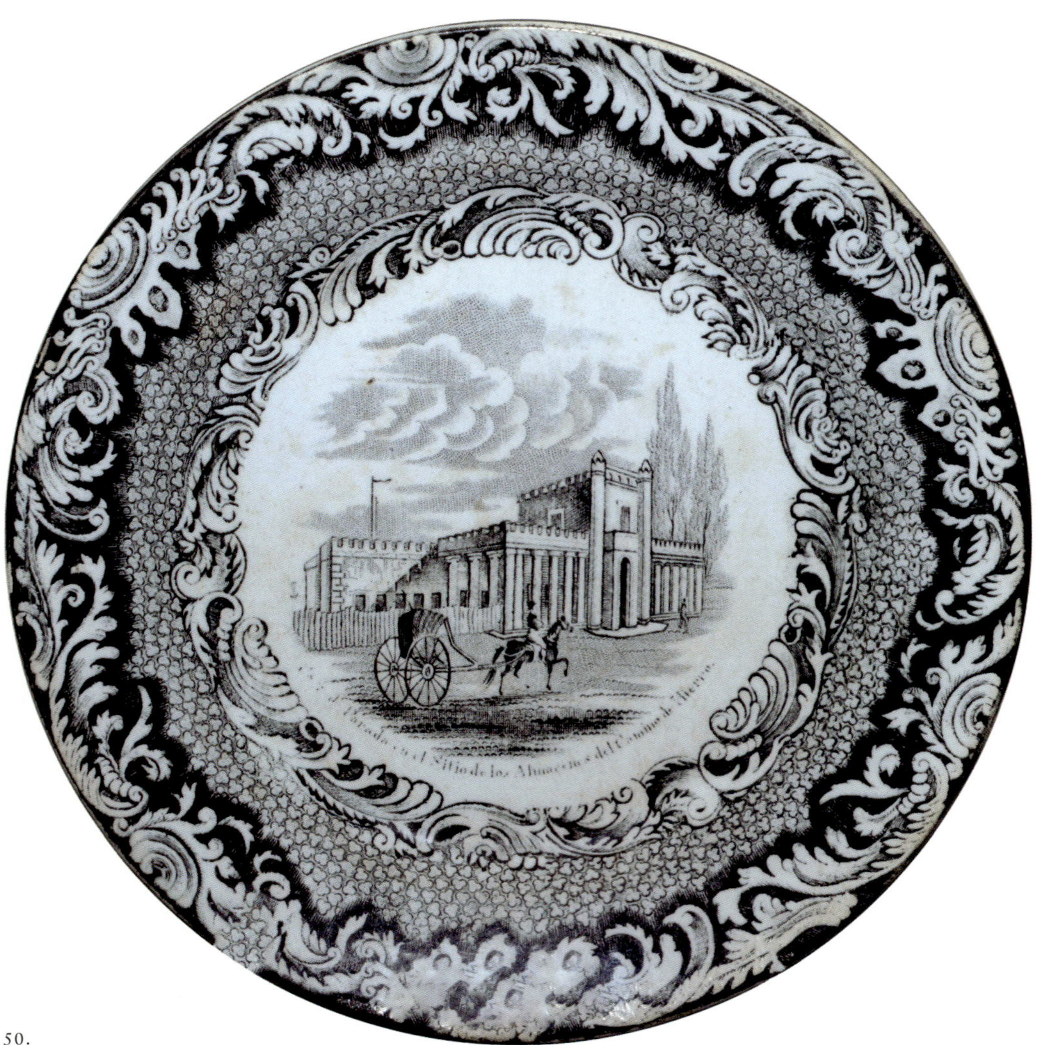

50.

· 50
Fernando Costa. Main Havana Railroad station. Sargadelos (Galicia, Spain), 1845-1862.
· 51
Fernando Costa. Almendares steamer passing Morro castle. Sargadelos (Galicia, Spain), 1845-1862.

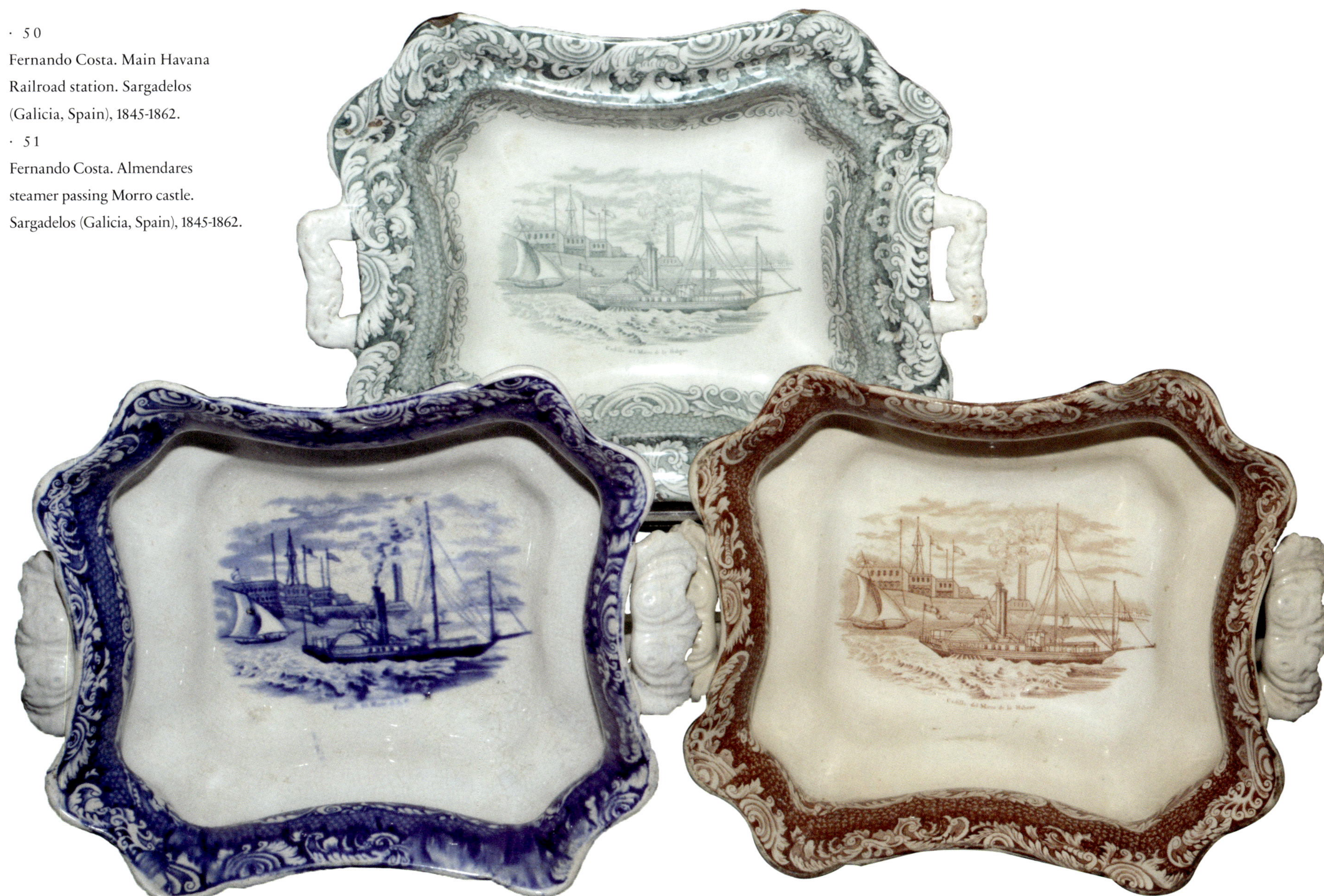

51.

· 52
Fernando Costa.
Navy headquarters.
Sargadelos (Galicia, Spain),
1845-1862.

· 53
Fernando Costa.
Railroad stop at Aguada.
Sargadelos (Galicia, Spain),
1845-1862.

· 54
Fernando Costa. Cemetery.
Sargadelos (Galicia, Spain),
1845-1862.

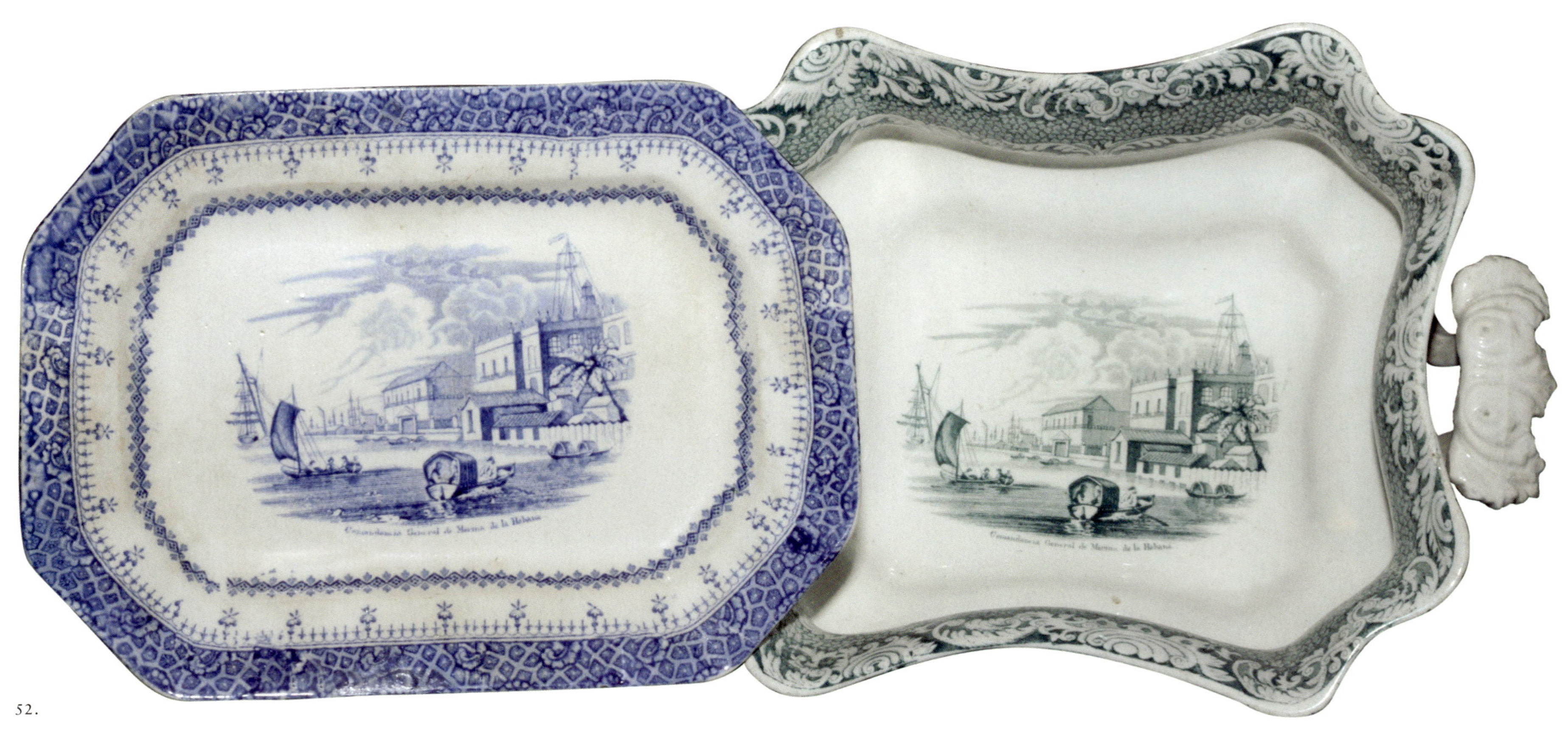

52.

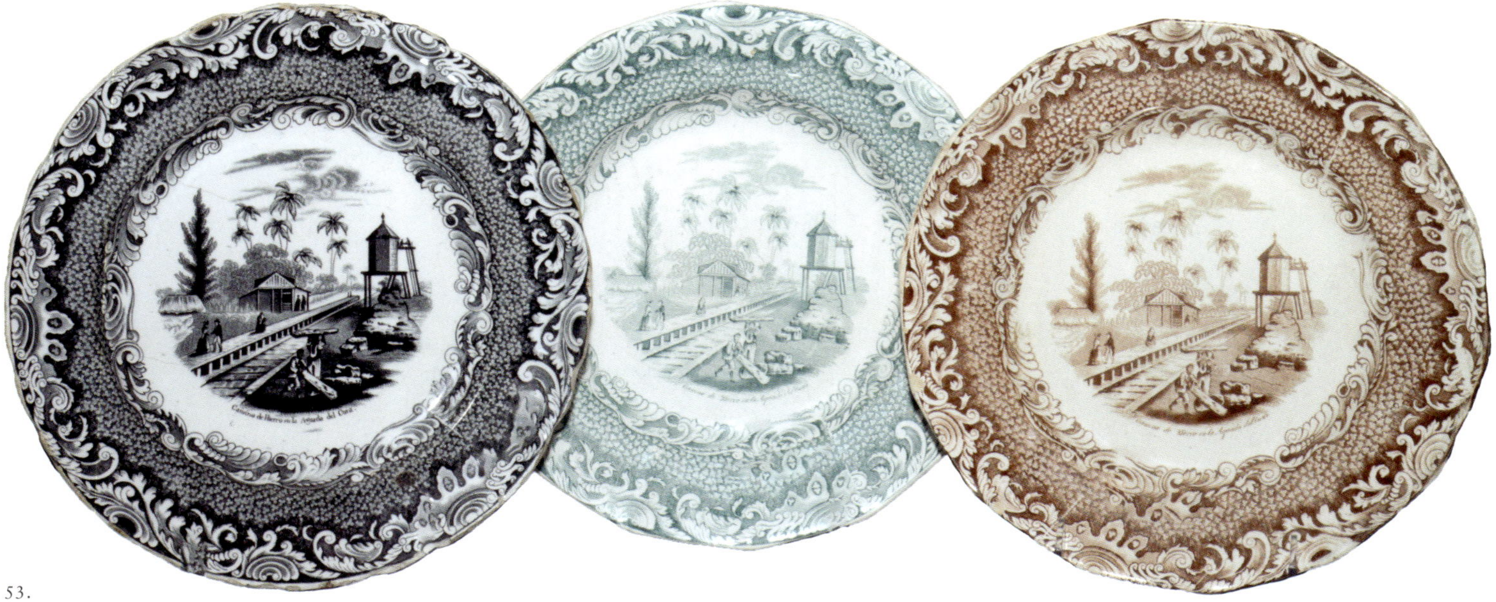

53.

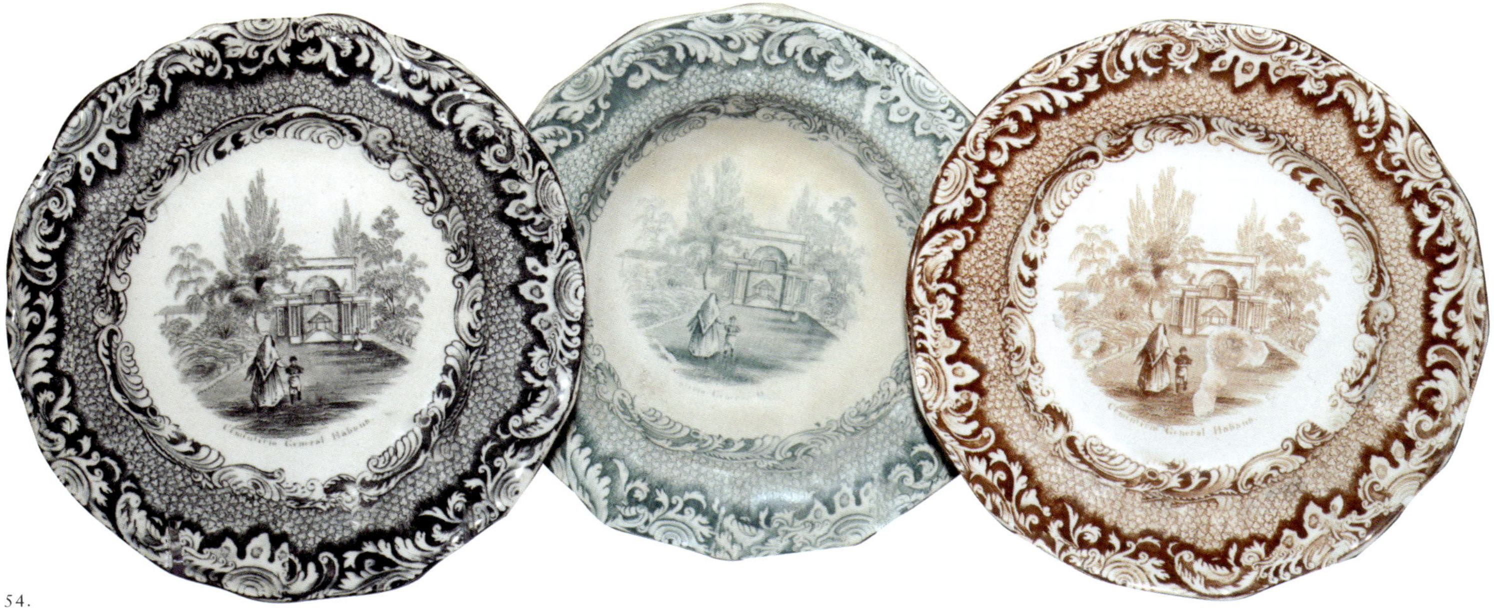

54.

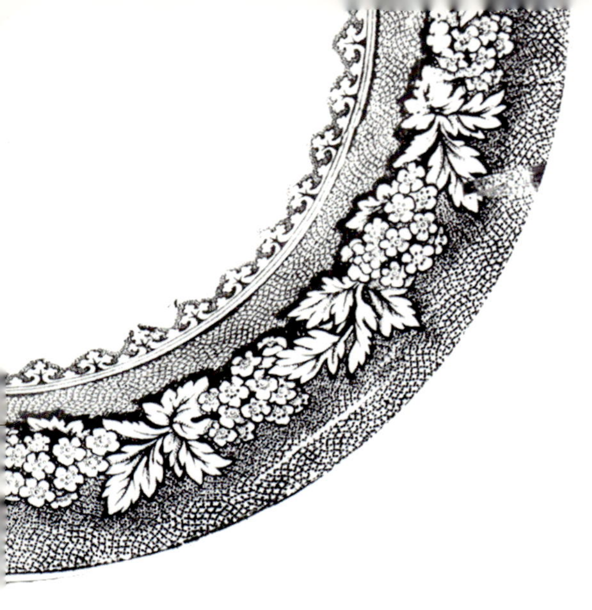

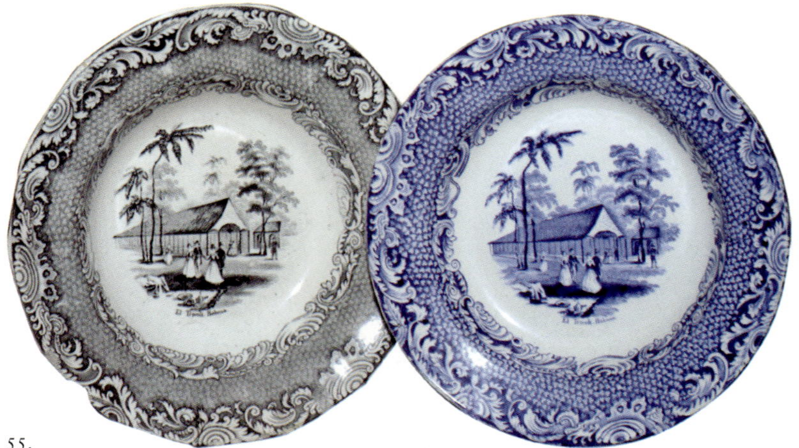

55.

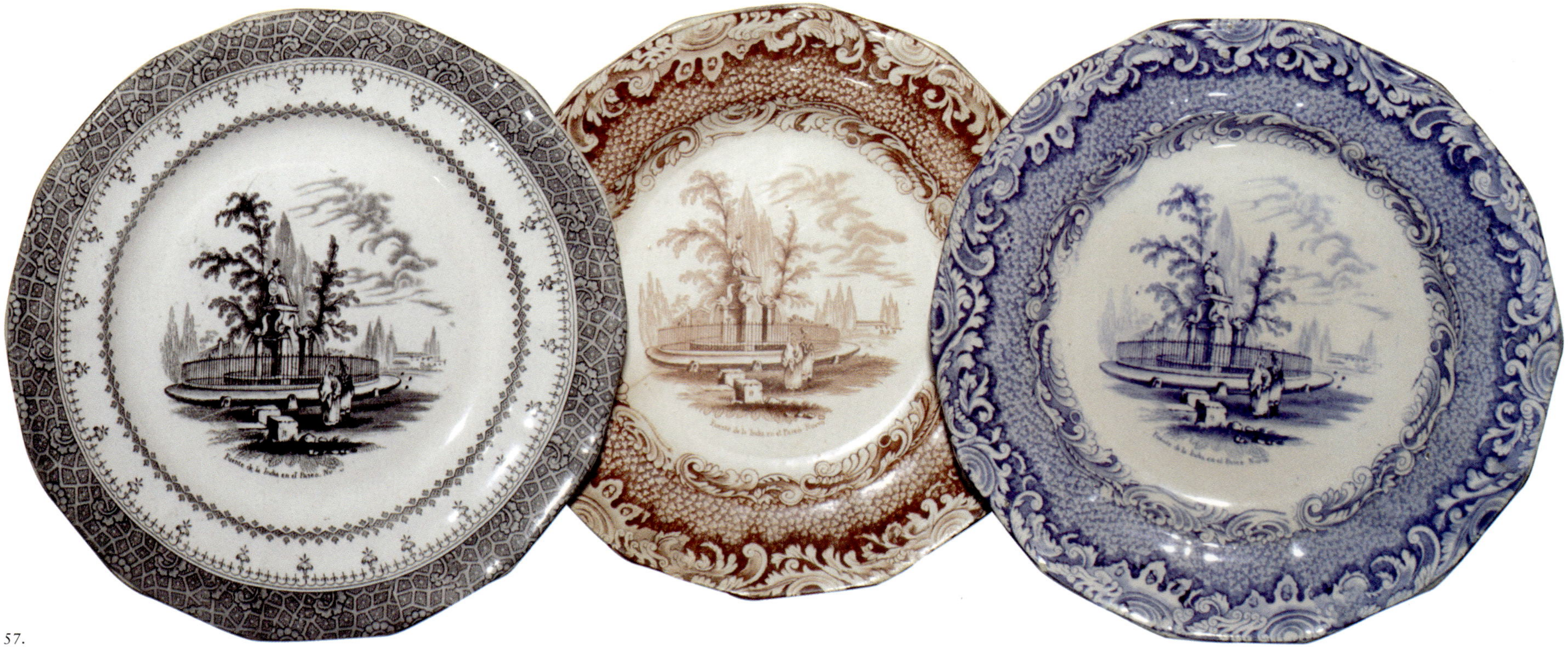

57.

Four of these images continue to puzzle me, two from Mialhe (Carnicería bridge, Fig. 58) and Tacón theater, Fig. 59), and two from Costa (Tivoli and San Francisco church).[30] They appear both in Sargadelos and in Staffordshire dinnerware, the only items to show up both in Spain and in England. Unfortunately, I have been unable to determine conclusively who copied whom.

I had originally assumed that the Sargadelos views were initially transferred onto ceramics in Spain, believing that Spain, being Cuba's *madre patria* (mother country), had obtained the lithographs directly from the island. But the discovery of these four matching pieces has added complexity and confusion to the subject.

My working hypothesis now is that, at least for the Mialhe views, the images came from England to Spain and not vice versa. This, for two reasons. The Enoch Wood borders for the two Tacón theater views (Figs. 15, 58) were copied exactly by the Sargadelos potters (Figs. 16-58). If they copied the border, they certainly had ample opportunity to copy the image also.[31] Furthermore, the English Carnicería bridge platter I own was found in Spain, not England. In fact, while many English plates are often found in Spanish museums and antique markets, I have yet to see a Galician plate in England.

30. I have seen the English matching pieces only in internet, have not been able to examine the pieces for marks or other clues and do not know their whereabouts.

31. Filgueiro Valverde has told us that, originally, many patterns used at Sargadelos were brought from England (*"Inicialmente muchos trabajos fuero traidos de Inglaterra"*), *op. cit.*, p. 21.

· 55

Fernando Costa. Tivoli. Sargadelos (Galicia, Spain), 1845-1862.

· 56

Fernando Costa. San Francisco Hospital. Sargadelos (Galicia, Spain), 1845-1862.

· 57

Fernando Costa. Indian Fountain Statue. Sargadelos (Galicia, Spain), 1845-1862.

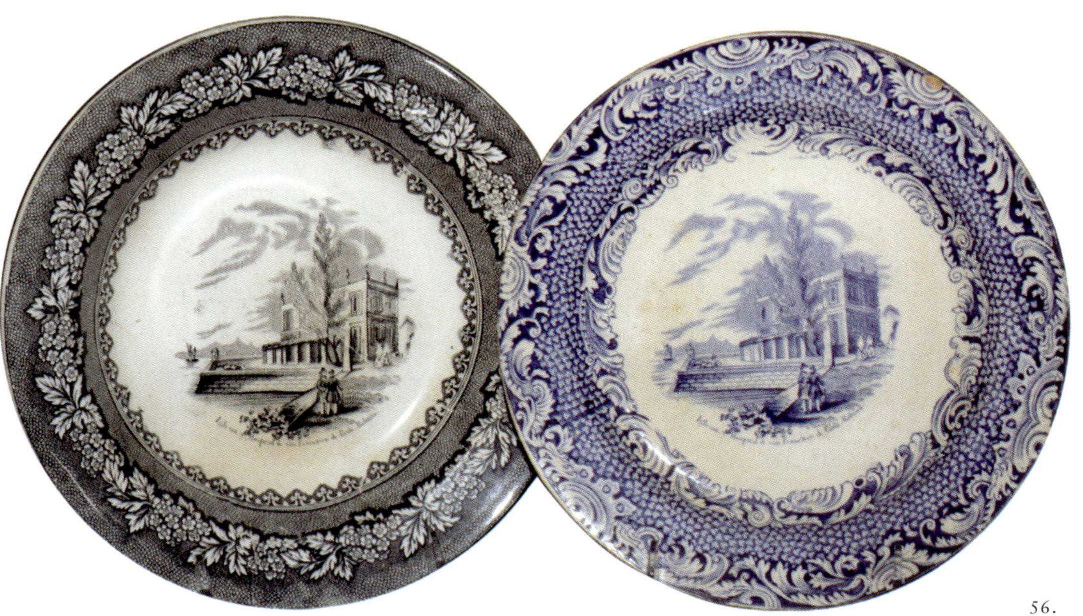

56.

With respect to Costa's Tivoli and San Francisco views, it is harder to make any conclusions since I have not physically examined the English pieces, nor have I been able to match their unique border with any particular Staffordshire potter. I do know, however, that the Paula view by Costa made it into the Habana pattern by Adams in 1845 discussed earlier (Fig. 20), so perhaps the English did get a hold of the Costa set of views first. Needless to say, I could be wrong. Perhaps in the future other researchers with access to commercial correspondence and other information will be able to conclusively solve the riddle.

The Carnicería bridge pattern has prompted additional concerns. I have seen one such platter in Philadelphia without a Sargadelos mark on the back. Its owner told me he had purchased it during the 1970s in Cuenca, Spain, and that the seller had suggested it was made at the Pickman factory in Seville.

According to Eloísa Vilar, when the Sargadelos factory disintegrated in 1875, Pickman did acquire some of its moulds and patterns.[32] And my friend's platter indeed bears the anchor mark of Pickman and a notation "porcelana opaca grantizada". In fact, Pickman copied another pattern from Sargadelos: Costa's Morro view. It appears as a small vignette in the border of one of its plates illustrating a Madrid view.[33]

One last note. Sargadelos ware is hard to find and quite expensive when you do locate it. Unlike the English factories, production in Galicia was in a much smaller scale, being mostly for domestic consumption. In fact, except in the home of collectors, I have never found a Sargadelos piece outside of Spain, and, even inside the Peninsula, they are almost always to be found within the small Galician province. During the 1950s interest in collecting these pieces spiked (I have been told that Generalísimo Francisco Franco's wife was an avid collector). Perhaps also the physical and chemical properties of these items made them more fragile (I have noticed they stain easier than others), and fewer have survived.

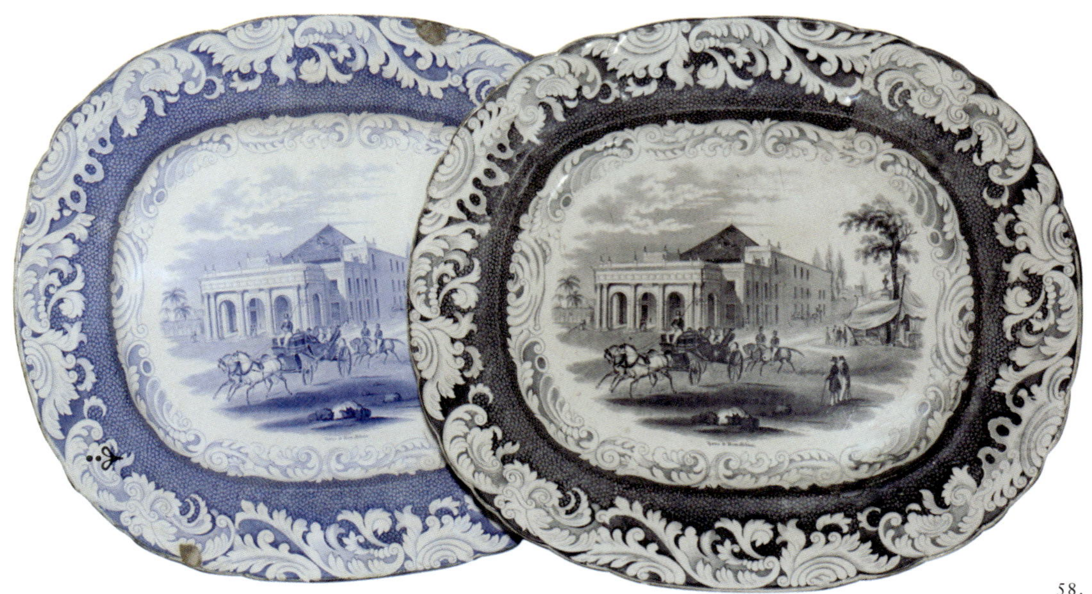

58.

---

[32] Eloísa Vilar Checa, *op. cit.*, p. 145.

[33] See Marcos Buelga. *Vistas de ciudades en la cerámica española del siglo XIX.* Oviedo, Museo de Bellas Artes de Asturias, 2005, figs. no. 41, p. 75 and no. 62, p. 103.

· 58
Frédéric Mialhe. Tacón Theater. Enoch Wood (Staffordshire, UK), 1840s, left and Sargadelos (Galicia, Spain), 1845-1862, right.
· 59
Frédéric Mialhe. Carnicería Bridge in Matanzas. Enoch Wood (Staffordshire, UK), 1840s, left and Sargadelos (Galicia, Spain), 1845-1862, right.

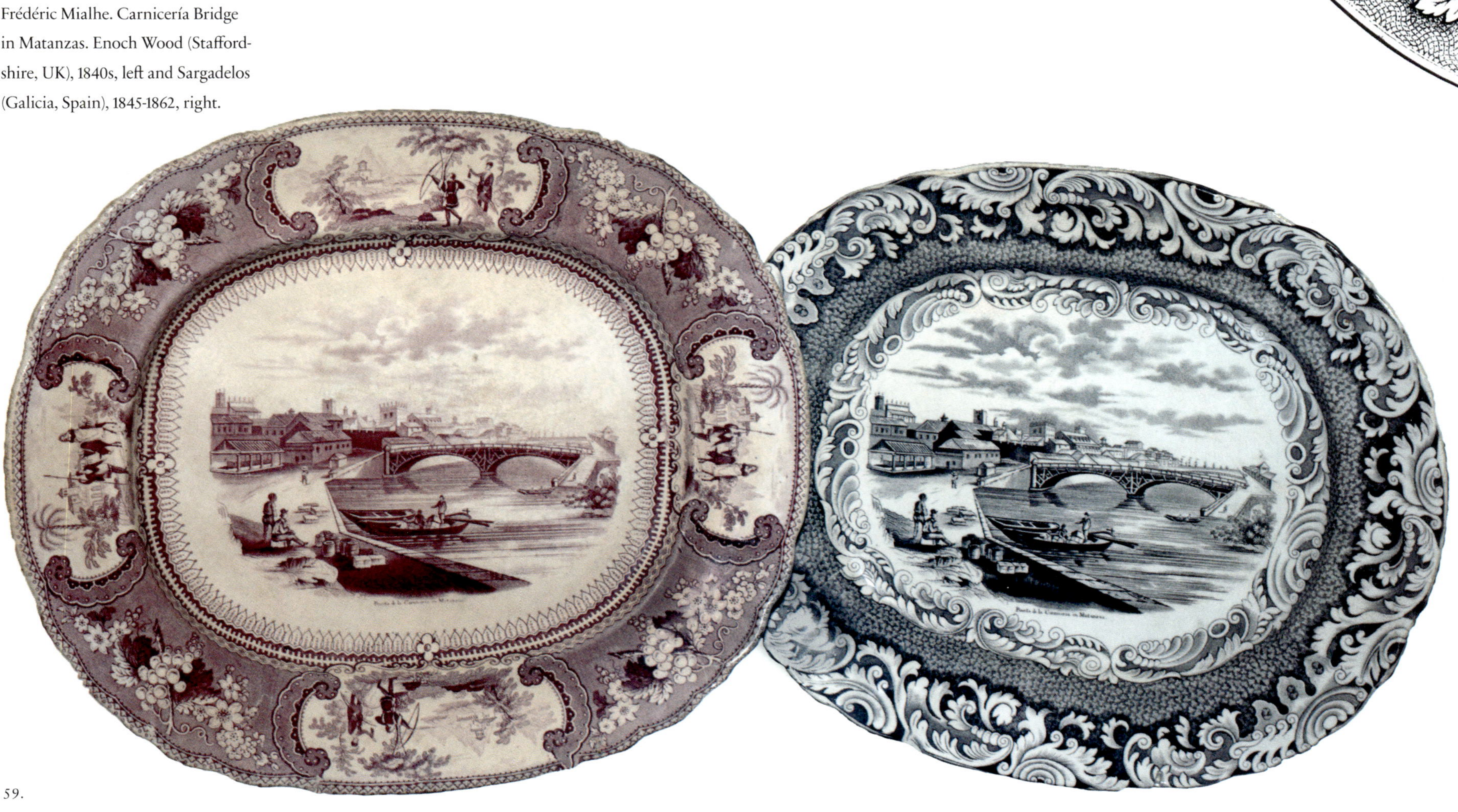

59.

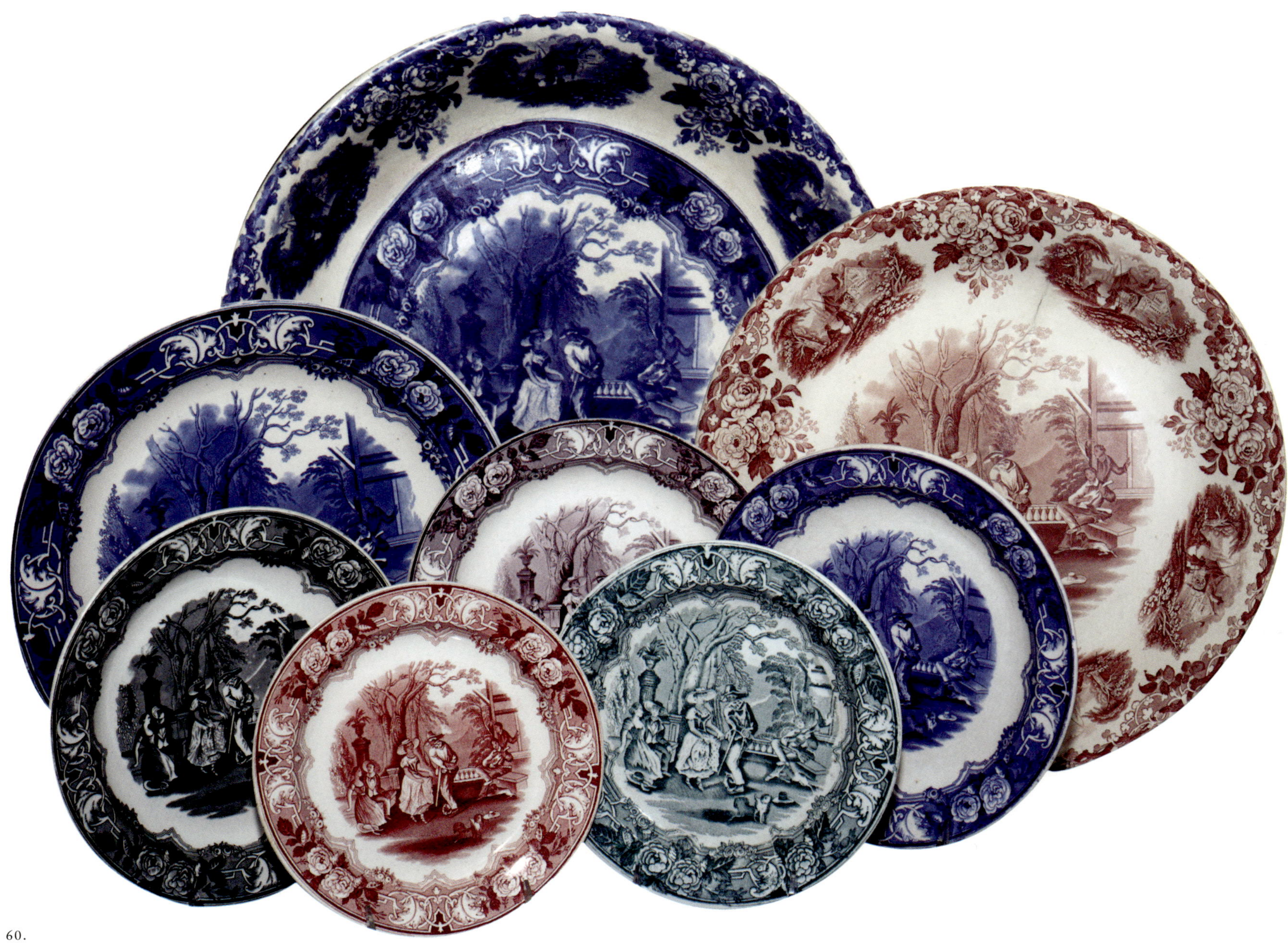

60.

Holland[34]

The Petrus Regout factory, founded in 1836 in Maastricht, Holland, also produced two Cuban views taken from Mialhe's second 1848 album.[35] The zapateado dance image was drawn in England on five occasions, by Th. Toft (1855), E. Pepper (1857), E. Pepper & Son (1874), J. Johnson (1876), and H. Toft (1881). The design was each time transferred in Holland and sold under the pattern name "Dancing" (Figs. 60-61). It is interesting to note that some of the characters in this Dutch zapateado image are positioned differently than in the original Mialhe view and the English ceramic plates of the "Spanish Festivities" family (compare Fig. 61 to Fig. 33).

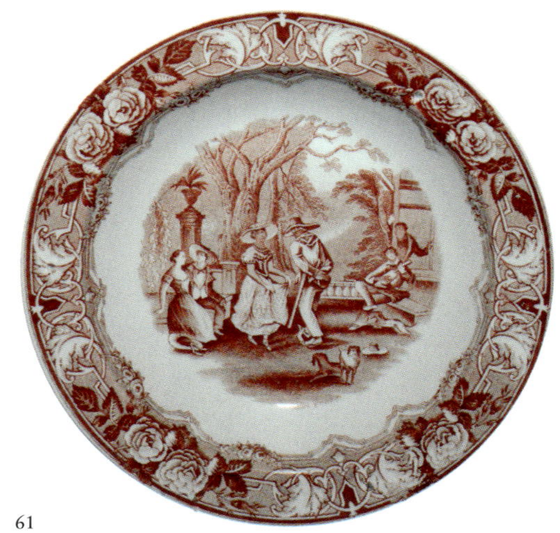

61

---

34. On Maastricht ceramics, see Pieter Beek, F Van Den Berge, Marie-Rose Bogaers, Hans Meulman, Joseph Regout, and J. B. M. Vercauteren, all cited in full in the Bibliography.

35. I discovered my first Regout piece quite by accident in 1983 inside a quaint New York City store named Cheese and Antiques (which, to my surprise, sold both!). Subsequently, I travelled to Holland and began to make contacts with various antique dealers.

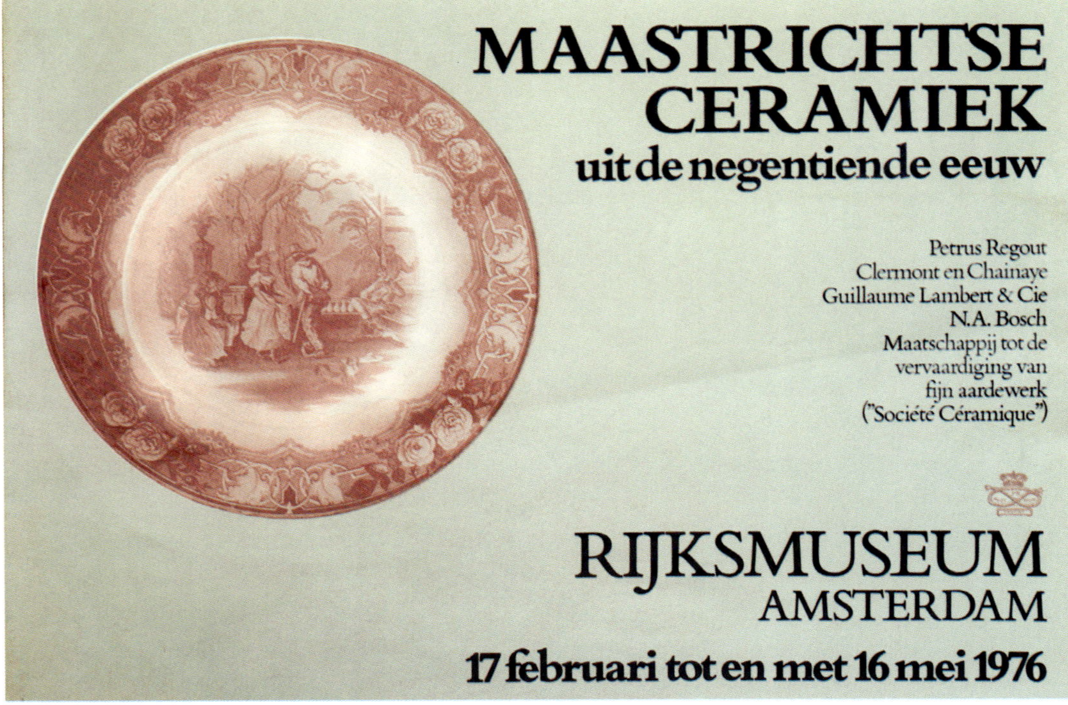

62.

· 60-61

Frédéric Mialhe. "Dancing". Regout (Maastricht, Holland), 1855-1890s.

· 62

Royal Museum, Amsterdam, Holland, 1976. Exhibition poster with "Dancing" pattern by Regout.

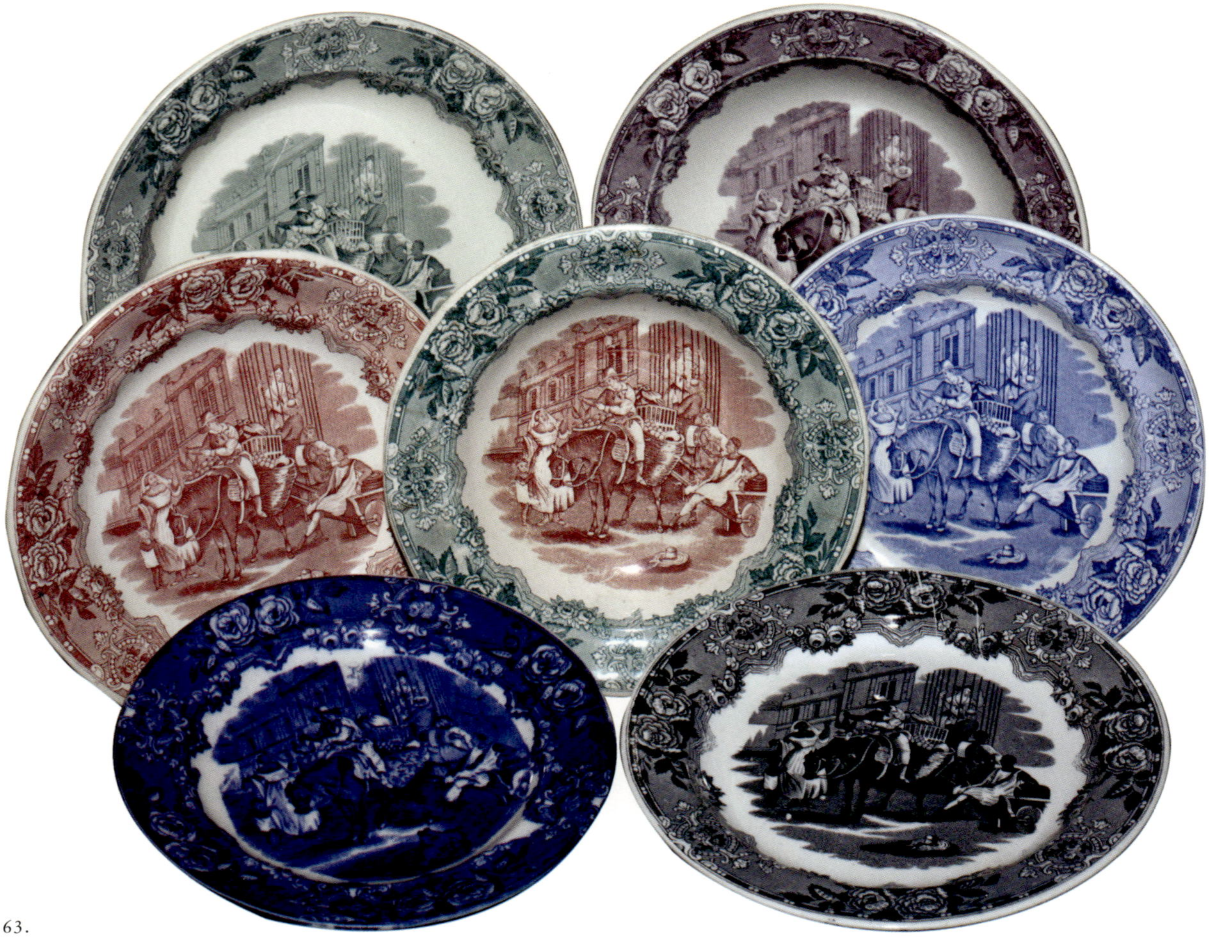

63.

· 63
Frédéric Mialhe. "Indian Trafic". Regout (Maastricht, Holland), 1874-1890s.

· 64
Frédéric Mialhe. "El Casero". Lithograph. Havana, 1848.

The second image was the poultry seller, sold under the pattern name of "Indian Trafic" (Fig. 63). A very knowledgeable Dutch dealer wrote to me in 1995 indicating that this pattern was used between 1859 and 1912. Like its "Dancing" counterpart, it was drafted in England, first in the 1850s, later by E. Pepper & Son (1874), and then by J. Johnson (1876), each time transferred in Holland.

A third image, the King's Day view depicting the black slaves parading on January 6th, was found among the factory papers, indicating that it had it had been drafted by Th. Toft in 1859 and was available for production. But I have never seen any such images and all Dutch antique dealers I have asked have assured me that such view was never produced. None has ever surfaced, to my knowledge.

Some Dutch pieces have Indonesian script on the back, suggesting they were also intended for that market (The Dutch East Indies were under Dutch administration between 1800 and 1949). They also exported these plates to Mexico, and the renowned Franz Mayer Museum in Mexico City owns and displays several pieces.[36] When I first visited their collection in the 1990s they were under the misimpression that they depicted Mexican, not Cuban, colonial views.

It is worth noting that when in 1976 the prestigious Rijksmuseum in Amsterdam offered its first retrospective on Maastricht ceramics, they chose for their poster the image of the Cuban peasant dance, not even knowing its origin and clearly having hundreds of images to choose from (Fig. 62). This is certainly the best tribute Frédéric Mialhe, and Cuba, could have hoped for.

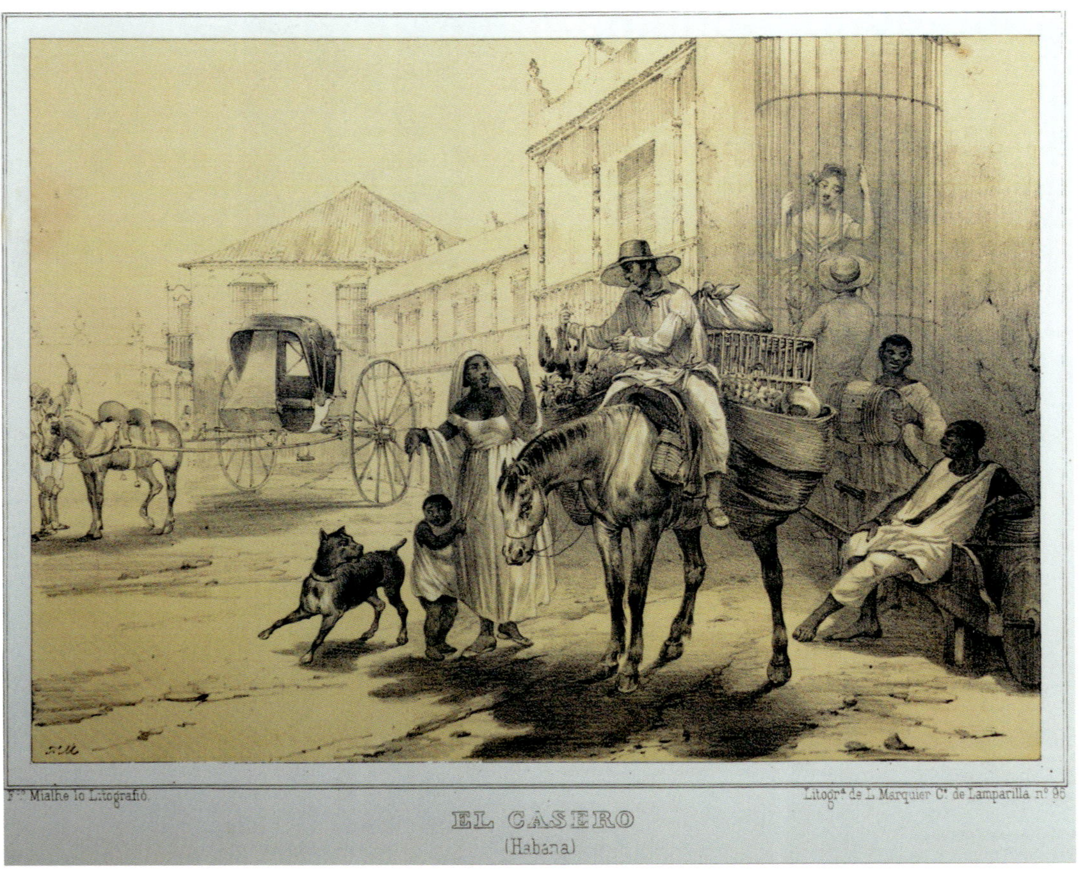

64.

[36]. See *Cerámica inglesa en México*. México, D.F., Museo Franz Mayer, The British Council: Artes de México, 1996 [Colección Uso y Estilo, 4], pp. 24-25.

One-of-a-Kind Sets

The Cuban elite, particularly those with nobility titles issued by the Crown, like its European counterparts, wanted to impress their visitors. And a good dinner around a splendidly arranged table would certainly be an excellent way to do so.

To that effect, Cuba's privileged class ordered their custom-made fine china, adorned with their respective coats of arms, from the best porcelain makers in England, France and China. The largest and best collection of such items I know is on display at the Sala Pedro Morales Coronado, Palacio Lombillo, in Havana's Cathedral Square.[37] There is also an important collection at the Museum of Decorative Arts in Vedado, Havana.[38]

Among the many families who are represented in these 19th and 20th century sets of dinnerware we mention: Álvarez Calderón family, Marqueses de Avilés y de Pinar del Río (C. Ahrenfeldt, Limoges, Fig. 65), Marqués de Almendares (China, 1840s, Fig. 66),[39] Marqués de Balboa, Marqués de Campo Florido, Marqués de Casa de Calderón, Conde de Casa Montalvo, Conde de Casa Morales, Conde de Casa Romero, Castellanos Perdomo family, Conde de Fernandina, Conde de Galarza, Marqués de la Gratitud, Conde de Ibáñez, Conde de Macurijes, Marqués de Larrinaga, Meyreles family, Conde de Moré, Conde de Pedroso, Pedroso y del Castillo family, Marqués de Peñalver, Pérez Piquero family, Marqués de Prado Ameno, Marqués de la Real Campiña, Marqués de la Real Proclamación, Marqués del Real Socorro, Conde de la Reunión de Cuba, Conde de Sagunto, Conde de San Ignacio, Marqués de Sandoval, Conde de Tardiff, Marquesa de Tiedra, Truffin family, Marqués de Valle Siciliana,

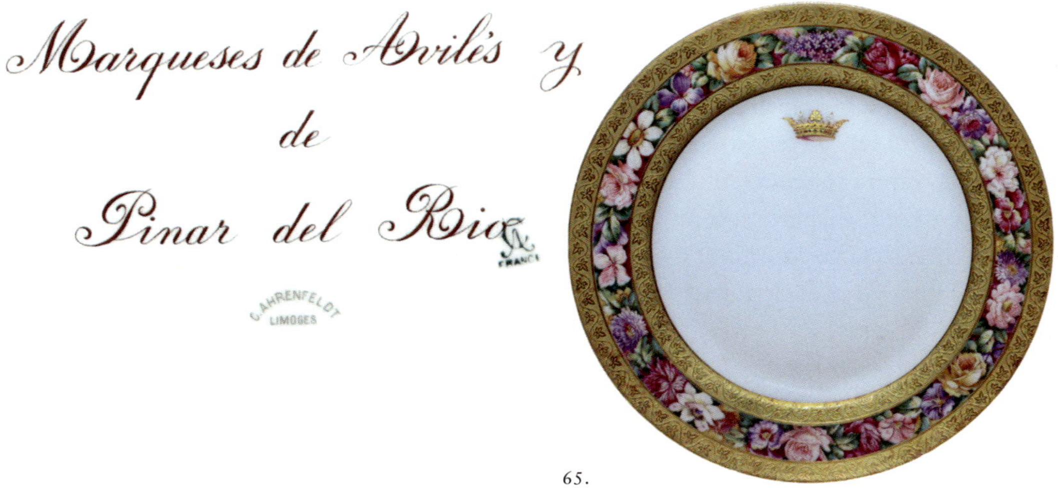

65.

37. My friend Pedro Morales was a Cuban-American living in New York who had inherited a sampling of such plates from his sister, a wealthy Cuban lady (how she got them in the first place is another story). Pedro donated his plates to the Office of the Historian in Havana and, at present, both Pedro's plates and a large collection from Havana's own museums (many of them probably confiscated from their original owners as they left the island in the 1960s) dazzle the visitor to the Palacio Lombillo.

38. See Esteban Llorach Ramos, *Ya está el café.* La Habana, Editorial Gente Nueva, 2011, pp. 115-118.

39. Somehow, several pieces from this magnificent set made their way to the US, where they occasionally show up in auction houses (where I was lucky enough to win my warmer plate).

40. See also *Diario de La Marina*, July 27, 1930, “La Exposición de porcelana”, *Carteles*, December 6, 1942 and Luis de Soto Sagarra, “El tesoro artístico nacional. La colección Osuna-Varela Zequeira”, *Carteles*, August 31, 1947.

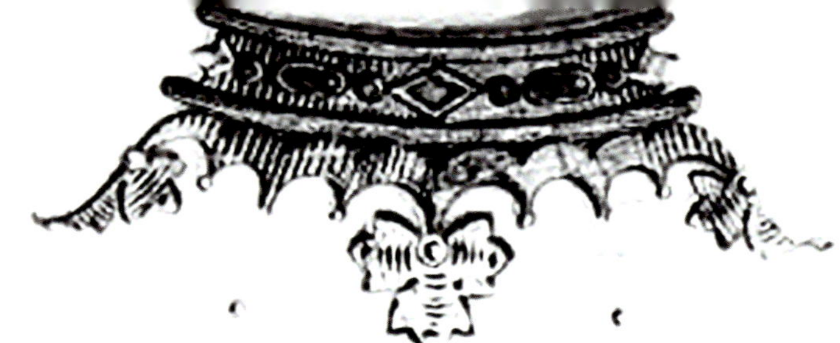

Marqués de Villalba, Marqués de Villalta, Conde de Villanueva, Marqués de Villavicencio and Zuazo family.

Other Cuban museums also display china purchased in the 19th and 20th centuries by wealthy Cuban families (some monogrammed, others not): The Museum of the City of Havana (Palacio de los Capitanes Generales); the Colonial Museum in Cathedral Square; the Casa de la Obra Pía; the Museum of Decorative Arts in Santa Clara; the Palacio Cantero and Romantic Museum in Trinidad; the Colonial Art Museum in Sancti Spíritus, the *Museo de Ambiente Histórico* in the old mansion of Diego Velázquez (ca. 1465-1524), in Santiago de Cuba, etc.[40]

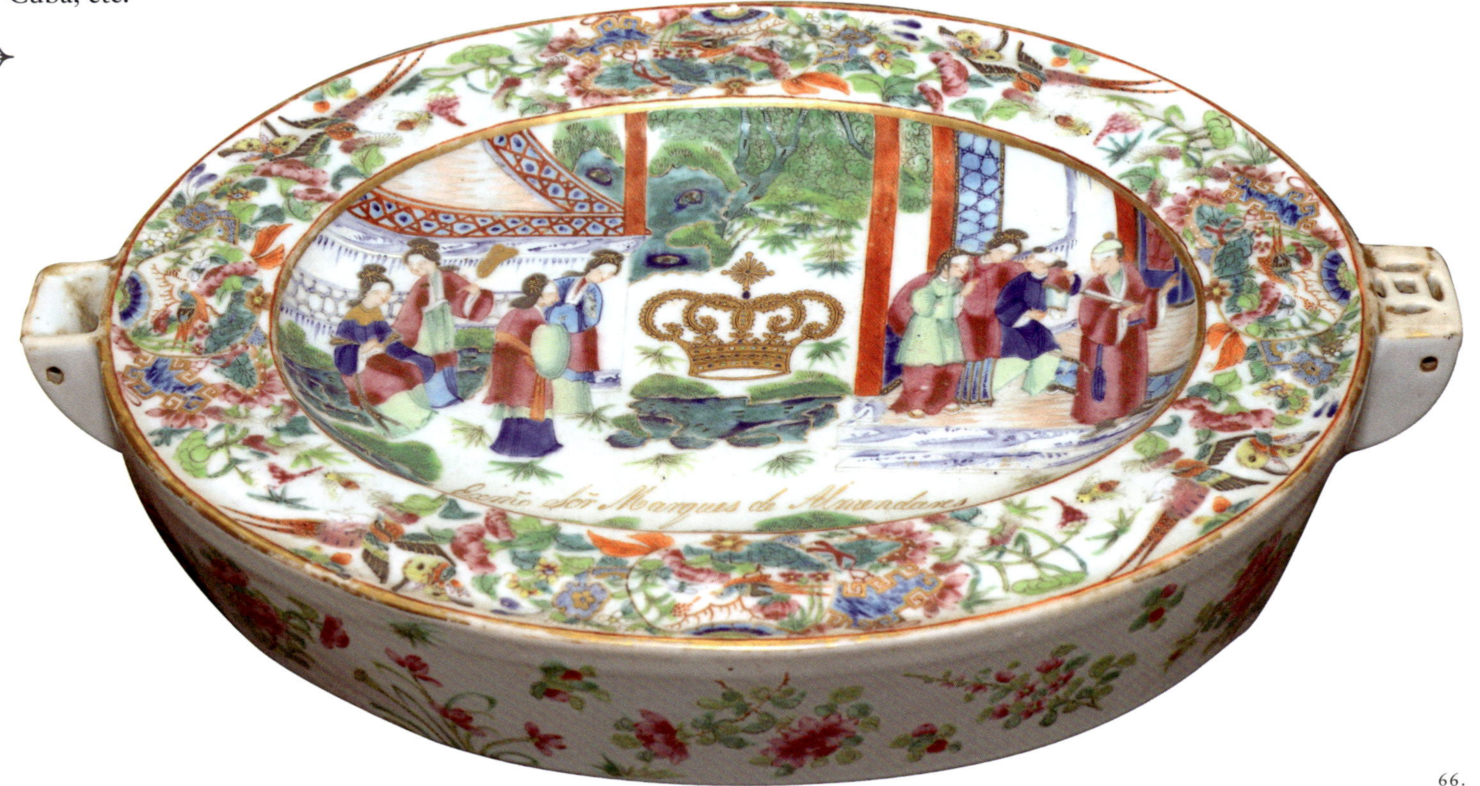

66.

· 65

Marquis of Avilés and Pinar del Río.

C. Ahrenfeldt (Limoges, France)

19--.

· 66

Marquis of Almendares.

Export trade (China), 1840s.

In addition to these pieces, there is another unique and splendid dinnerware set which remains shrouded in mystery. I first noticed it the Miami shop ("Museo Cubano") of my friend Julián Valdés in 1993, but, even though it was on display at the store, it was not for sale. Twelve years later, the set was still there. This time I was able to convince him to sell it to me.

The pieces were hand painted ("pintado a mão") by Brazilian artist N. Kislanski[41] on porcelain plates from the famous Schmidt factory in Pomerode, Santa Catarina, Brazil. They were probably made in the late 1940s or early 1950s.

Which Cuban family had it made? How did they learn about the Brazilian factory (most Cubans look to US and Europe, not to South America, for inspiration and culture). Did it belong to a Cuban diplomat or businessman living abroad? Why did they sell it?

It is abundantly clear that the family who ordered the set had both money and great taste. They were also familiar with the prints of Frédéric Mialhe, as the majority of the pieces were inspired by the French lithographer. Among the images used were the Husillo waterfalls, the Almendares bridge (Fig. 67), Arms Square, Havana's Cathedral (Fig. 68), Viñales Valley (Figs. 69), Belén convent (Fig. 73), Tacón theater, and the popular Quitrín open carriage. Other views include the Fuerza castle, St. Francis Convent, Havana's City Hall, the *Maine*'s Monument (Fig. 70), The Capitol, Havana's Morro Castle, Santiago's Morro Castle (Fig. 71), El Cobre Shrine (Fig. 74), and an old bridge in Sancti Spíritus (Fig. 75).

Let us hope that, through the circulation of these images in this book someone will come forward to unlock the secrets behind this great *vajilla*.

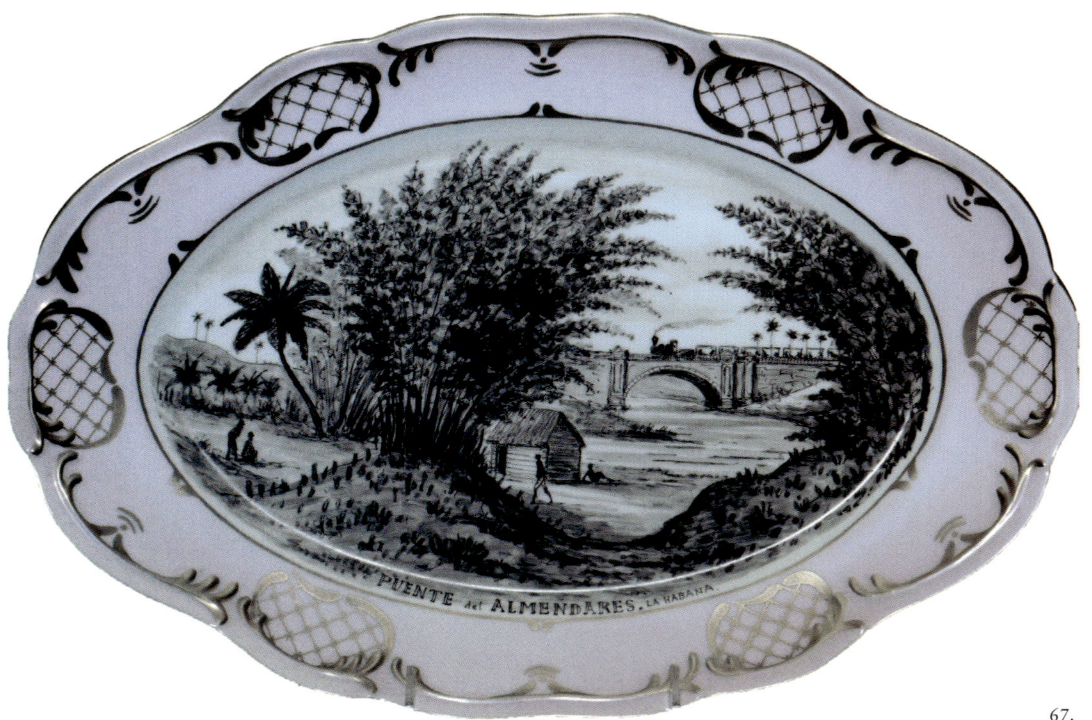

67.

41. There is an Israel Kislanky who is a sculptor in Brazil nowadays. Perhaps both are related.

· 67

N. Kislanski, after Frédéric Mialhe. Almendares bridge. Porcelana Schmidt (Pomerode, Santa Catarina, Brazil), 1950s.

· 68

N. Kislanski, after Frédéric Mialhe. Havana's cathedral. Porcelana Schmidt (Pomerode, Santa Catarina, Brazil), 1950s.

· 69

N. Kislanski. Viñales valley. Porcelana Schmidt (Pomerode, Santa Catarina, Brazil), 1950s.

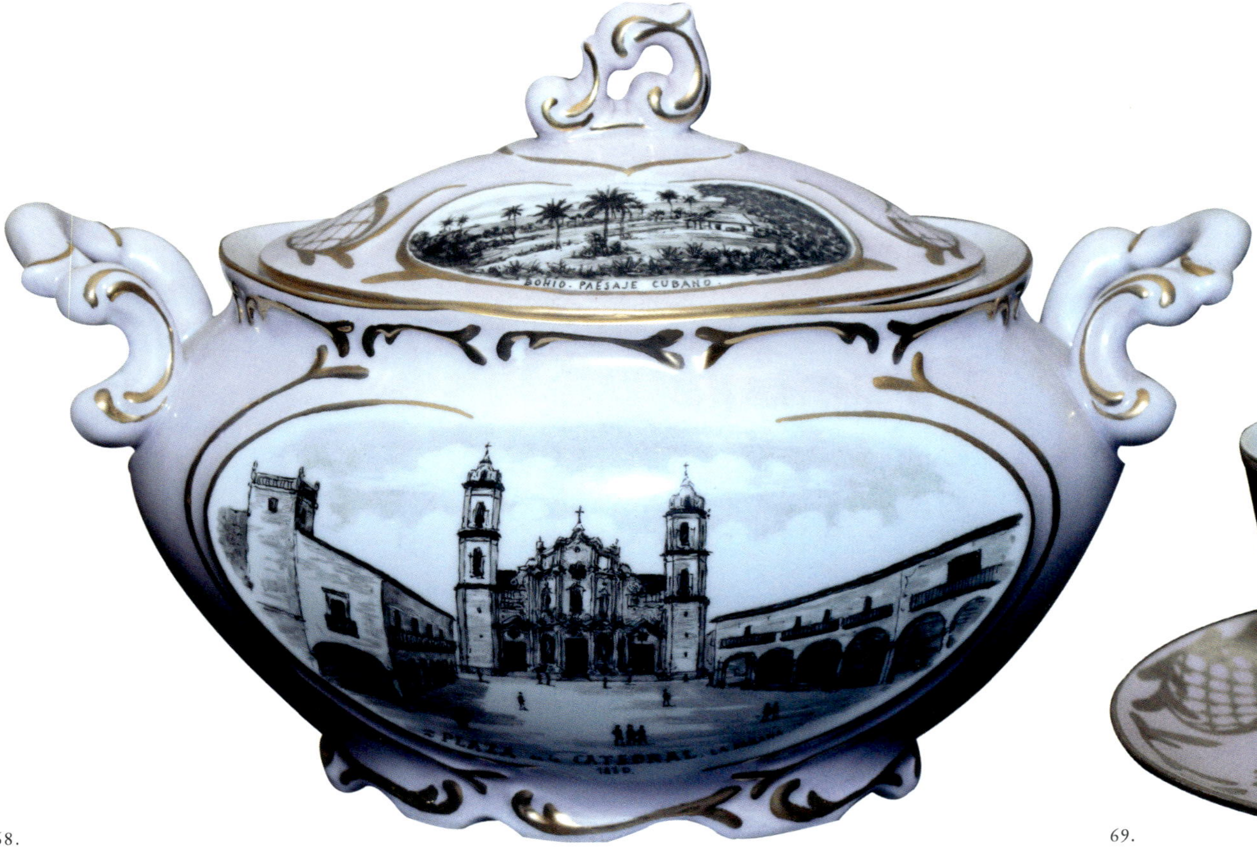

68.

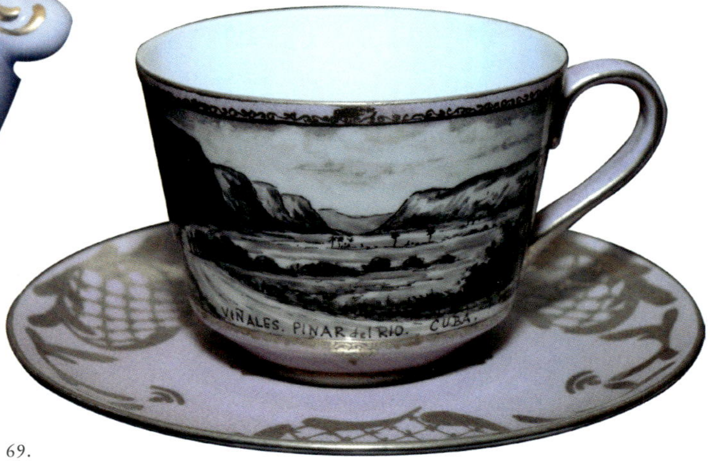

69.

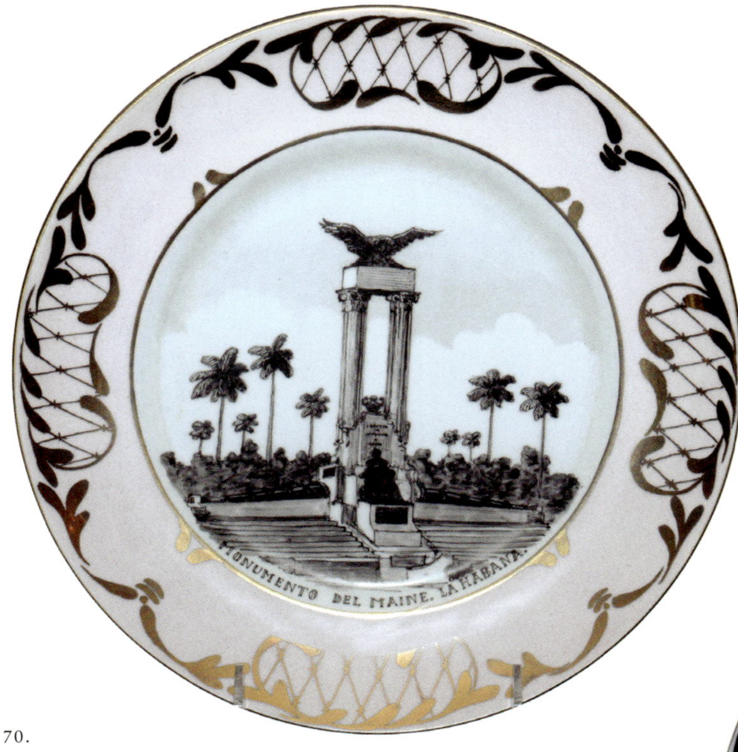

70.

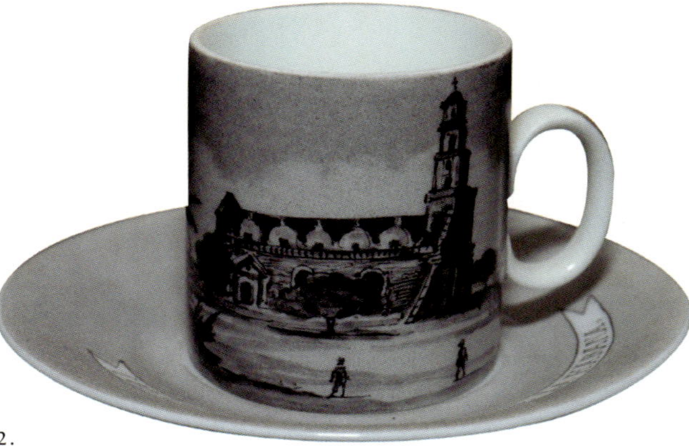

72.

· 70

N. Kislanski, after photograph. The Maine monument. Porcelana Schmidt (Pomerode, Santa Catarina, Brazil), 1950s.

· 71

N. Kislanski. Santiago's Morro Castle. Porcelana Schmidt (Pomerode, Santa Catarina, Brazil), 1950s.

· 72

N. Kislanski. St. Francis Convent. Porcelana Schmidt (Pomerode, Santa Catarina, Brazil), 1950s.

71.

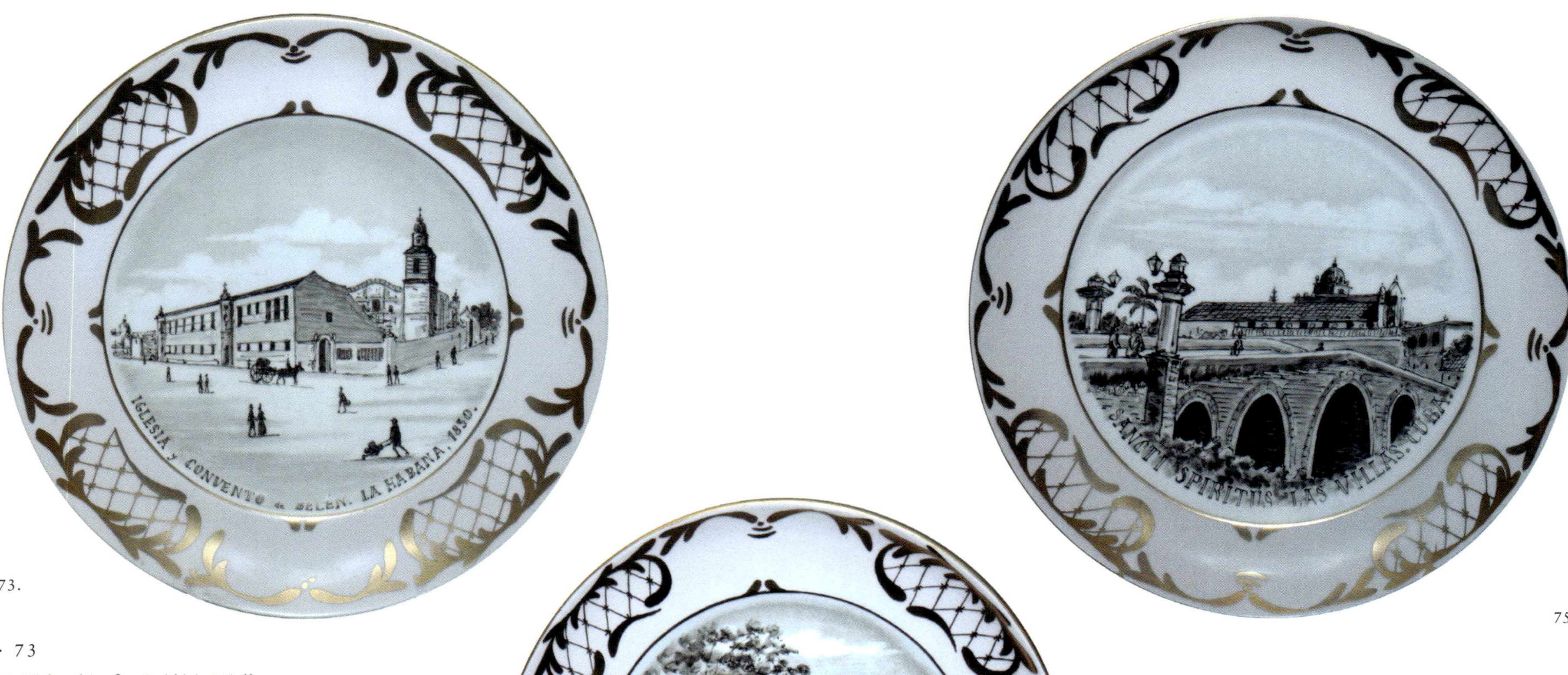

73.

74.

75.

· 73

N. Kislanski, after Frédéric Mialhe. Belén convent. Porcelana Schmidt (Pomerode, Santa Catarina, Brazil), 1950s.

· 74

N. Kislanski. Our Lady of Charity Shrine at El Cobre. Porcelana Schmidt (Pomerode, Santa Catarina, Brazil), 1950s.

· 75

N. Kislanski. Sancti Spíritus old bridge. Porcelana Schmidt (Pomerode, Santa Catarina, Brazil), 1950s.

Business use: Dinnerware and propaganda items with Cuban logos and trade names

The earliest 19th century commercial pieces I am aware of are two plates from Havana's Locería El Globo, one unmarked, and one marked (Fig. 76) by Wm. Adams, Turnstall, England, a multi-colored piece advertising the Villar and Gutiérrez chocolate factory (Fig. 77) and a dark blue plate decorated with a map of Cuba (the word "Cubanas" written across) and a poem praising the beautiful Cuban girls, made for La Cafetera, Almacén de Gamba y Co. Habana.[42] I am not aware of any 19th century hotel or restaurant ceramic pieces, though it would not surprise me if a few have survived and will eventually surface.

Because of their very nature, hotels, restaurants and clubs are important users of dinnerware (and other items such as candlesticks, ashtrays, etc.). In addition to the establishments in the island, outside of Cuba there are dozens of restaurants and coffee shops (and several hotels) bearing Cuba-related names and/or serving Cuban food. Other associations and groups may find themselves in need for ceramic pieces, and a few products do advertise their brand by way of ceramic items.

———

42. See A. W. Coyish, *et. al. Dictionary, op. cit.*, (vol 1), p. 20. One copy was sold by Garths Auctioneers (Delaware, Ohio) around 2008 and another one, from Coyish's own collection, was auctioned by Andrew Smith & Son, Itchen Stoke, Winchester, UK, on February 6, 2018, lot 200.

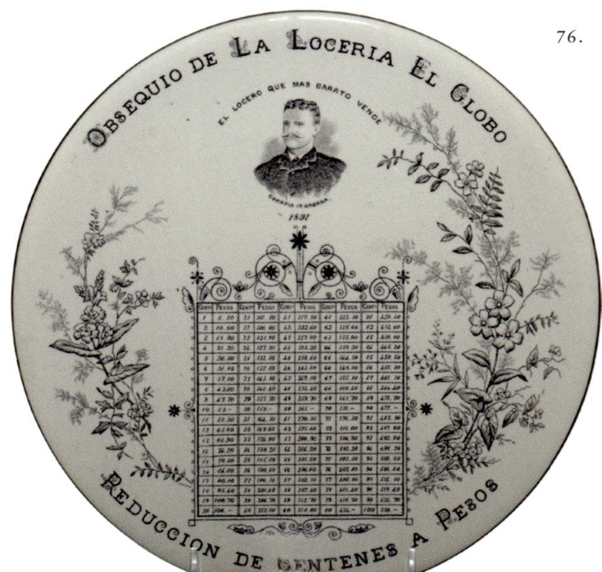

76.

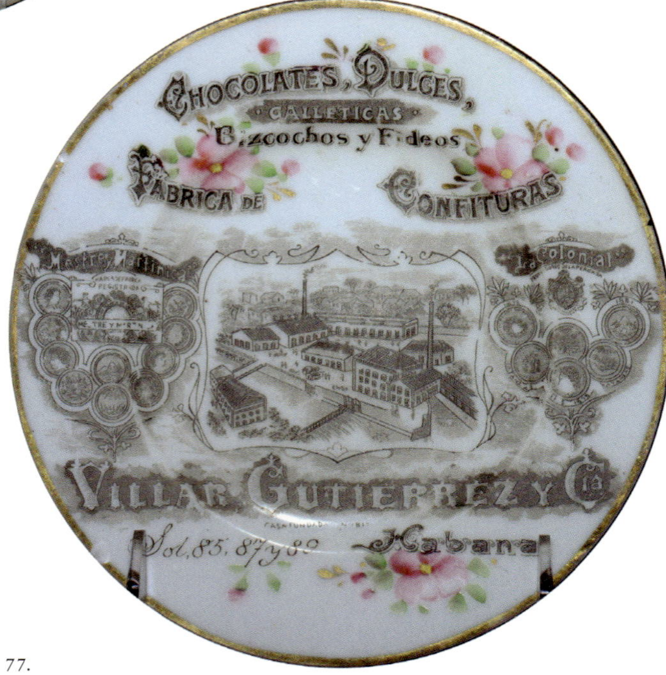

77.

· 76
El Globo ceramics factory. Unmarked (probably Wm. Adams & Co., UK) 1881.

· 77
Villar and Gutiérrez chocolate factory. Unmarked (?), 19th century.

· 78
Florida. Bauscher (Weiden, Germany), 1940s?

· 79
Inglaterra. Liberty Park, Matanzas. Bauscher (Weiden, Germany), 1920s.

Hotels

The Bauscher firm in Weiden, Germany, appears to have been well-known in the island and furnished items for various Havana hotels: Florida (Fig. 78), Inglaterra (Fig. 79), Pasaje, Plaza (Fig. 80) and Sevilla Biltmore. Another Bavarian porcelain factory, Black Knight, provided the Hotel Presidente with its 1927 colorful service (Fig. 81). Salón Trotcha's clientele dined on French Limoges porcelain by Jean Pouyat (Fig. 82); the Ambos Mundos ordered items from Buffalo, New York through Albert Pick & Co (Fig. 84); Riviera's ware came from Elephant Brand, in Staffordshire; La Unión preferred Shenango, from New Castle, Pennsylvania (Fig. 85); the Nacional shopped at one point at the Verbano establishment in Buenos Aires (Fig. 83) and Capri's ware was furnished by Royal China, in Sebring, Ohio. Quite a world tour.

I have not been able to locate any items from establishments in other Cuban cities. Outisde of Cuba, the Hotel Habana in Barcelona had some of its pieces marked with the name of the Barcelona Gallery Griffé y Escoda (Fig. 86). I stayed there. You guessed it!

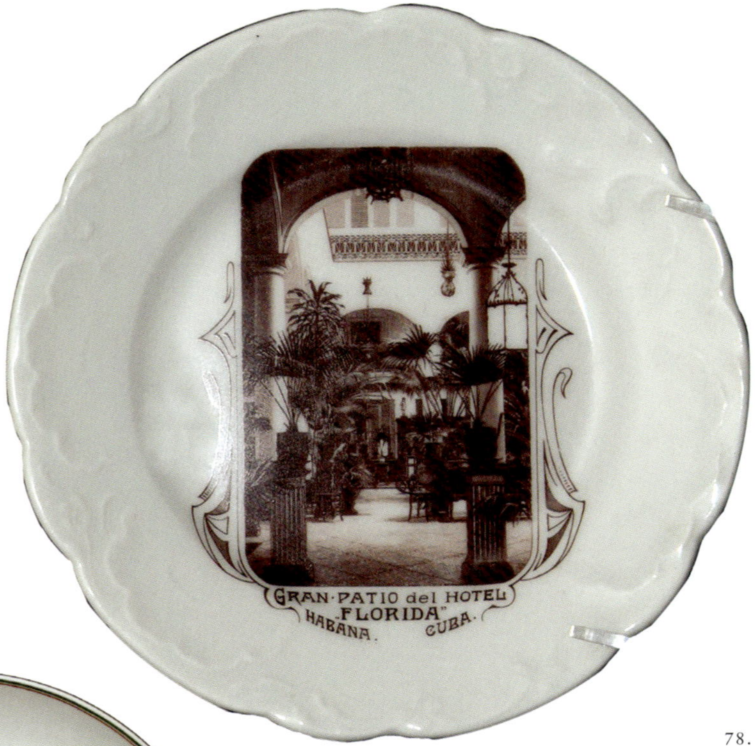

78.

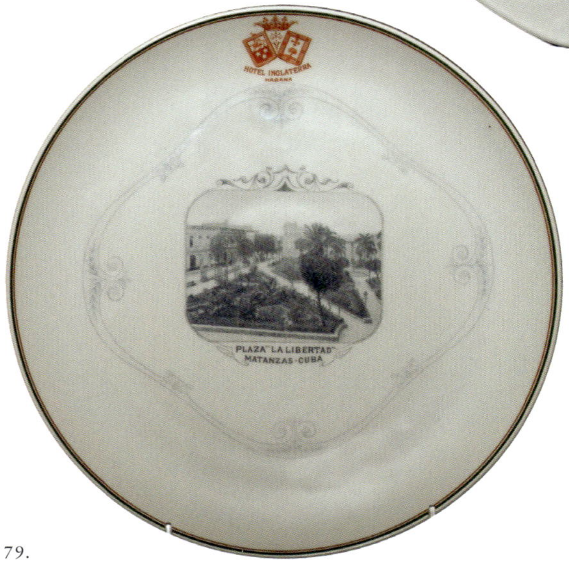

79.

· 80

Plaza. Bauscher
(Weiden, Germany), 1920s.

· 81

Presidente. Black Knight
(Selb, Germany), 1927.

· 82

Salón Trotcha. Jean Pouyat
(Limoges, France), 1910s?

· 83

Nacional. Verbano
(Argentina), 1990s.

· 84

Ambos Mundos. Albert Pick & Co.
(Buffalo, New York, US), 1927.

· 85

La Unión. Shenango (New Castle,
Pennsylvania, US), 1940s?

· 86

Habana. Barcelona. Grifé y Escoda
(Barcelona, Spain), 1970s.

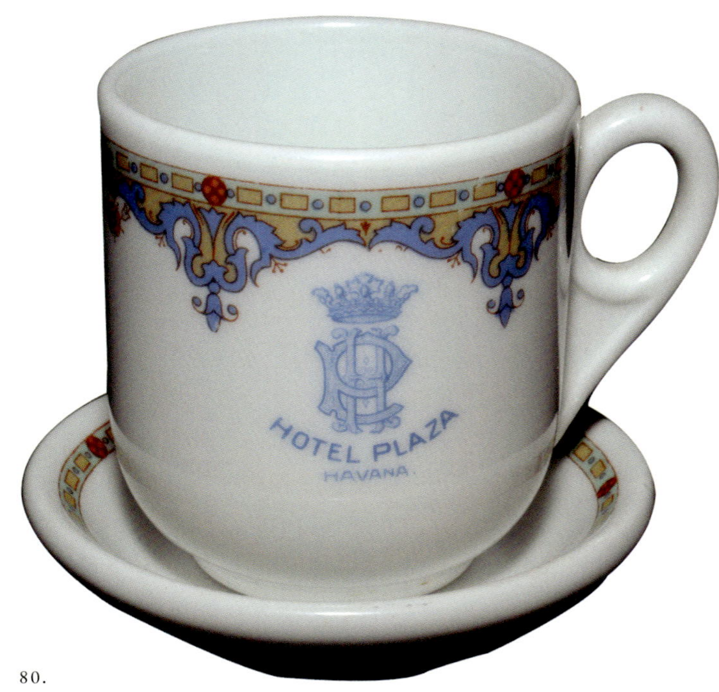

80.

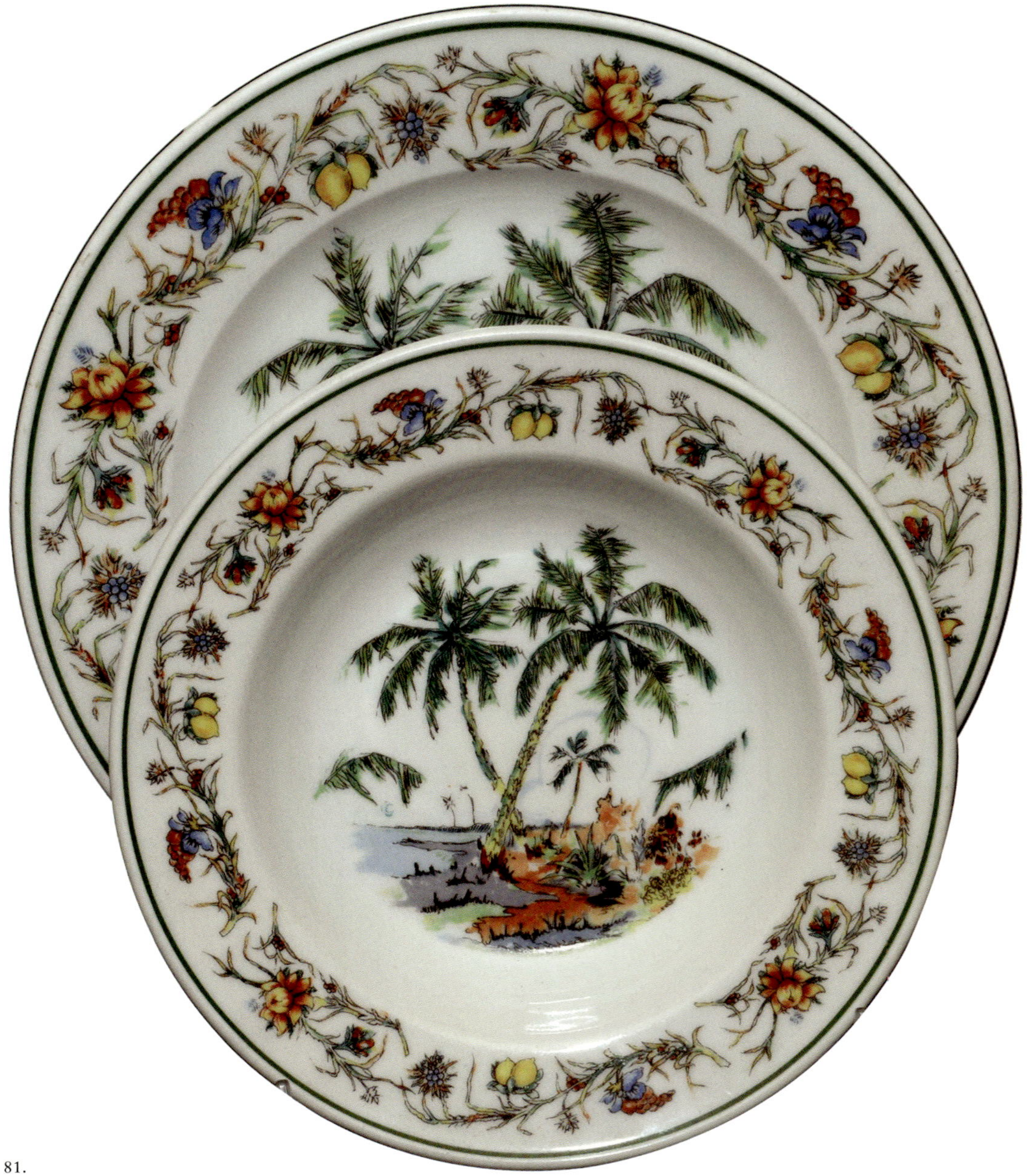

81.

SALON
TROTCHA
J.P.
L.
FRANCE
ALBERT PICK & COMPANY
Vitrified China
CHICAGO
BUFFALO
CHINA
1927

82.

84.

83.

Hotel La Union

85.

Hotel Habana

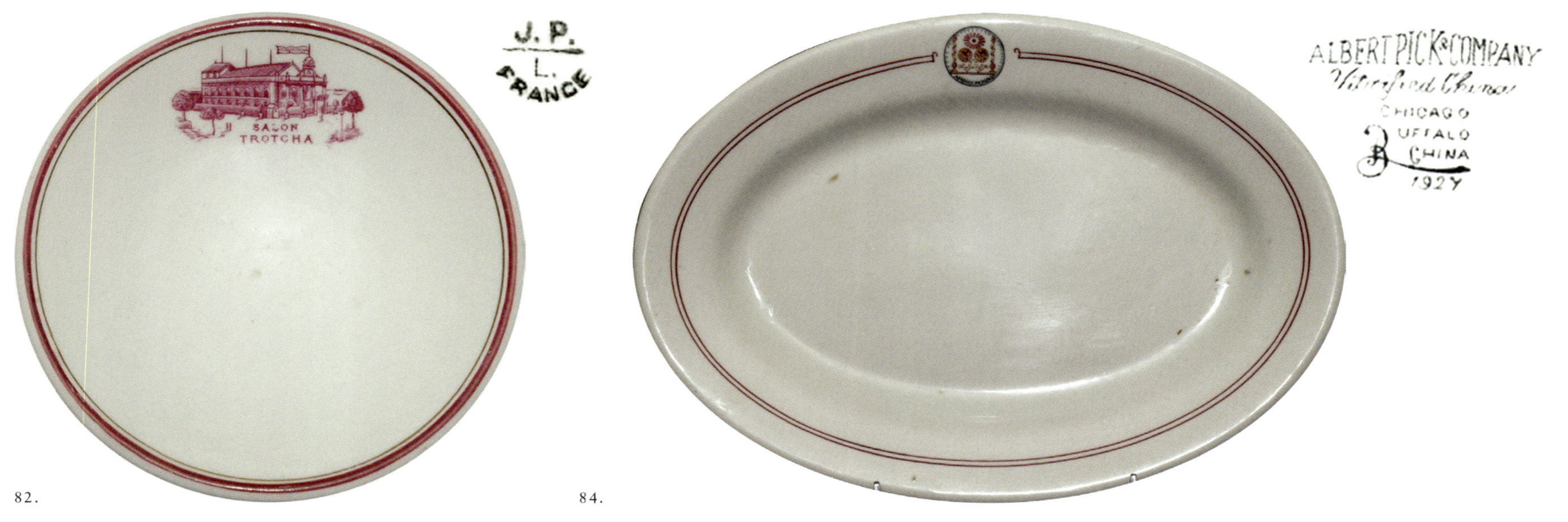

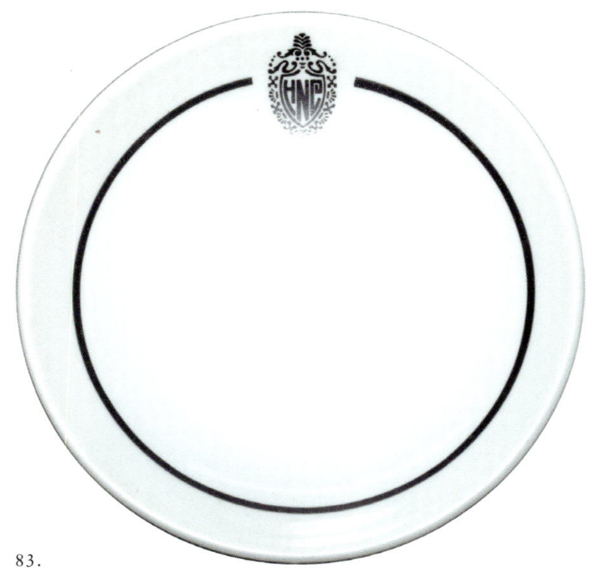

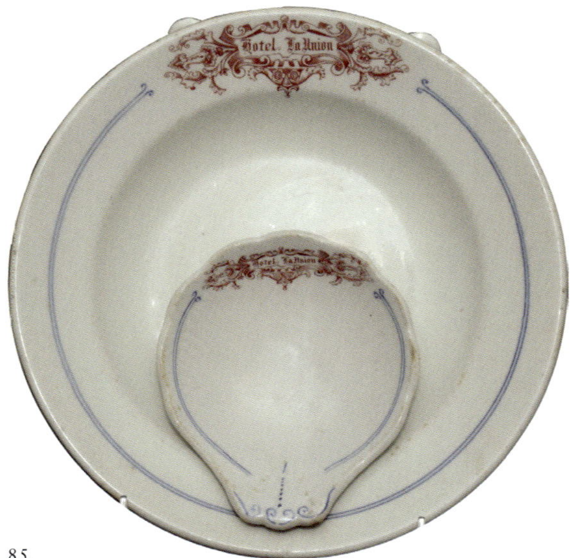

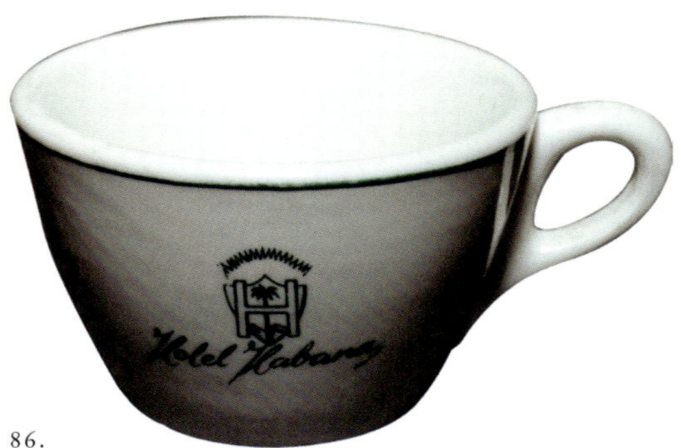

86.

Clubs and restaurants

The Havana establishments represented in my collection and elsewhere include: El Anón (unknown); Chateau-Madrid Fibah (unmarked); El Country Club de La Habana (Wood & Sons, Burslem, England and Walker China (Bedford, Ohio); La Dominica ("Plaza de la Catedral", Habaguanex, Churchill, England); Emperador (Jackson china, Falls Creek, Pennsylvania); La Florida (unmarked); Havana Biltmore & Yacht Club (Dunn, Burnett & Co., England, Fig. 87); La Roca (Sterling, East Liverpool, Ohio); Moneda Cubana (Dudson, Stoke-on-Trent, England, Fig. 88); Paris (Iroquois, Solvay, New York); Sloppy Joe's (Warwick China, Wheeling, West Virginia, Fig. 89); Tropicana (Jackson china, Falls Creek, Pa., Fig. 90), and Zaragozana 1830 (Bauscher, Weiden, Germany).

Outside of Cuba, my holdings include samples from Bongo, in Orlando, Florida (stamped Ruben Estefan); Club Cubano de España, in Madrid (Fig. 91); Columbia Café, in Tampa (Mayer China, Beaver Falls, Pennsylvania and Syracuse China, Syracuse, New York); Cuba Libre, in Washington, D.C. (Tuxton, China, Fig. 92); Estefan Kitchen, in Miami (Steelite, England); Havana Harry's, in Miami (Victoria, El Nepe, Venezuela); Havana-Madrid, in New York City (Inca Ware, Shenango China, New Castle, Pennsylvania); Kuba-Kuba, in Richmond, Virginia (SS, China, Fig. 94); Tocororo, in Buenos Aires (Schmidt, Pomerode, Brazil, Fig. 93) and Victor's Café 52, in New York City (Syracuse China, Syracuse, New York, Fig. 95).

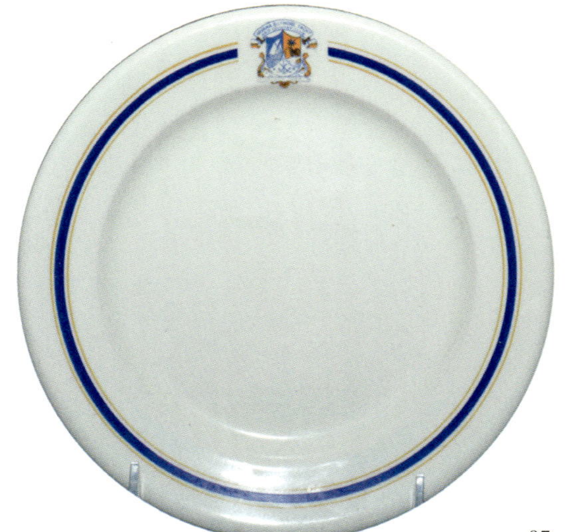
87.

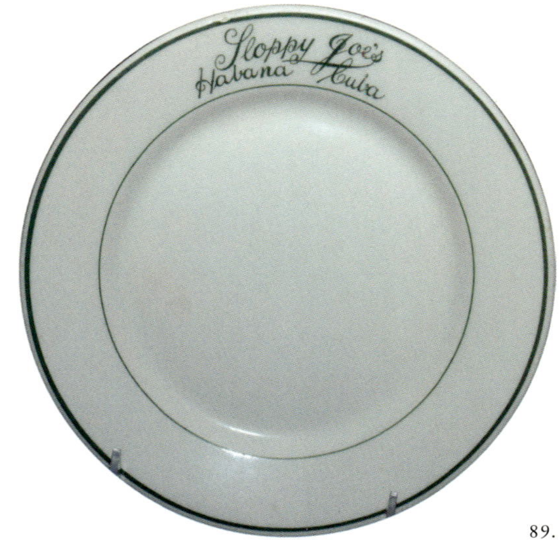

89.

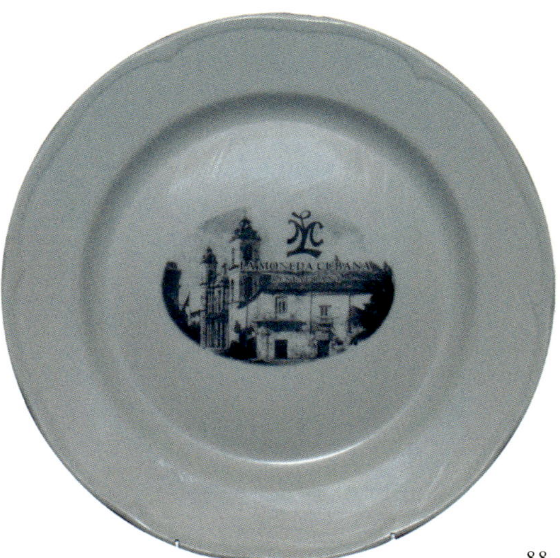
88.

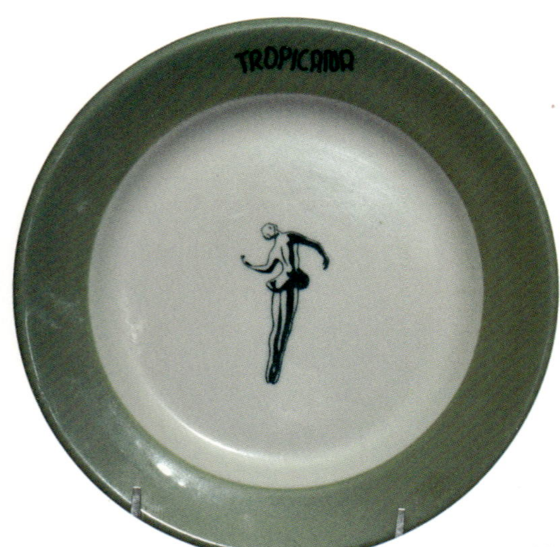

90.

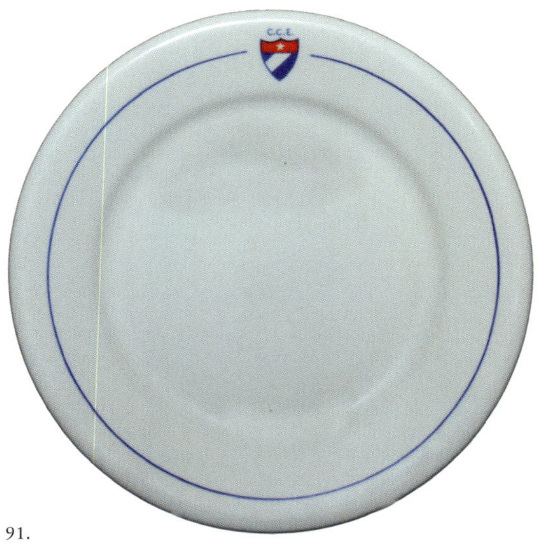

91.

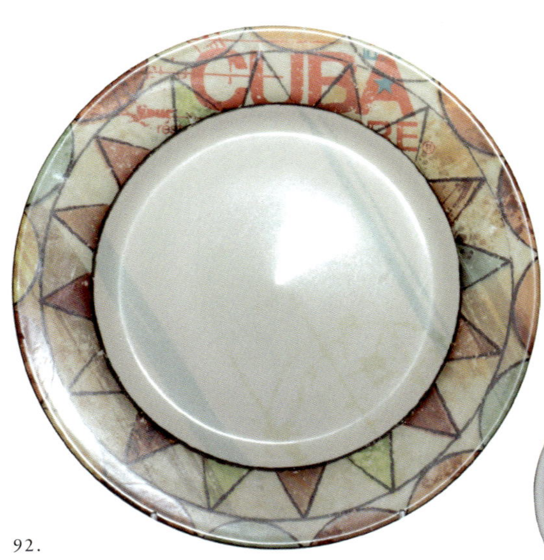

92.

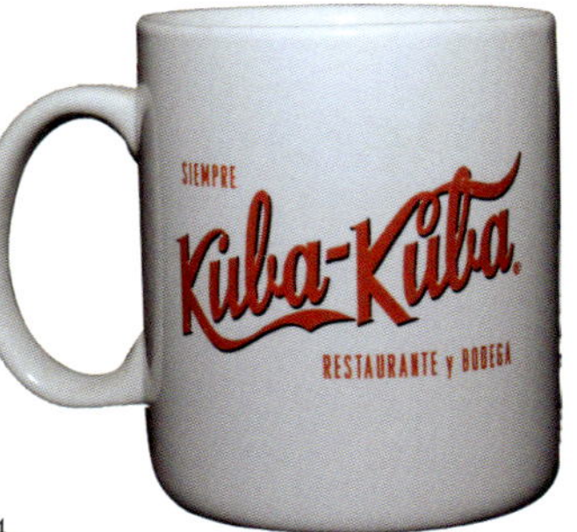

94.

93.

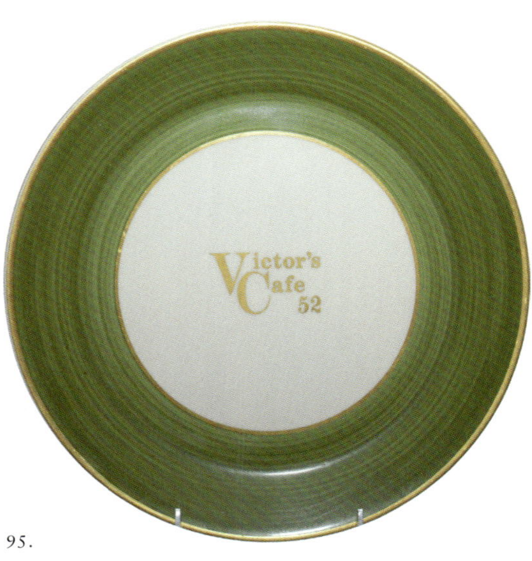

95.

· 87

Havana Biltmore & Yacht Club. Dunn, Burnett & Co. (UK), 1950s.

· 88

Moneda Cubana. Dudson (Stoke-on-Trent, UK), 2014.

· 89

Sloppy Joe's Warwick China (Wheeling, West Virginia, US), 1950s.

· 90

Tropicana. Jackson china (Falls Creek, Pennsylvania), Sampedro y Puig (Barcelona, Spain), 1950s.

· 91

Club Cubano de España. Madrid. Unmarked (Spain?), 1980s.

· 92

Cuba Libre. Washington, D.C. Tuxton (China). 2010.

· 93

Tocororo. Buenos Aires, Argentina. Schmidt (Pomerode, Brazil), 1990s.

· 94

Kuba-Kuba, in Richmond, Virginia. S.S. (China), 2000s.

· 95

Victor's Café 52. New York City. Syracuse China. (New York, US), 1990s.

Commercial Companies, Products and Brands

I already mentioned the El Globo ceramics workshop, Villar and Gutiérrez chocolate factory and Almacenes Gamba. Other items include pieces from: Bacardi (a pitcher (Fig. 97) and a plate (CGP Porcelain by Victoria); Cubana de Aviación (Wedgwood, England); Esso oil company (Fig. 96); Habana 1791 perfume; Hatuey beer (Fig. 98); Matusalem rum (Fig. 99), and La Flor Cubana.[43]

I have also seen another "Cervecería Hatuey" stein made by the Milchspeiser & Katscher brewery in Vyškov (Wischau) Czechoslovaquia; a small ceramic car advertising La Cruz Verde, owned by Pomar, Chao and Co; a plate illustrating the FOCSA Havana skyscraper; and an "Isla del Tesoro" rum jar.

---

[43] The La Flor Cubana plate, and three other commercial pieces from the late nineteenth to early twentieth century are illustrated in Dioelis Delgado Machado, "Sueño de Porcelana", *Opus Habana* (Havana), No 3, 2003, breviario section.

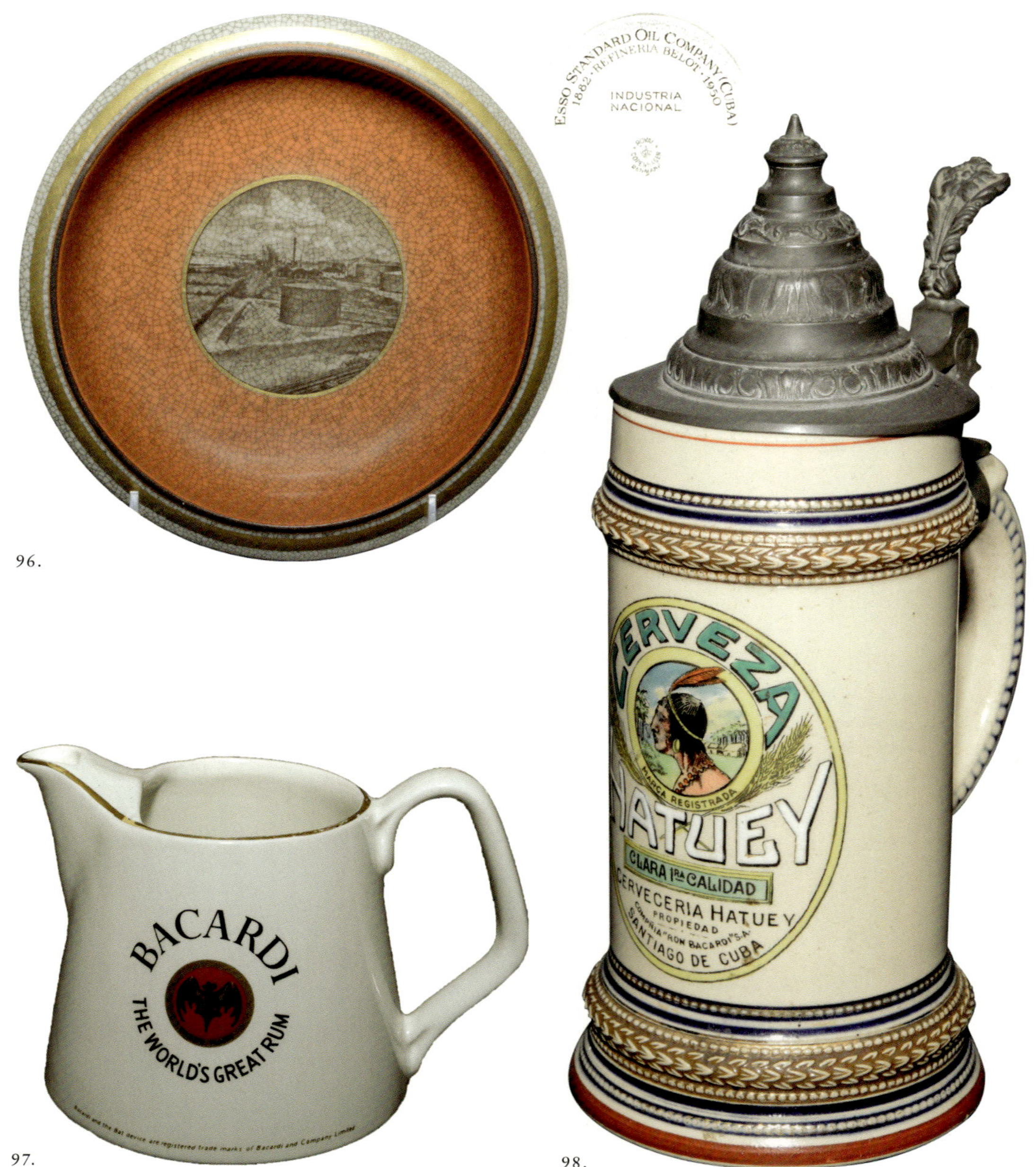

96.

97.

98.

· 96

Esso oil company.
Royal Copenhagen (Denmark),
1950.

· 97

Bacardi rum. Arklow
(Arklow, County Wiclow, Ireland),
1990s?

· 98

Hatuey beer stein. Unmarked,
1930s?

Associations and Other Groups

My collection treasures items from the American Dominican Academy Alumnae (Fig. 100); Belen Jesuit School, in Miami (Fig. 101); and the *Spanish War Veterans* (Fig. 102).

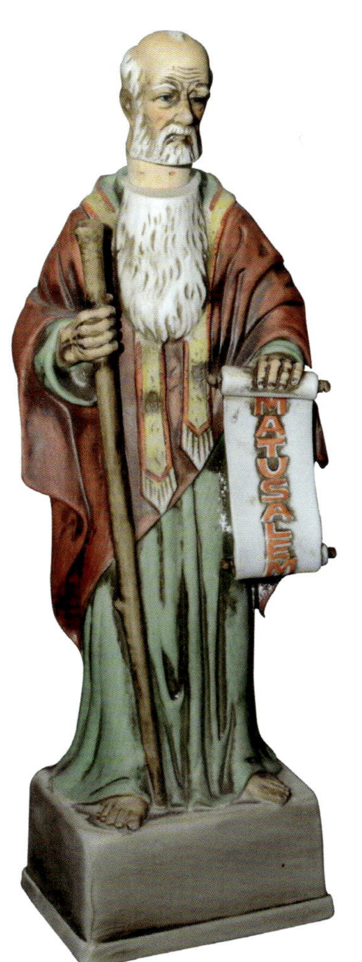

99.

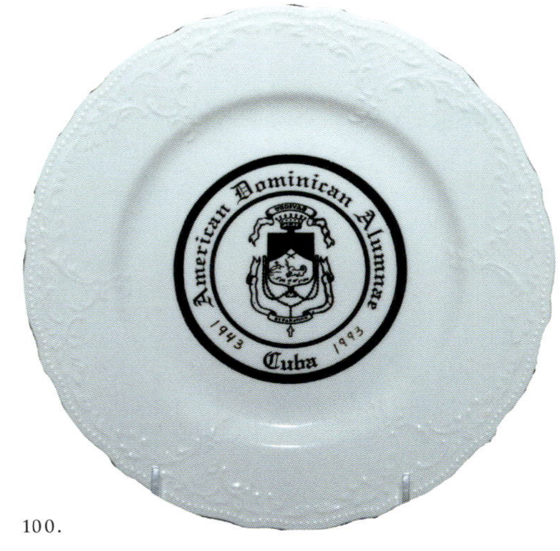

100.

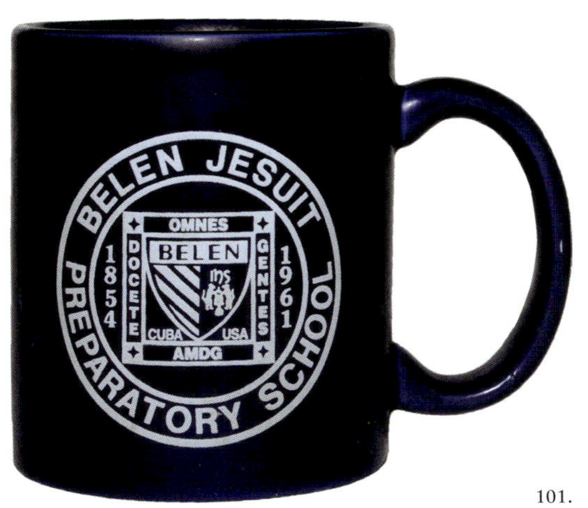

101.

· 99

Matusalem rum. Unmarked, 1950s?

· 100

American Dominican Academy Alumnae. US. Unmarked (US?), 1993.

· 101

Belen Jesuit School. Miami. Unmarked (China), 1990s.

· 102

Spanish War Veterans. B. E. McNicol (Clarksburg, West Virginia, US), 1910s-30s?

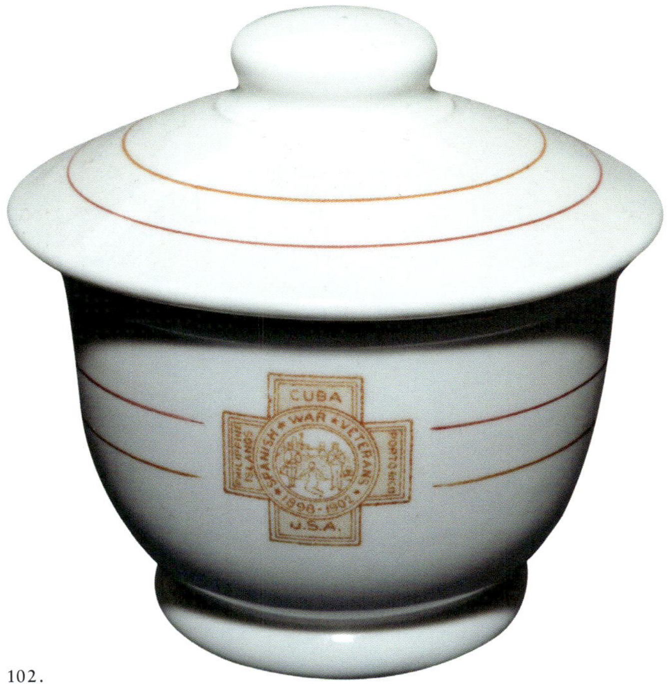

102.

The Cuban war of independence (1895-1898)

Ever since the various colonies in the American continent became independent from their respective European masters (US, 1776; Haiti, 1804; Mexico, 1821; Brazil, 1822; Argentina 1818; Peru, 1828), Cuba had also longed to be a free and sovereign state.

Nineteenth-century Cuba witnessed several attempts at emancipation (notably 1850s and 1860s), but it was only during the 1895-1898 War of Independence, that Cuba could finally see the light at the end of the tunnel.

During these years, and particularly after the warship *Maine* exploded in Havana Bay on February 15, 1898 and the subsequent invasion and occupation of Cuba by American voluntary and regular forces, the US market was flooded with ceramic pieces celebrating these events. Perhaps some pieces also reached the Cuban consumer.

A few of these plates, made by Adams and Clementson in England and by Société Céramique in Holland, depict the busts of the most revered Cuban leaders: José Martí (1853-1895, Fig. 103), Antonio Maceo (1845-1896, Fig. 103, 104), Máximo Gómez (1836-1905, Fig. 103, 1540-42) and Calixto García (1839-1898, Fig. 103). A white and green English plate showing Maceo on horseback was displayed in the Bacardí Museum when I visited it on December 2008. Cuba's symbols (flag and coat of arms) have also been reproduced in commemorative plates (Figs. 105 and 106).[44]

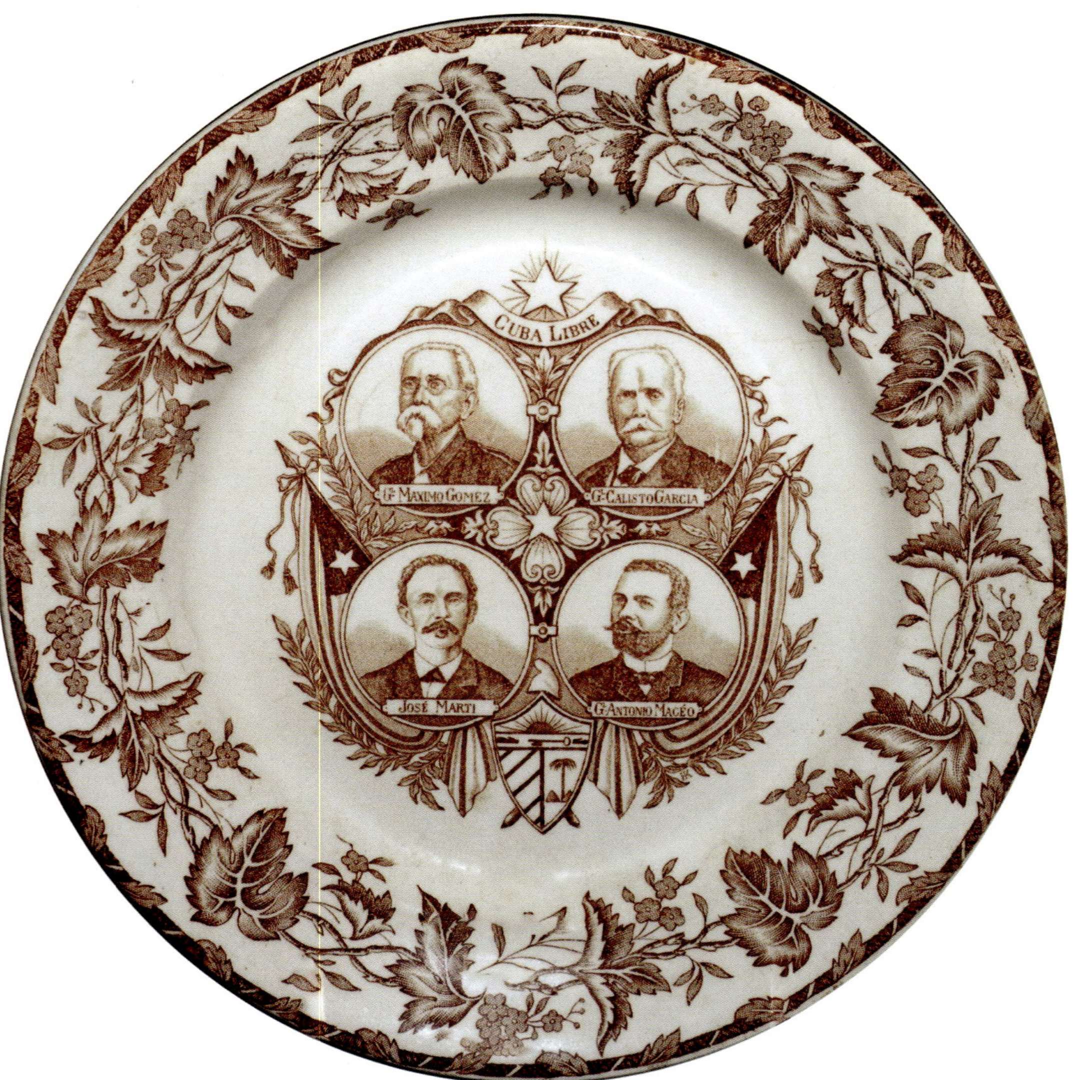

103.

44. Ezequiel García had a large collection of these items, which was featured in *El Fígaro* (Havana), on May 24 1908, p. 276. I presume it has been dispersed since. I have seen a few of the patriotic plates in the Museum of the City of Havana (former Palace of the Captains General in Old Havana) and the Maceo plate at the Bacardí Museum in Santiago de Cuba.

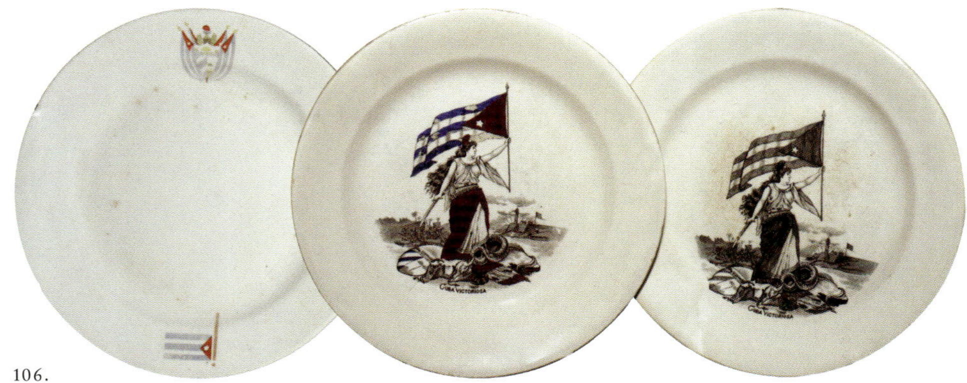

106.

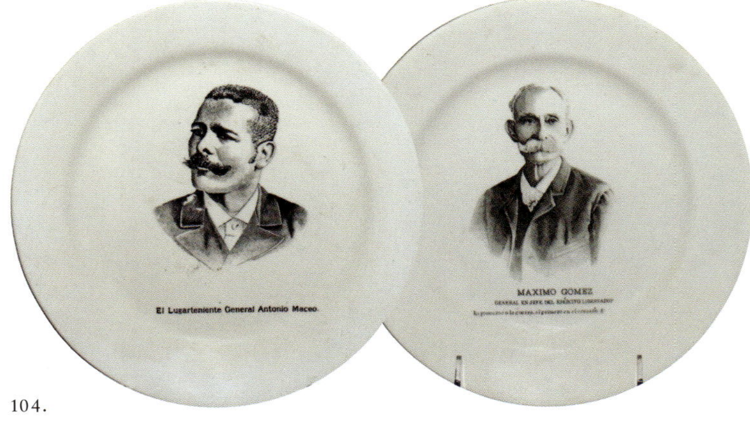

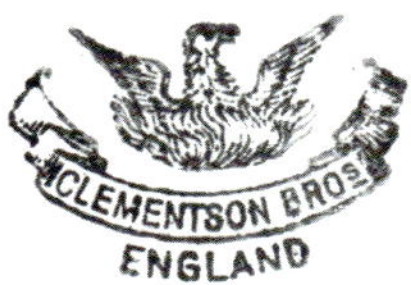

104.

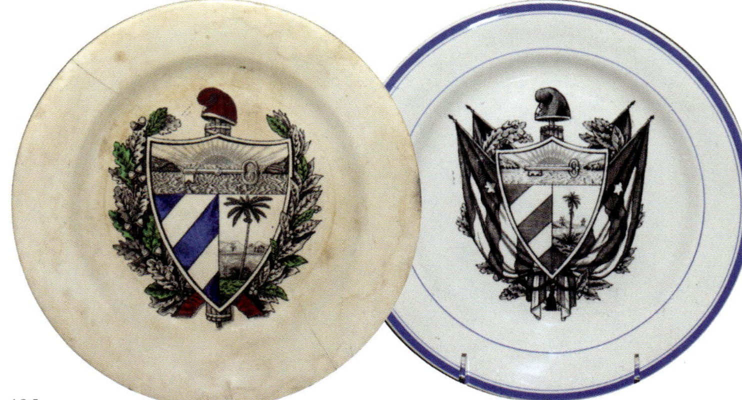

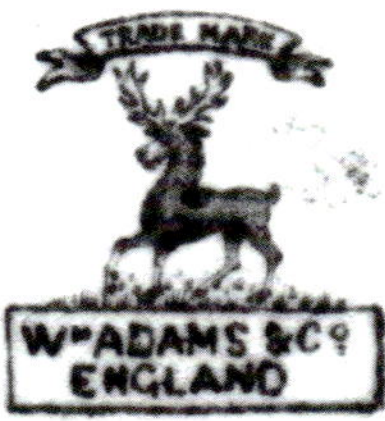

105.

· 103
José Martí, Antonio Maceo, Máximo Gómez and Calixto García. Unmarked (UK?), ca. 1898.

· 104
Antonio Maceo / Máximo Gómez. Clementson Brothers (Shelton, Hanley, UK), ca. 1898.

· 105
Cuban coat of arms. William Adams & Co. (Staffordshire, UK), ca. 1898.

· 106
Left plate: Cuban coat of arms and flag. Société Céramique (Maastricht, Holland), ca. 1898.
Center & right: Victorious Cuba with flag. William Adams & Co. (Staffordshire, UK), ca. 1898.

Other ceramic items honor American leaders —Rough Rider Theodore Roosevelt (1858-1919) (Rowland & Marsellus, UK, Figs. 107 and 108), Commodore Winfield Scott Schley (1839-1911), and Admiral William Thomas Sampson (1840-1902) (Coalport, UK, Fig. 109). Schley, Sampson and US Consul in Havana, Fithugh Lee, (1835-1905) also appeared in a 1900 German stein marked "1258". Fithugh Lee made it into a Vienna porcelain plate painted at the studio of Josef Ahne (1830-1909). For its part, the famous retailer R.H. Macy sold plates with the busts of Schley, Sampson and Lt. Richard Hobson (1870-1937). Hobson was also depicted in a plate by American China Company in Toronto, Ohio.

Other pieces depict US ships, particularly the *Maine:* Taliafero & Thomas (Baltimore, Maryland, Fig. 110); The Sebring (Sebring, Ohio, Fig. 111); La Belle (Wheeling, West Virginia); La Francaise (Sebring, Ohio); Ohio China Co. (East Palestine, Ohio); Vodrey and Brothers (East Liverpool, Ohio); French China Co. (East Liverpool, Ohio); Waco China, E.L.P. (East Liverpool Pottery Co. of Ohio); Dresden Ironstone China (East Liverpool, Ohio); Webber Brothers (Gardiner, Maine) as well as unmarked pieces mostly from the US and Germany (Figs. 111-114).

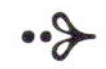

· 107

Rough Rider Theodore Roosevelt. Rowland & Marsellus (Staffordshire, UK), ca. 1900s.

· 108

Battle of San Juan Hill (detail of Fig. 107). Rowland & Marsellus (Staffordshire, UK), ca. 1900s.

· 109

Admiral William Sampson / Commodore Winfield Scott Schley. Coalport (Coalport, UK), ca. 1898.

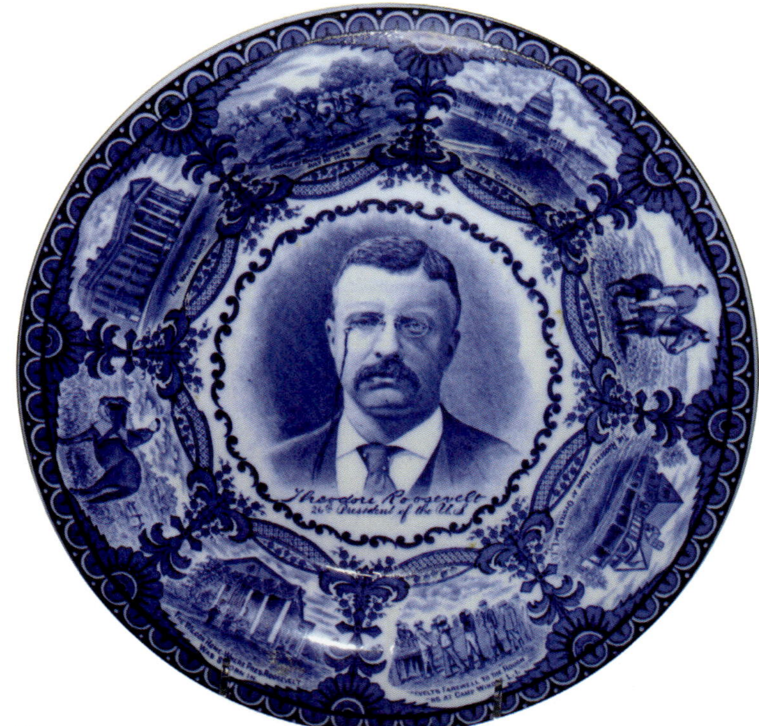

107.

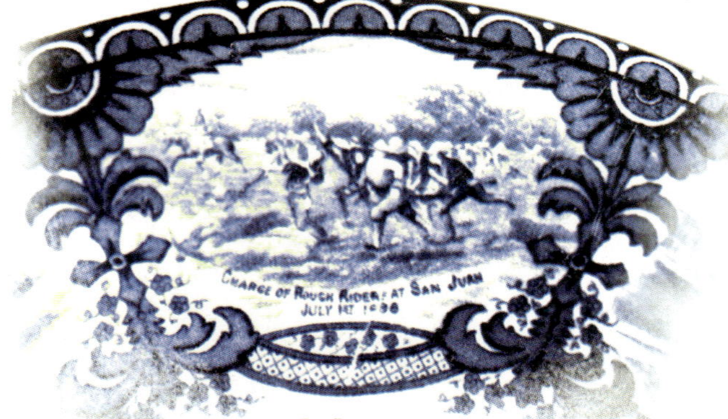

108.

MASSACHUSETTS
NEW YORK
SANTIAGO
SAMPSON
NEW ORLEANS
JULY
1898
ERICSSON
VIXEN
TEXAS
BROOKLYN
SANTIAGO
SCHLEY
INDIANA
OREGON
JULY
1898
IOWA
GLOUCESTER

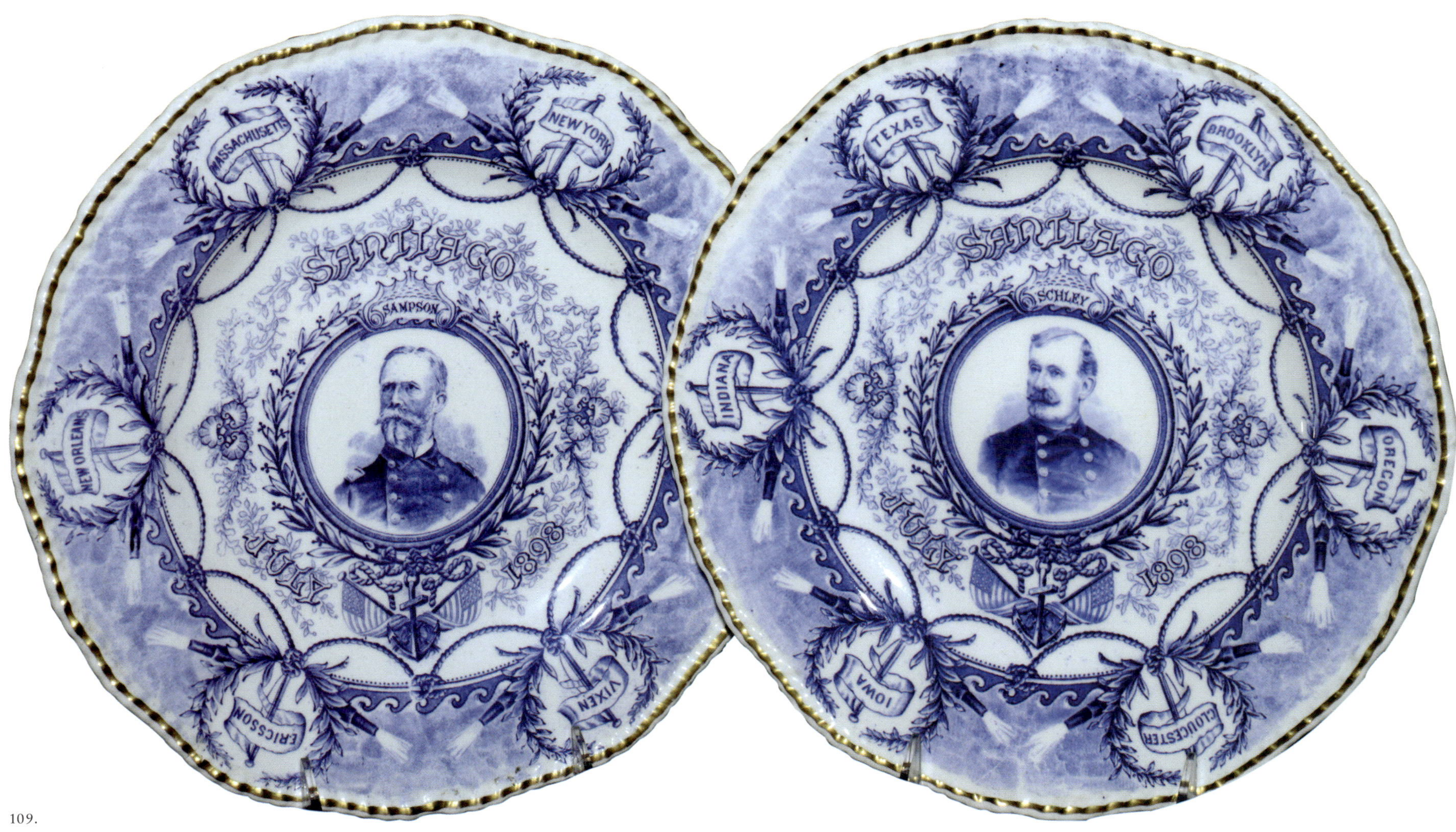

109.

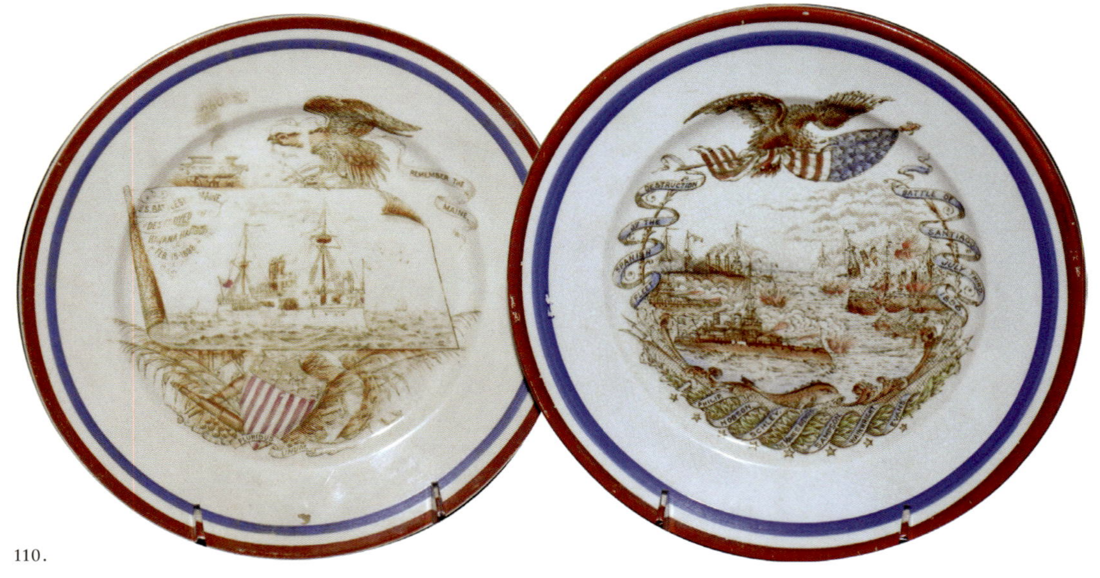

110.

· 110
The Maine, left. Taliafero & Thomas (Baltimore, Maryland, US); Naval battle of Santiago. Edwin Bennett Pottery (Baltimore, Maryland, US), ca. 1898, right.

· 111
The Maine, surrounded by victorious ships at Santiago de Cuba: Nashville, the New York and the Vesuvius. The Sebring (Sebring, Ohio, US), ca. 1898.

· 112
US & Cuban flags. Unmarked (US), ca. 1898.

· 113
The Maine. Unmarked (Dresden, Germany), ca. 1898.

· 114
US & Cuban flags. Columbia (US), ca. 1898.

· 115
"There is room for one more star". Danbury, Connecticut Fair (US), October 3, 1898.

· 116
Fritz Kredel. "Cuban expedition 1898" [Soldiers of the American Army]. Abercrombie & Fitch (New York, US), 1940s.

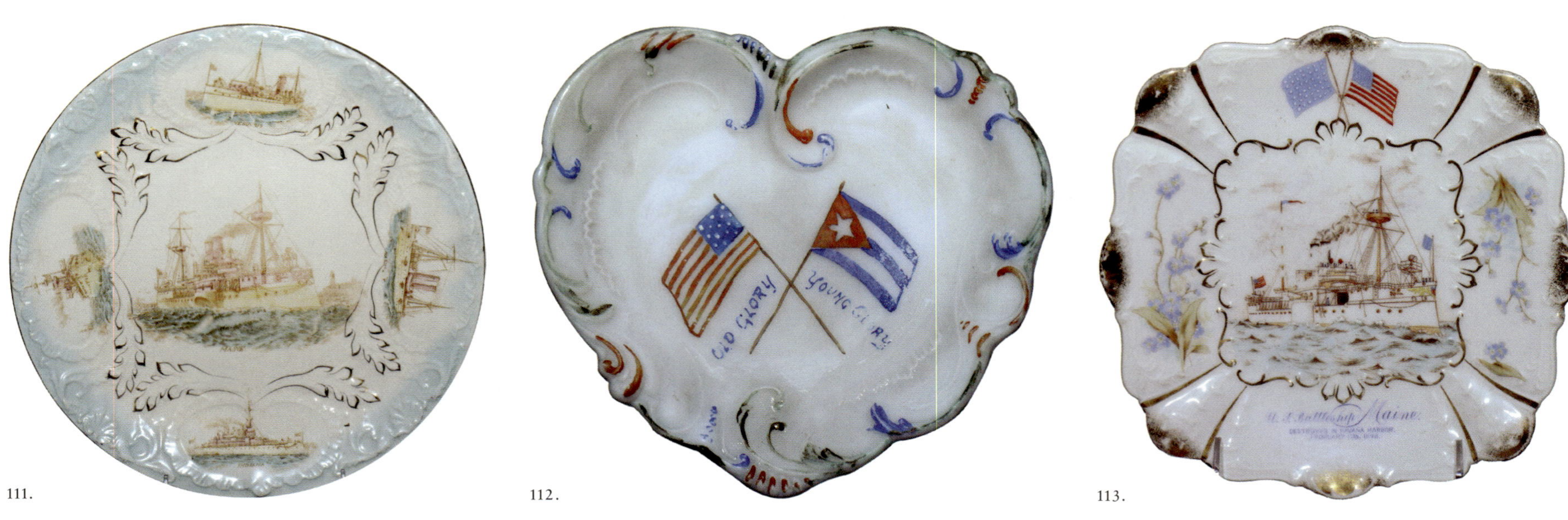

111.

112.

113.

One particularly interesting piece is a planter/jardinière depicting the members of the Court of Inquiry investigating the causes of the *Maine* explosion. It also includes images of the fallen ship, as well as those of Captain Charles Sigsbee (1845-1923) and US Consul Fitzhugh Lee. I have seen it in green and purple colors.

A few plates remember the naval battle of Santiago (Fig. 110) and some of the US ships — *Nashville*, *New York* and *Vesuvius* — which took part therein (Fig. 111). Other pieces show the US and Cuban flag side by side (Figs. 112-115), including one hand-painted bell reminding us of the annexationist sentiment prevalent in the US in 1898 (Fig. 115). Another pitcher with crossing US and Cuban flags was made by the Mercer Pottery Company "Ironstone China Nassau" mark, from Trenton, New Jersey.

In 1901 the Dutch Regout firm registered a pattern with a scroll proclaiming "Cuba Libre", but I have only seen an image of the decoration, not an actual plate. Even four decades after the end of that war, the famous New York store Abercrombie & Fitch had transferred onto plates the "Cuban expedition 1898" design by Fritz Kredel (Fig. 116).

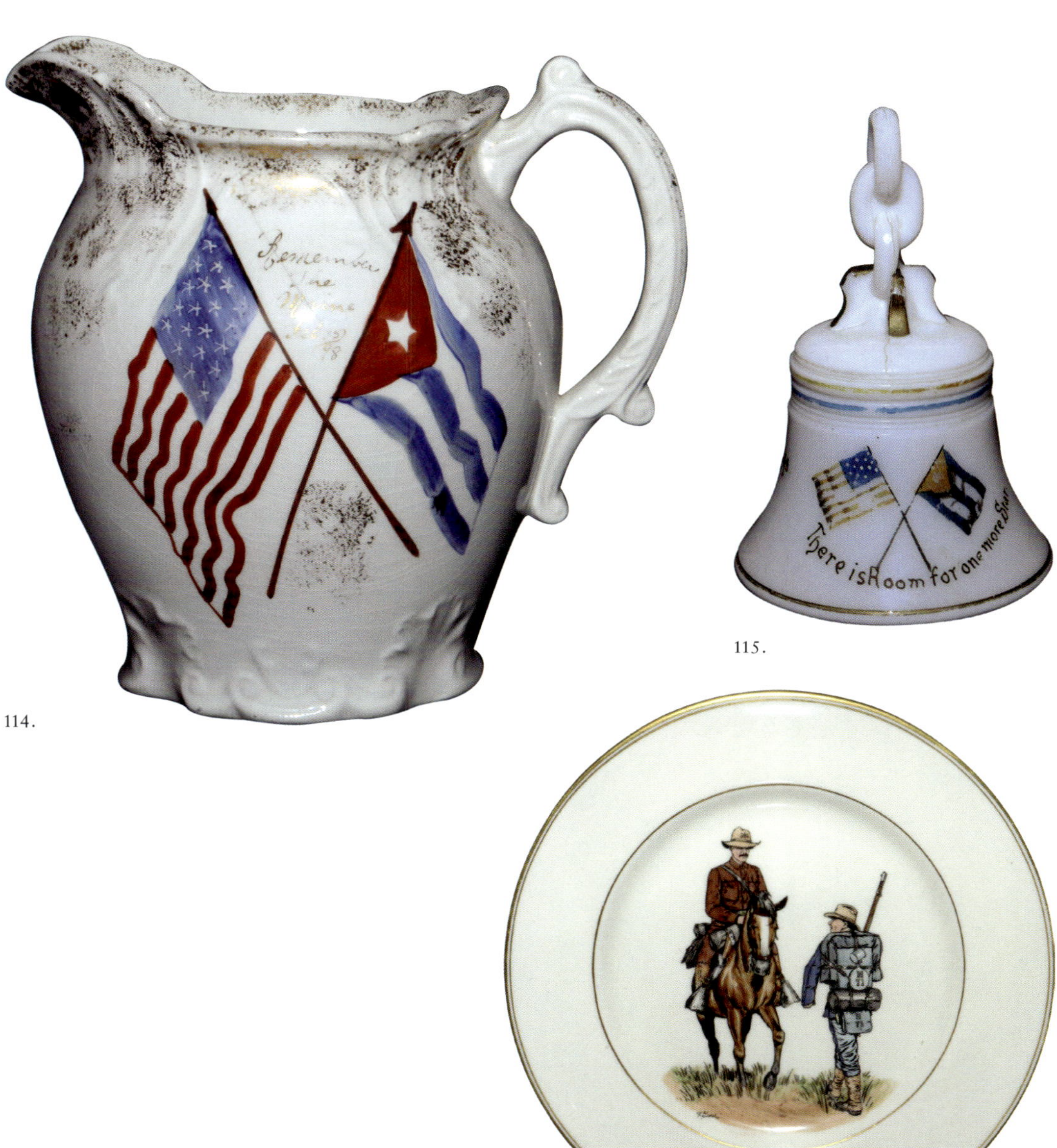

114.

115.

116.

Tobacco items

Christopher Columbus made a fascinating entry in his *Diary* on Tuesday, November 6 1492: "The two Christians [Rodrigo de Jerez and Luis de Torres] found many people, men and women, on their journey who were on their way to their villages carrying a smouldering brand of herbs which they are accustomed to smoke". Since that fortuitous day, Cuba (particularly Havana) and tobacco have been inseparable.

And the connection between tobacco and ceramics is truly impressive. In order to extend the shelf life of the product (which must be kept in dry, humid places), the Dutch produced magnificently decorated tobacco jars for storing snuff tobacco dating from the 1760s (Figs. 117, 118 and 119) to this day (Fig. 120).

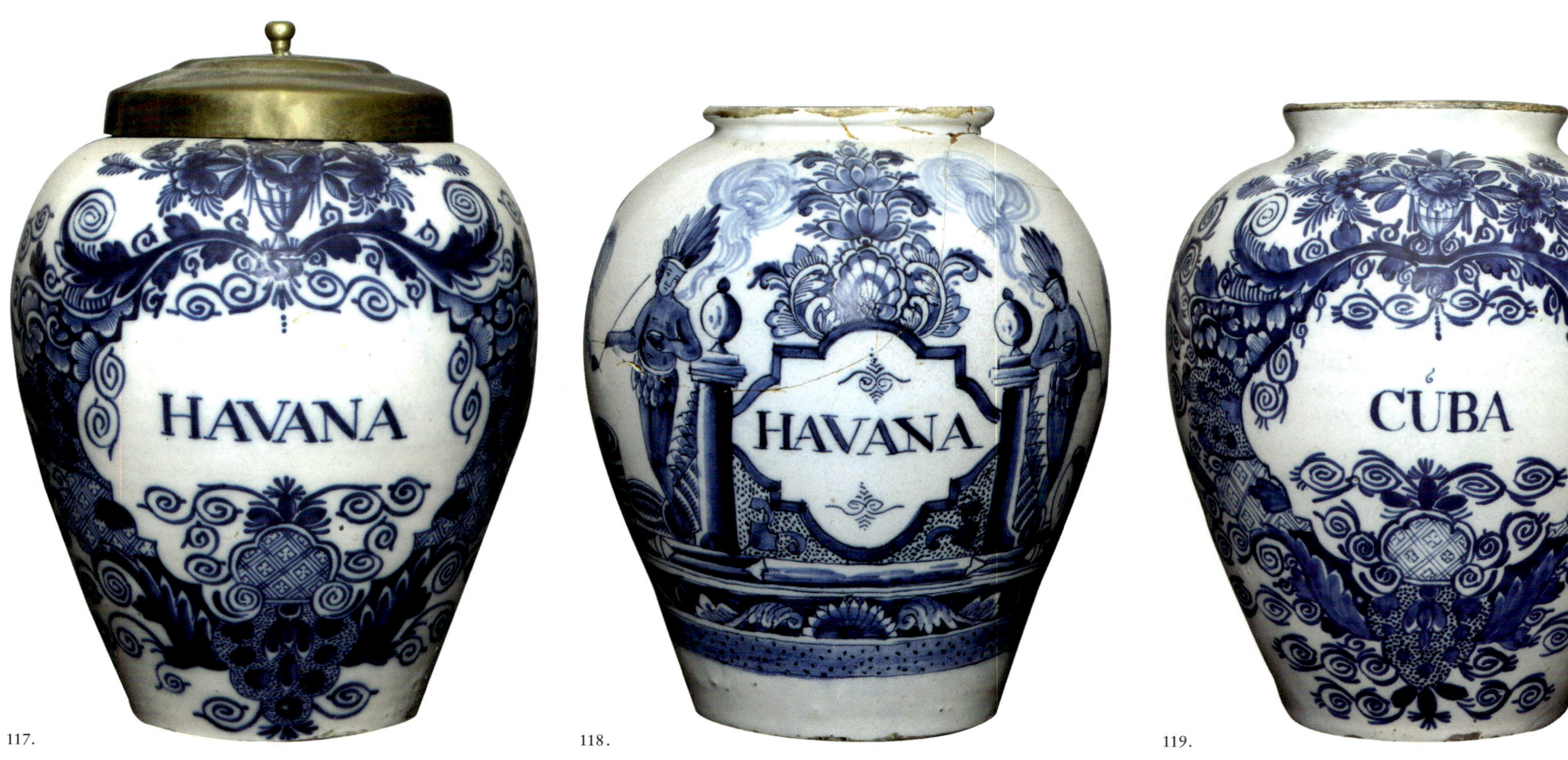

117. 118. 119.

These pieces were hand painted and no two decorations are similar. Inside the cartouche, the name of a country or city would be added so that the seller of tobacco could easily recognize the provenance from the outside label. Museums and antique shops often display these jars bearing the names of Portorico, St Vincent, Barinas (Venezuela), Virginia (US), St Omer (France), Manilla (Philippines), and of course "Cuba" and "Havana", which are the ones I do collect and the only ones discussed in this book.

Most of these jars were produced in the city of Delft, well known for its decorations in blue and white. Among the most famous Delft potteries of tobacco jars we can cite De Blompot (Figs. 117 and 118), Quirinus Mesch (Fig. 119), and De Drije Klokken (the three bells) (Figs. 121 and 122). These jars were also made in Nijmegen by Oud Delft (Figs. 123, 124 and 125) and in Gouda by Royal Goedewaagen (Fig. 120).

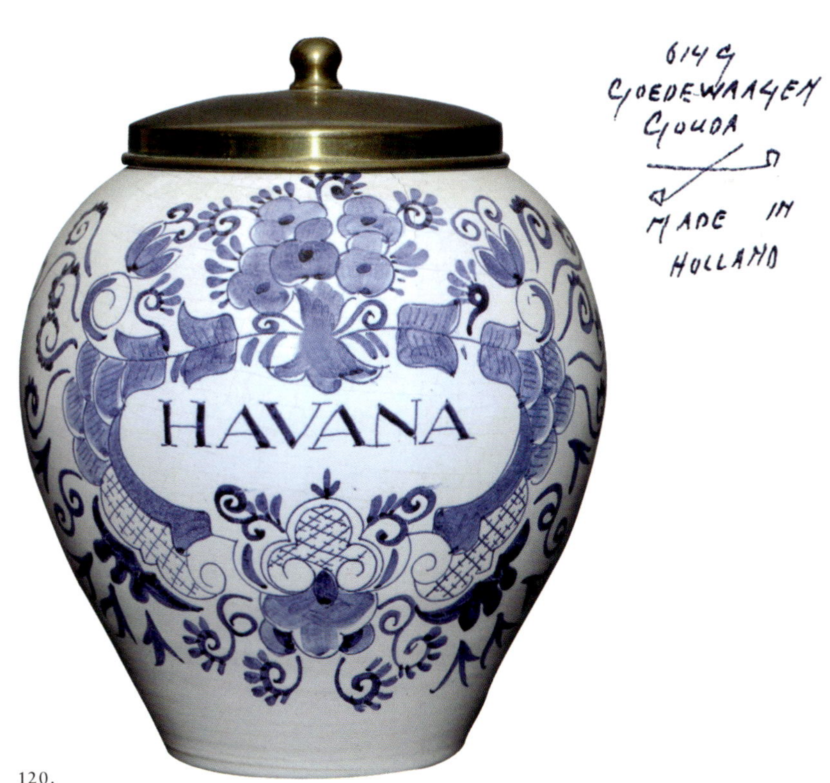

120.

· 117
Havana. De Blompot
(Delft, Holland), 18th century.

· 118
Havana. De Blompot
(Delft, Holland), 18th century.

· 119
Cuba. Quirinus Mesch
(Delft, Holland), 18th century.

· 120
Havana. Royal Goedewaagen
(Gouda/ Nieuw-Buinen, Holland),
20th-21st century.

121.

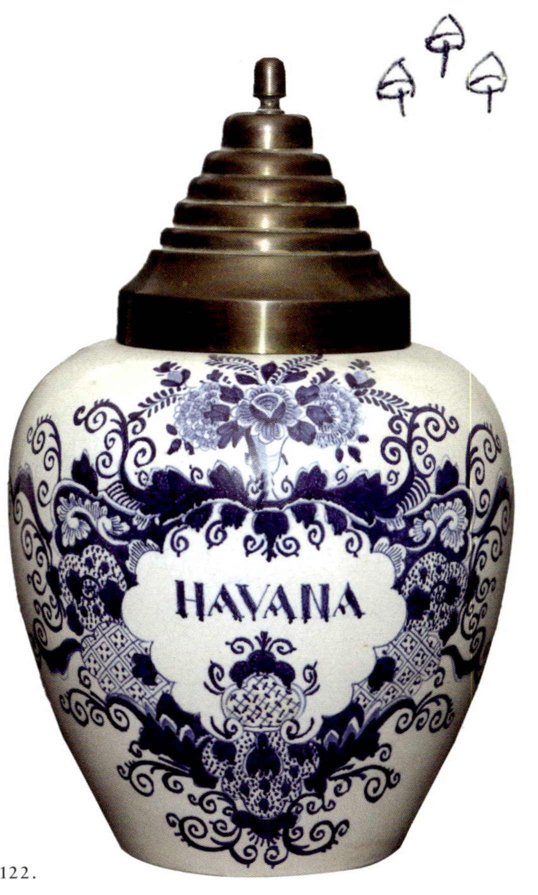

122.

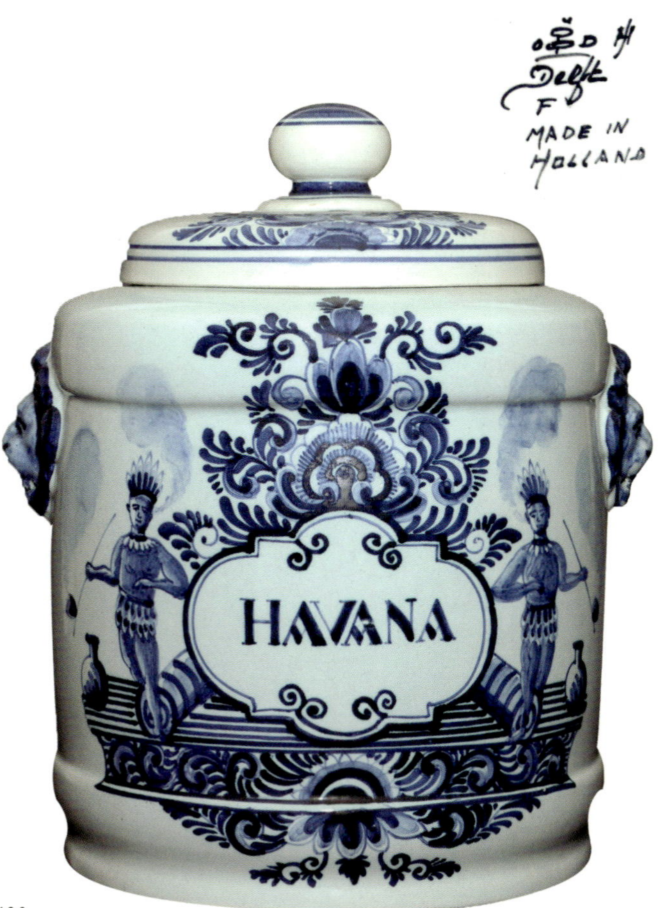

123.

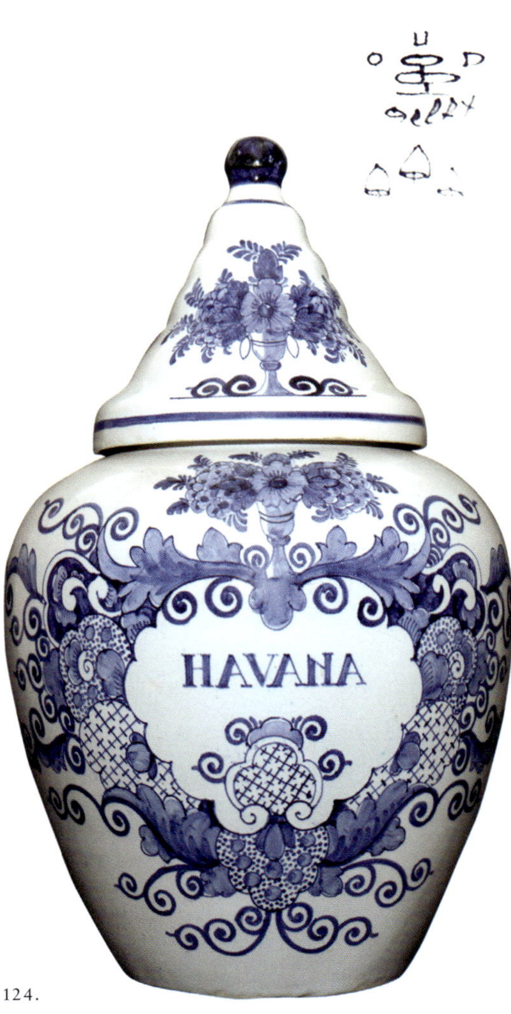

124.

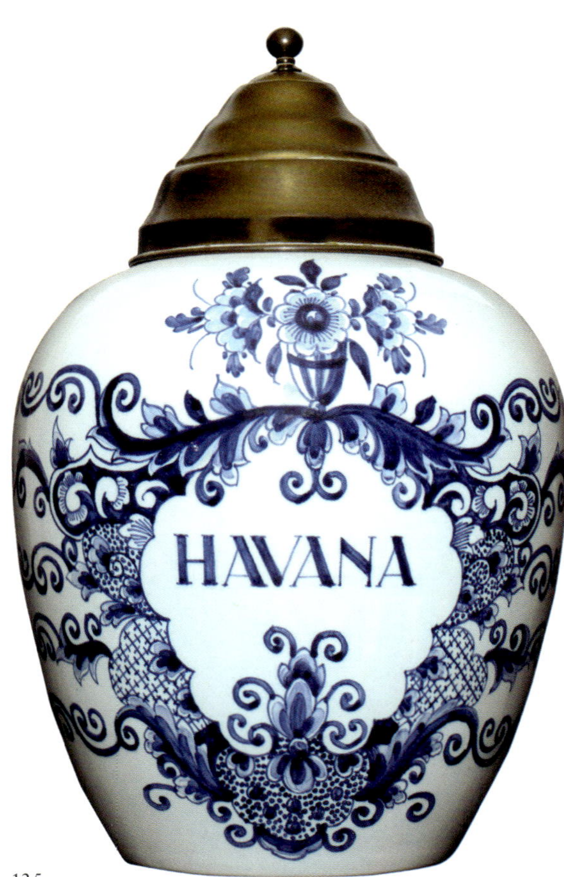

125.

· 121

Havana. De Drije Klokken
(Delft, Holland), 18th-19th century.

· 122

De Drije Klokken
(Delft, Holland), 18th-19th century.

· 123

Havana. Oud Delft
(Nijmegen/ Waddinxveen, Holland),
20th century.

· 124

Havana. Oud Delft
(Nijmegen/ Waddinxveen, Holland),
20th century.

· 125

Havana. Oud Delft
(Nijmegen/ Waddinxveen, Holland),
20th century.

During the first half of the 20th century (1940s?), very attractive multi-colored tobacco jars were produced by the Koninklijke Tichelaar Makkum factory in the Frisian part of Holland, bearing the labels of both "Cuba" (Figs. 126, 127) and "Havana" (Figs. 128, 129, 130).

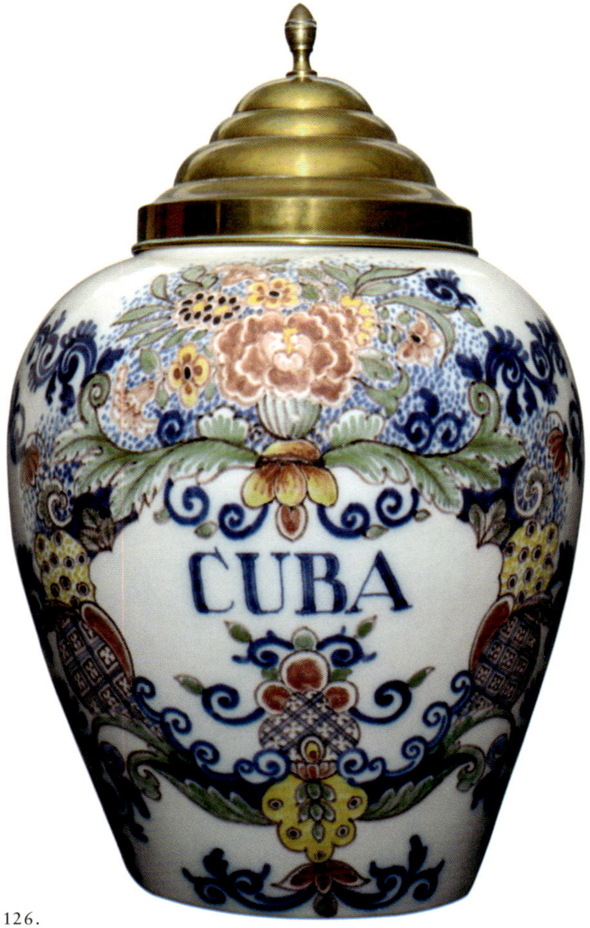

126.

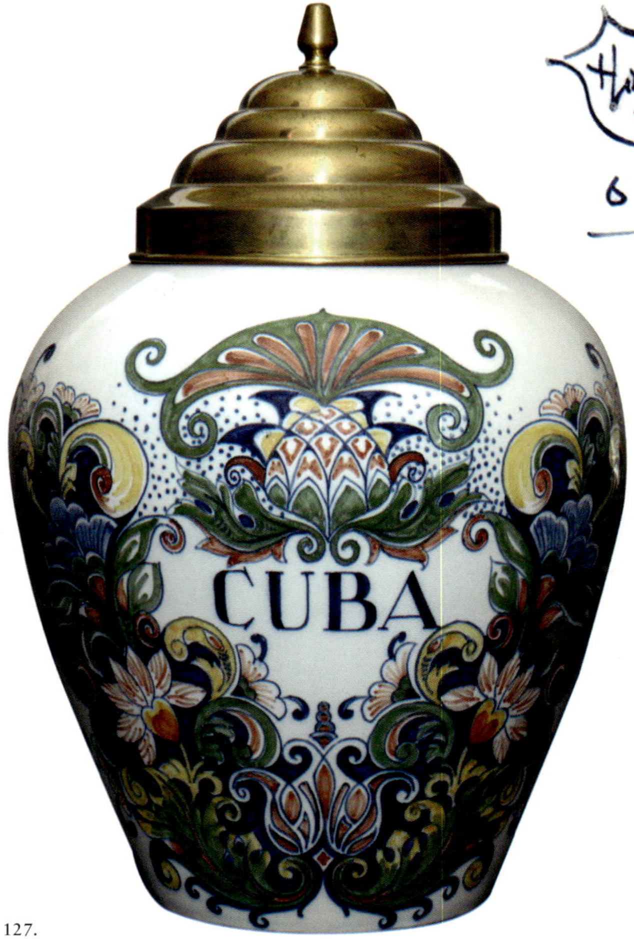

127.

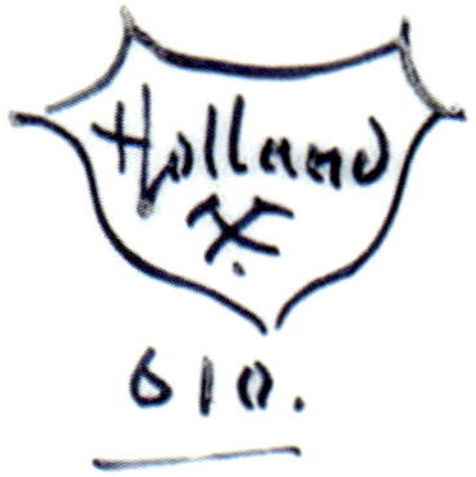

· 126
Cuba. Koninklijke Tichelaar (Makkum, Holland), 1940s?

· 127
Cuba. Koninklijke Tichelaar (Makkum, Holland), 1940s?

· 128
Havana. Koninklijke Tichelaar (Makkum, Holland), 1960s?

· 129
Havana. Koninklijke Tichelaar (Makkum, Holland), 1940s?

· 130
Havana. Koninklijke Tichelaar (Makkum, Holland), 1940s?

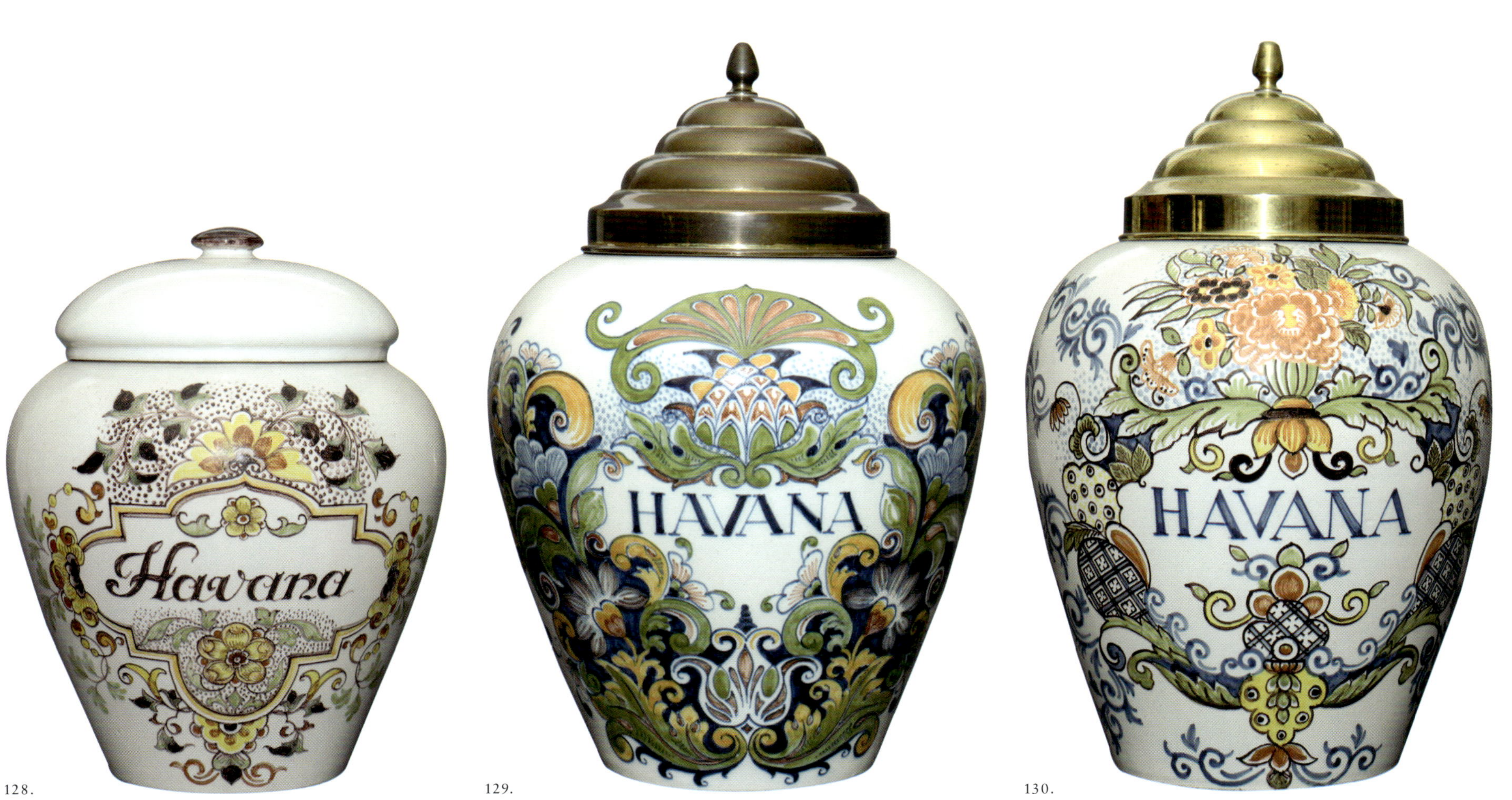

128.

129.

130.

Other humidors designed to preserve the aroma of the Havana cigars have been produced at various times and places. Foremost among these pieces are the well-crafted items by Johann Maresch (1821-1914) in then Aussig, Bohemia—today's Ústí nad Labem in the Czech Republic (Figs. 131, 132, 133), as well as more recent and cheaper imitations thereof. Other interesting vintage humidors include an unmarked 1920s "Havannah Segars" piece (Fig. 134), a 1920s Partagás cigar brand jar made in Talavera, Spain, and mid-1920s-1930s items by the Pickman (La Cartuja) factory in Seville, Spain, for both the Partagás (Fig. 135) and Ramón Allones factories. More contemporary pieces come from France (Fig. 136) and Mexico (Fig. 137). Cuban artist Nelson Alfonso is responsible for the design of the Gloria Cubana humidors.[45]

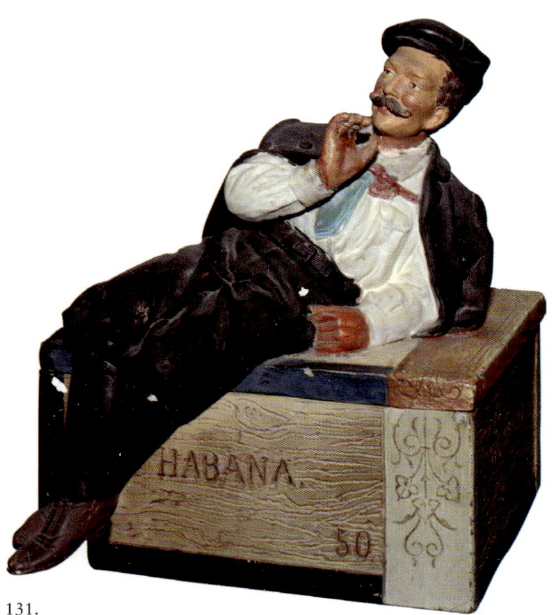

131.

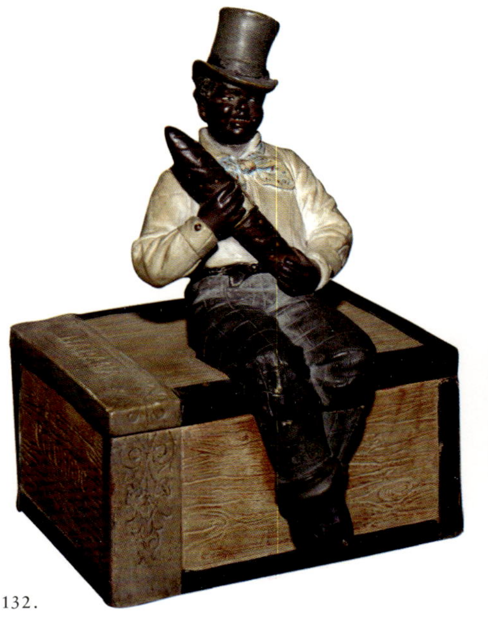

132.

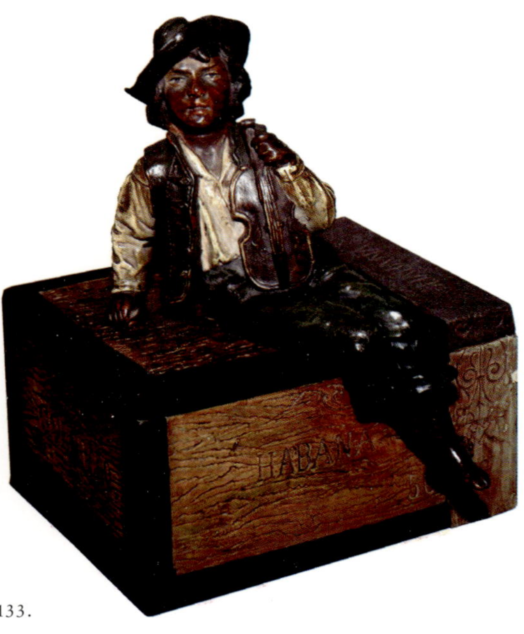

133.

45. Old Havana's Cigar Museum holds a variety of tobacco-related materials, including a set of vintage humidors. See Leonardo Depestre Catony, "El Museo del Tabaco", *Correo de Cuba* (Havana), 4º trimestre, 2002, pp. 50-51.

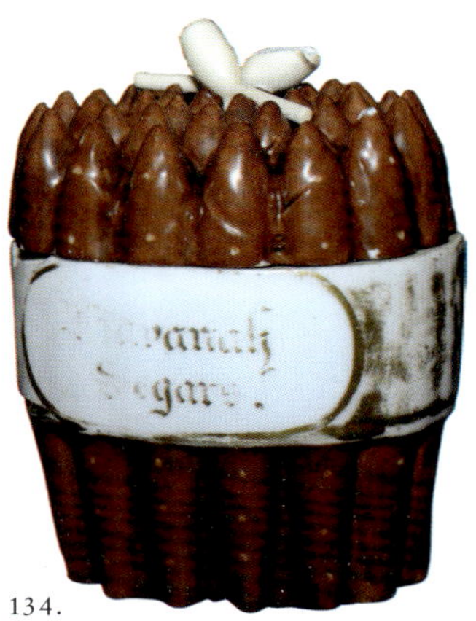

134.

135.
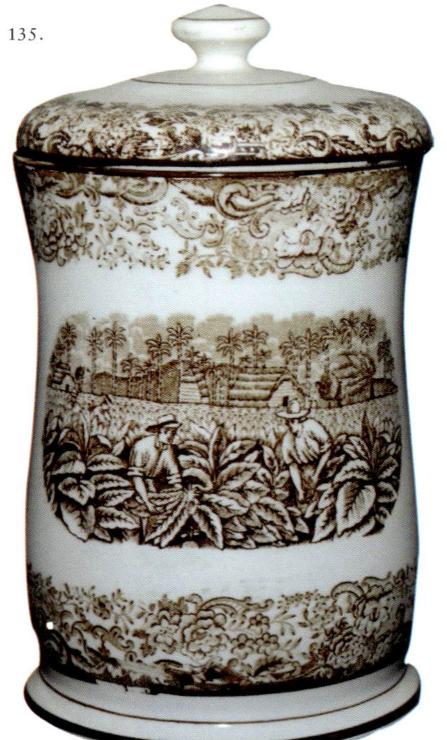

136.
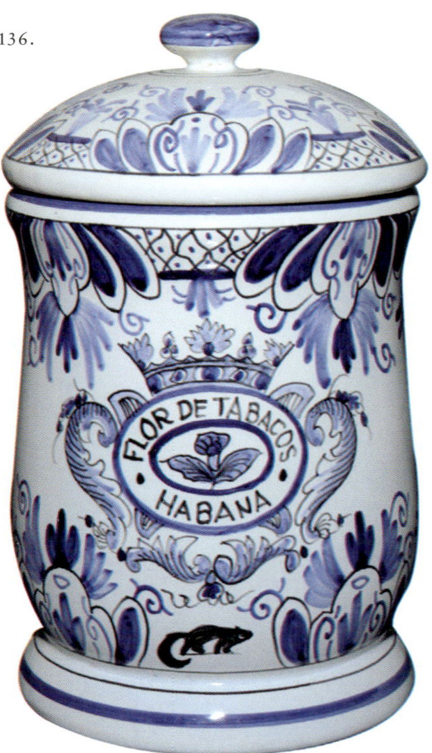

137.
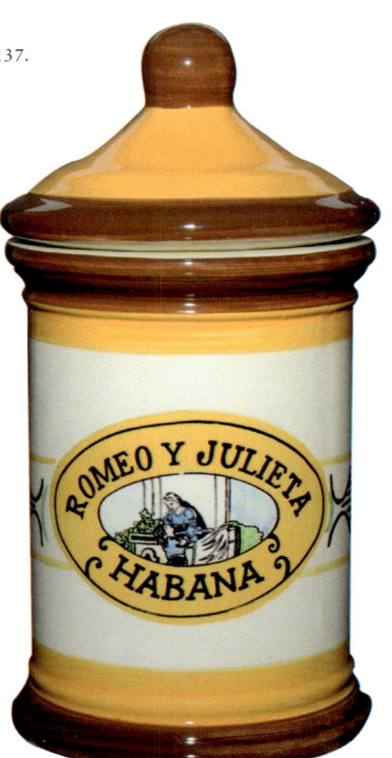

· 131-133
Johann Maresch (Ústí nad Labem, Czech Republic), ca. 1900.
· 134
Havannah Segars. Unmarked (UK?). 1920s?
· 135
Partagás. Pickman/La Cartuja (Seville, Spain), 1930s.
· 136
À la Civette (Paris, France), 1990s?
· 137
Romeo y Julieta. Unmarked (Mexico). 200-.

Smoking produces ashes, and a spent cigar must be disposed of, so the ashtray was born. Ashtrays used to be everywhere… because we smoked everywhere: inside the home, in restaurants and hotels, in airplanes, in waiting rooms, even in doctor's offices and hospitals. They were also purchased as souvenirs from trips abroad.[46]

As would be expected, Cuba-themed ashtrays come in all shapes, colors and sizes: A Batista propaganda piece displaying some of the buildings completed during his mandate (Fig. 138), the silhouette of the island (Fig. 139), a souvenir of the typical Cuban hut (Fig. 140), a colorful rendition by Ruben Estefan (Fig. 141) and an ashtray for the Asociación de Dependientes clinic in Havana by Clementson (Hanley, UK). Recently, large ashtrays displaying the Punch and Cohiba brands have been produced by White Ash/ Xonex (Cleveland, Ohio), and Tabacalera de García in La Romana, Dominican Republic, has issued a splendid Romeo y Julieta piece.

Of particular importance is a piece (I have been told it is Austrian) dating from the Cuba War of Independence (1898) showing Cuba in the shape of a cigar being torn apart by the forces of Spain and the U.S. (Fig. 143).

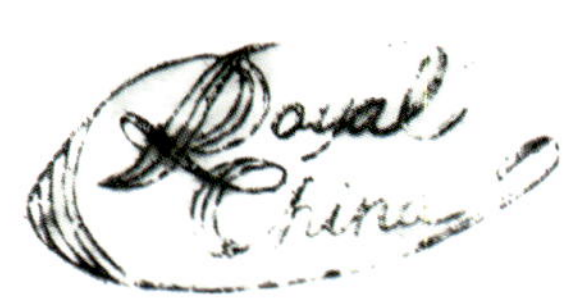

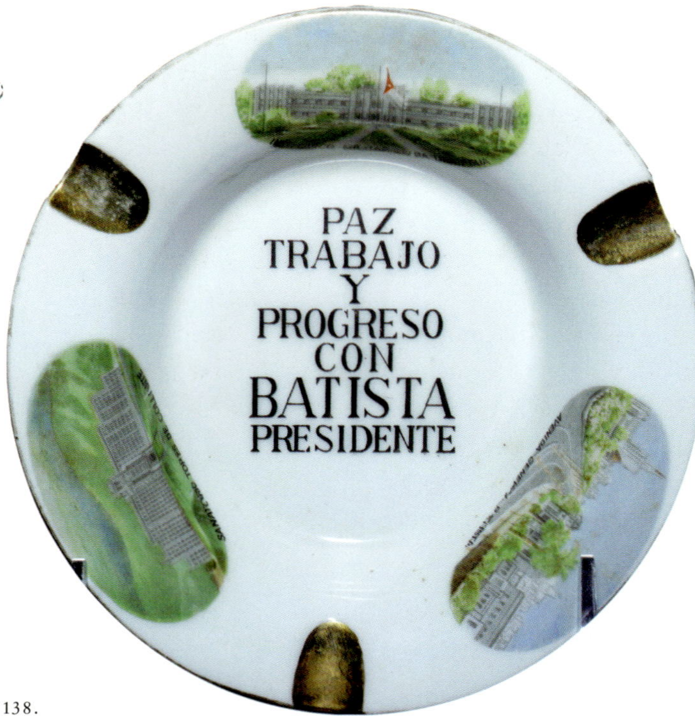

138.

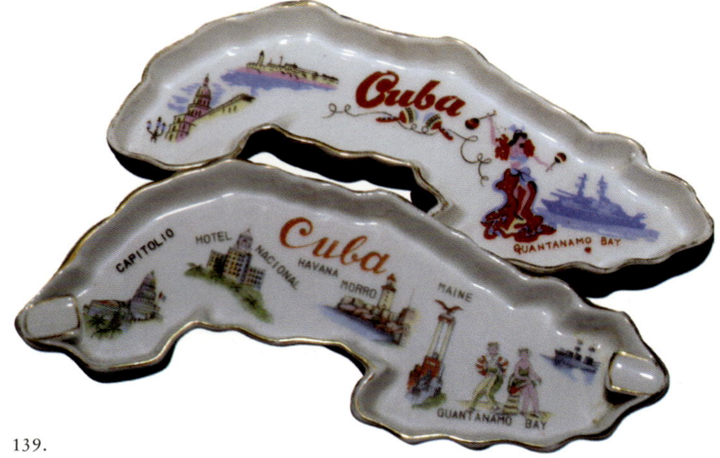

139.

46. For several decades now (one key element was the US Surgeon General's Report on smoking and health issued in 1964), tobacco use has been regulated in public spaces and many hotel rooms, restaurants, apartment buildings and even homes are now smoke-free. This appears to have led to a considerable decrease in the production of ashtrays, as they seem to be more difficult to find as souvenirs or as propaganda items.

There are many more tobacco items around, including a splendid cigarette and match holder piece advertising the Cuba brand, perhaps late nineteenth century-1910s (Fig. 144). Much later, in 2004 American Atelier issued a set of colorful Havana cigar plates (Fig. 142). French artists in the region of Limoges, France, well known for its porcelain, have been recently producing miniature Cuban-themed hand-painted cigar boxes (Figs. 145, 146).

One curious English tea pot in a whimsical shape depicting the Churchill Habana tobacco brand has caught our attention (Fig. 147). On a similar note, there is a colorful Cigar stein ("The bulldog") made by Albert Stahl & Co (Rudolstadt, Thuringia, Germany). Another striking novelty piece: a Havana cigar shop in New York City during Christmas, which lights up from the inside (Fig. 148).

· 138

Batista propaganda. Royal China (Sebring, Ohio, US), 1950s.

· 139

Map of Cuba. Princesa (Spain?), 1950s.

· 140

Typical bohio/ Cuban hut. Unmarked (US?), ca. 1940s.

· 141

Ruben Estefan (US), 201-?

· 142

American Atelier (New York, US; China), 2004.

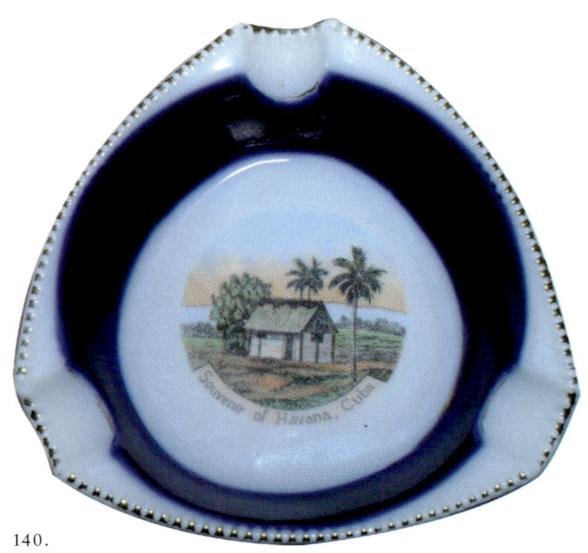

140.

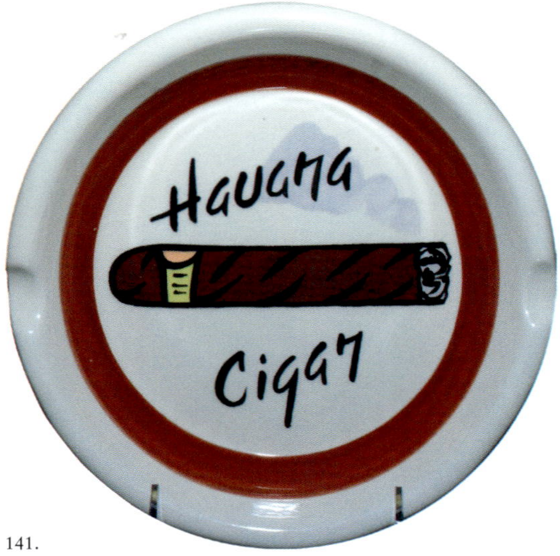

141.

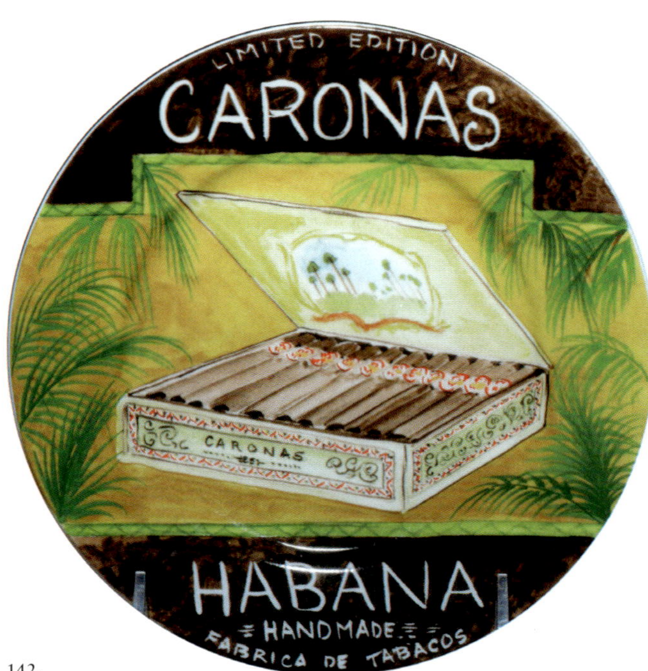

142.

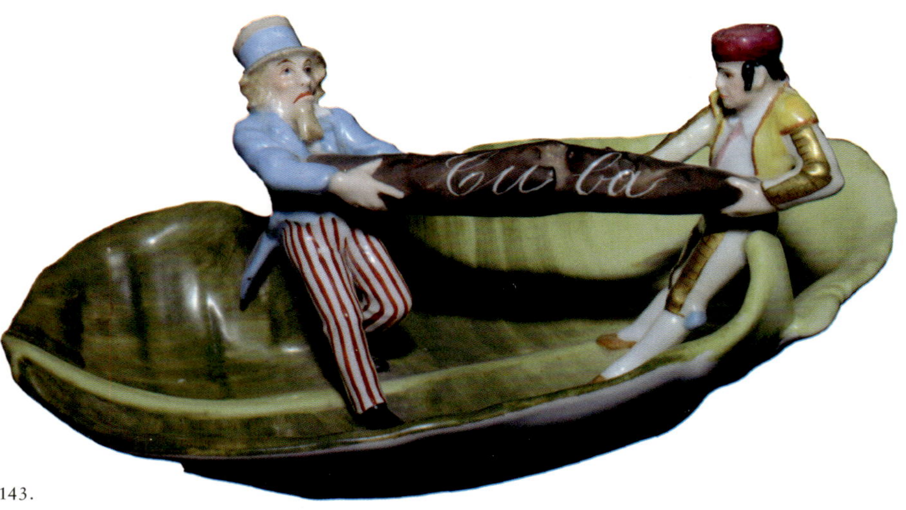

143.

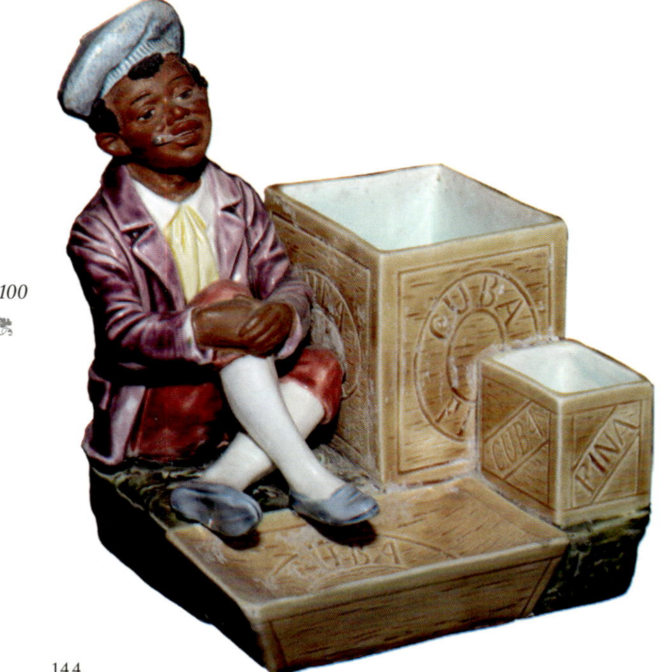

144.

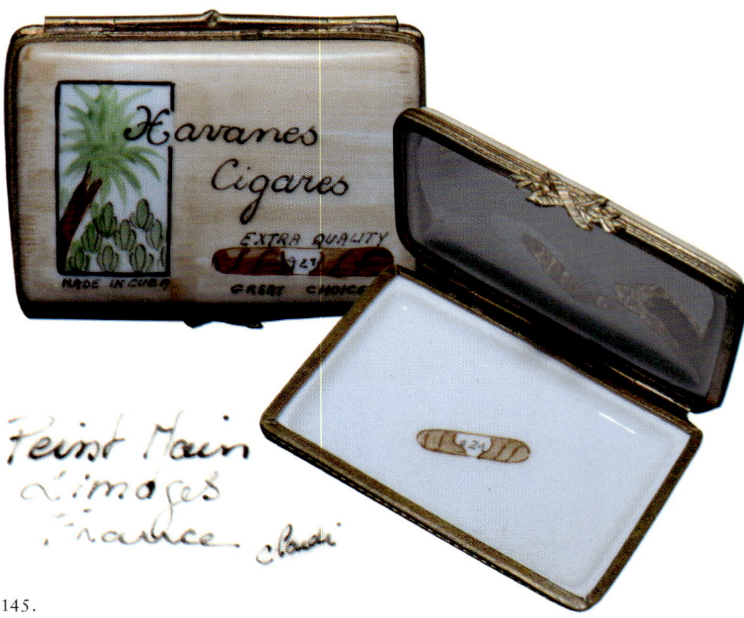

145.

· 143
Spain vs. Uncle Sam over Cuba.
Unmarked (Austria?), ca. 1898.

· 144
Cigarrete and match holder.
Unmarked (UK?), late 19th century-1910s.

· 145
Clardi? Hand painted
(Limoges, France), 200-.

· 146
G.P. Hand painted
(Limoges, France), 200-.

· 147
Swineside Teapottery (Leyburn, North Yorkshire, UK), 200-.

· 148
Havana's cigar shop.
Department 56 (Eden Prairie, Minnesota, US; China), 2008.

COHIBA
LEGITIMO TABACO IMPORTADO DE LA HAB
CUBA

146.

SWINESIDE ©
Teapottery
MADE IN ENGLAND
CHURCHILL
HECHO A MANO
IMPORTED
CHURCHILL
HECHO A MANO
HABANA

147.

CHRISTMAS IN THE CITY® SERIES
"HAVANA'S CIGAR SHOP"
DEPARTMENT 2008
56®
CIGAR
HAVANA'S
SHOP
FINEST QUALITY
HAVANA CIGARS

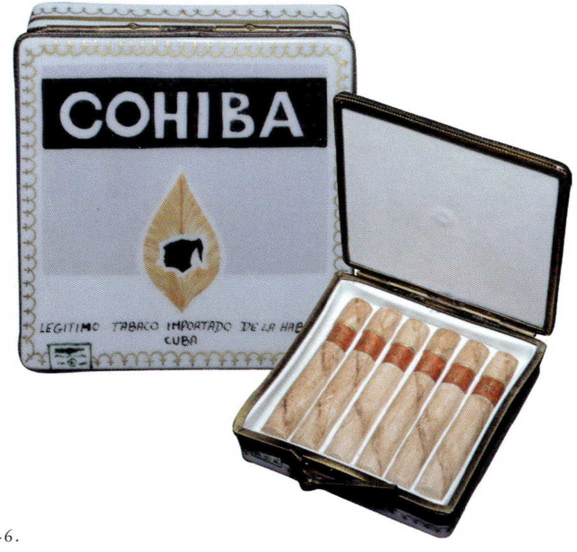

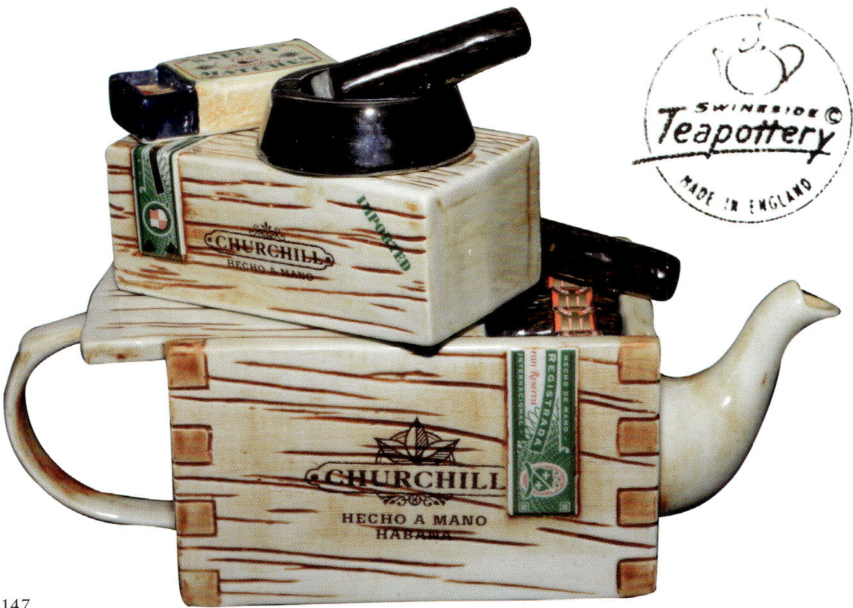

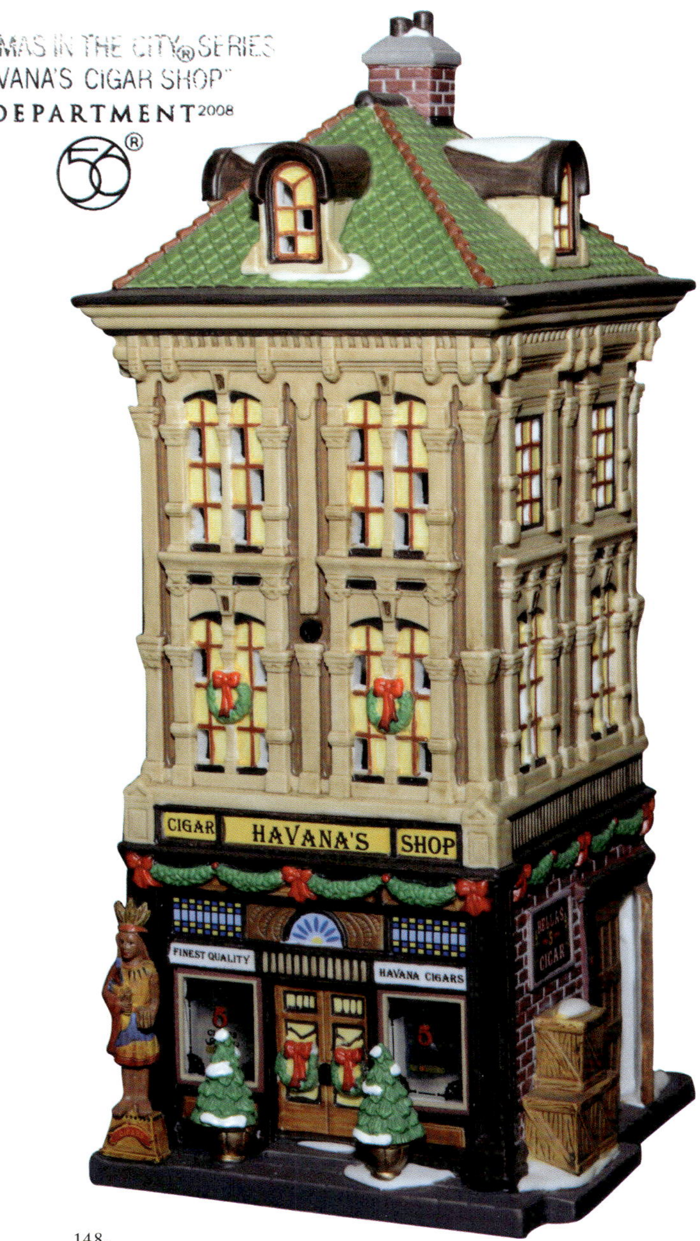

148.

Baseball memorabilia

At the end of the Summer of 1864 Nemesio and Esteban Guillot, two brothers who had been studying in Spring Hill College, run by Jesuit priests in Mobile, Alabama, returned to Havana. Nemesio had learned to play baseball in the US and packed a glove and a bat in his suitcase. Soon, Cubans, too, were playing baseball. A few years later, another Jesuit-trained Cuban student, Esteban Bellán (1849-1932), who had learned to play the game at St John's (today Fordham, in New York), also returned to Cuba and participated in the legendary game played on December 27 1874 at the *Palmar del Junco* stadium in Matanzas.

Baseball soon replaced bull fights as the favorite pastime of Cubans and is today considered to be the island's national sport (although, recently, football has made important advances among Cuban youth). During the next decades four teams dominated the field.[47]

Sometime during the 1940s or 1950s coffee sets and other ceramic objects (candle sticks, vases, book ends, lamps, etc.) were produced depicting the logos of each the four teams (Fig. 149).

They were collected, enjoyed and displayed by their respective fans: Almendares (Letter A, blue color, scorpion mascot, Fig. 150); Cienfuegos (Letter C, green color, elephant mascot, Fig. 151); Marianao (Letter M, orange color, tiger mascot, Fig. 152); and Habana (Letter H, red color, lion mascot, Fig. 153). I have not been able to ascertain if the initiative originated with the teams themselves or with the anonymous manufacturers, nor where the pieces were made.

· 149
4-club grouping. Unmarked, ca. 1940s-50s.

· 150
Club Almendares. Unmarked, ca. 1940s-50s.

· 151
Club Cienfuegos. Unmarked, ca. 1940s-50s.

· 152
Club Marianao. Unmarked, ca. 1940s-50s.

· 153
Club Habana. Unmarked, ca. 1940s-50s.

47. See Félix Julio Alfonso López, “Arqueología del béisbol cubano”. *Béisbol y nación en Cuba*. La Habana, Editorial Científico-Técnica, 2015, pp. 3-23; Roberto González Echevarría, *The Pride of Havana: a History of Cuban Baseball*. New York, Oxford University Press, 2001.

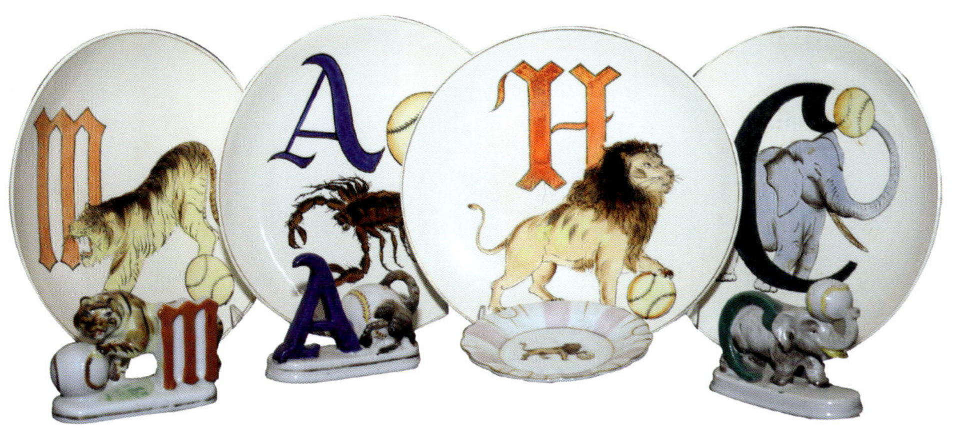

149.

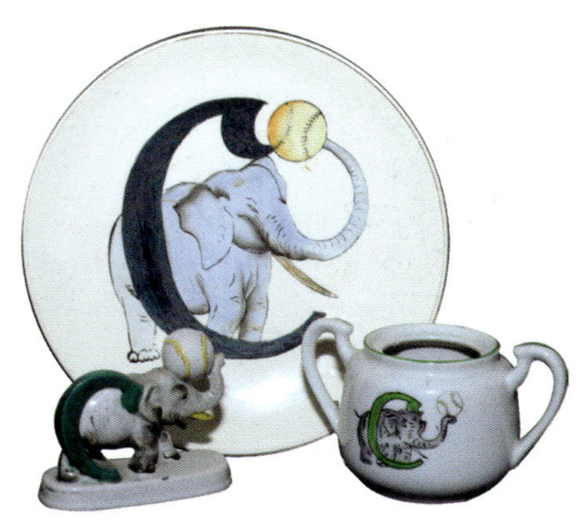

151.

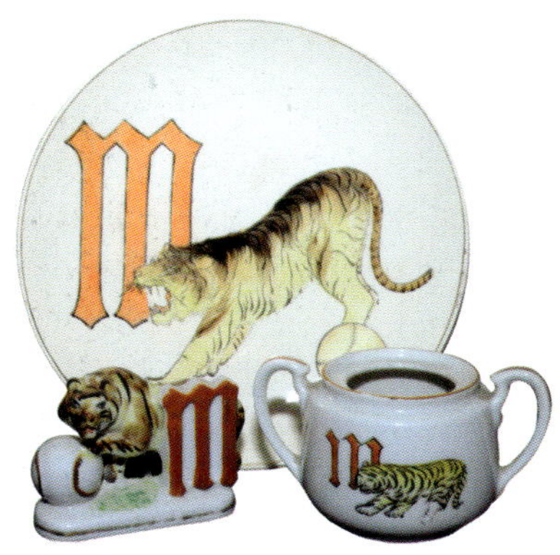

152.

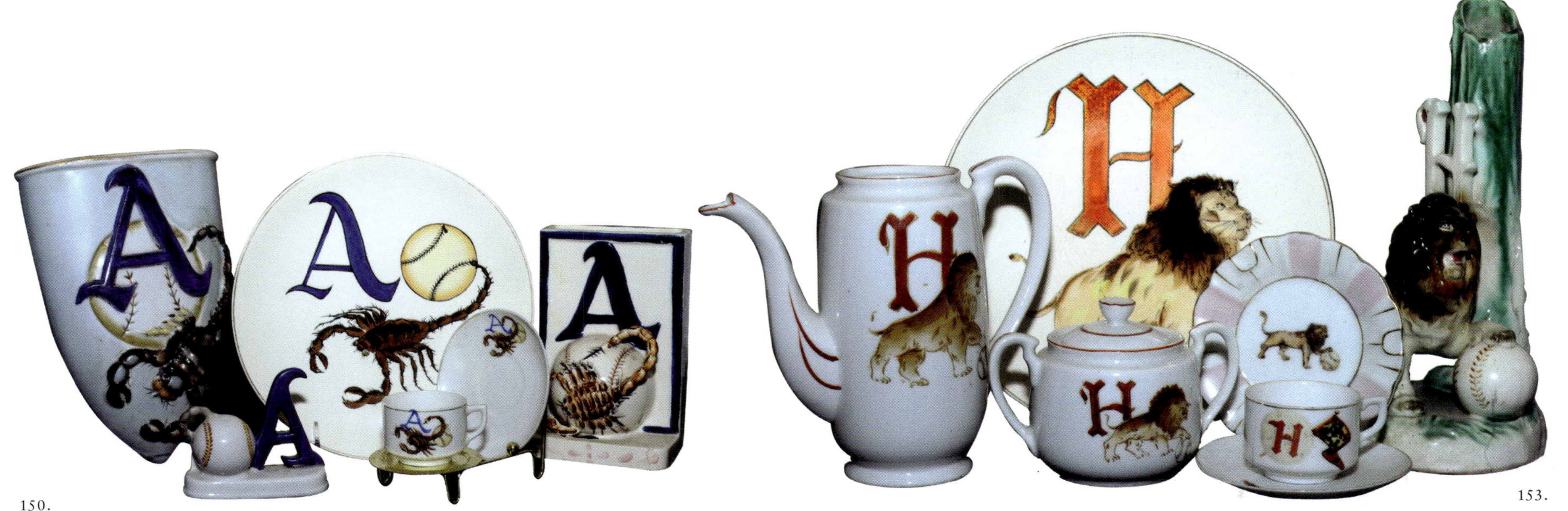

150.

153.

Religious images

A colony of Spain, early in the 16th century Cuba saw the arrival Catholic priests who began converting the natives and tended to the spiritual needs of the Spaniards and their offspring. As is well known, Catholics show special devotion to Saints, who they believe can intercede with God for favors on earth and beyond.

This practice generated the manufacture of statues, many on wood (later plastic) but also in ceramic, not only for display on the altars of churches but also to be kept at home for private devotion.

Foremost among Cuban devotions is that of our Lady of Charity, Cuba's patron saint.[48] A particularly interesting piece is the 1995 porcelain statue by the Valencia-based Lladró factory (Fig. 155). One popular plate with the image of La Virgen de la Caridad was distributed throughout Cuba during the 1940s (Fig. 154). Other items in my collection include works by Camagüey artist Maydelina Pérez Lezcano; a mosaic by my talented friend Rael Rodríguez Capote (Fig. 156), who also donated a larger piece to Pope Benedict XVI during his visit to Cuba in 2012.

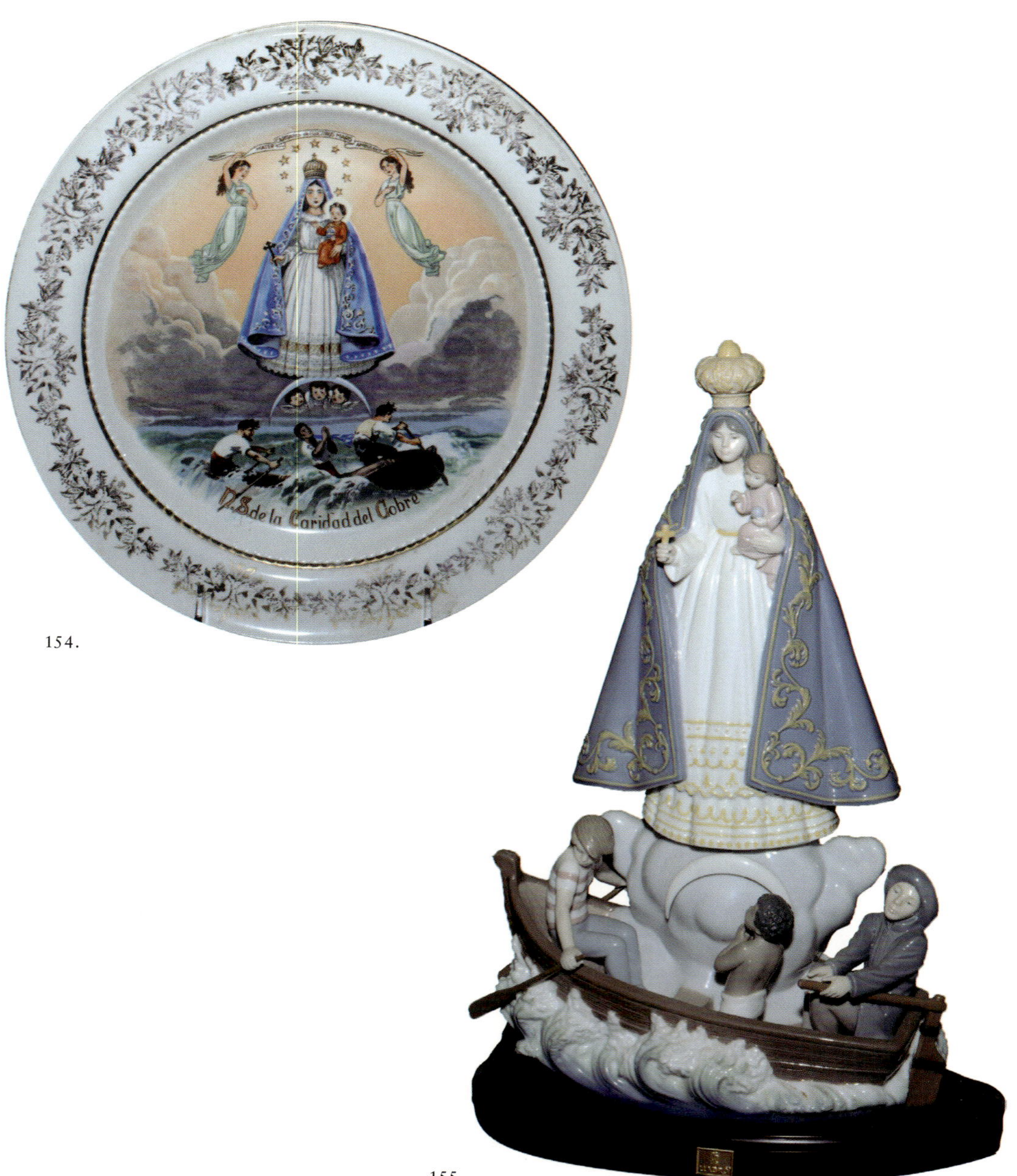

154.

155.

---

48. See Olga Portuondo, *La virgen de la Caridad del Cobre: símbolo de cubanía*. Santiago de Cuba, Editorial Oriente, 1995 and Emilio Cueto, *La Virgen de la Caridad del Cobre en el alma del pueblo cubano*. Ciudad de Guatemala, Guatemala, Ediciones Polymita, 2014.

I also display at home a plate by Sagua-born, Miami resident Emilio Falero, an innovative piece by Bernardo Cueto, also in the US (Fig. 157), sculptures by Venezuelan artists Luis Acosta (Fig. 158) and Bris (Fig. 161), a statute from the Luciana Collection made in China (Fig. 159), a charming, funny piece by the St Andrew's Abbey in California (Fig. 160) an unmarked Cuban vase (Fig. 162), and several other pieces, many of which are illustrated in my book *La Virgen de la Caridad del Cobre* already cited. Cubans, like all other Catholics around the world, also

156.

157.

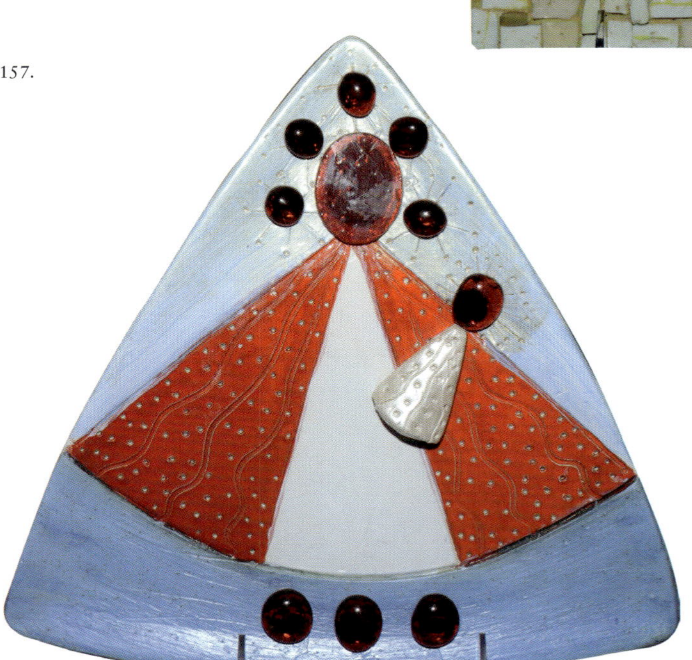

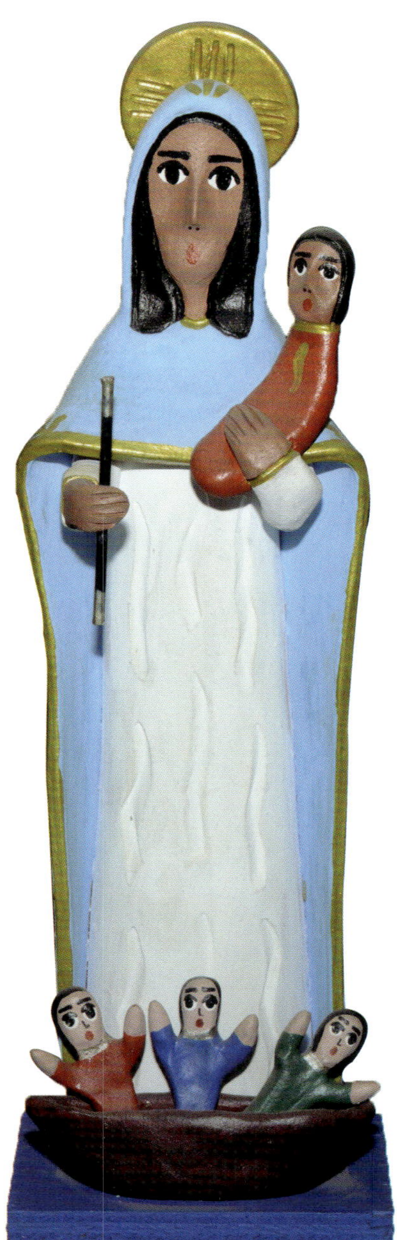

158.

· 154

Anonymous (Cuba?), 1940s?

· 155

Lladró (Tavernes Blanques, Valencia, Spain), 1995.

· 156

Rael Rodríguez Capote (Bauta, Artemisa, Cuba), 2015.

· 157

Bernardo Cueto (US), 21st century.

· 158

Luis Acosta (Caracas, Venezuela), 1991.

pray to many other saints, both in churches and at home. Therefore, Cuban churches (and Catholics schools, before their confiscation by the Government in 1961) are filled with holy statutes, many of which are surely made out of some form of clay. And in many Cuban houses and apartments one may find sacred spaces with ceramic images or ritual items. Finally, we should mention the coats of arms of various Cuban bishops appearing in ceramic pieces. That of Monsignor Guerra, already mentioned, is at the Santiago Archdiocesan museum. That of Havana's Cardinal Jaime Ortega ended up in tiles made at El Cotorro's suburb in Havana.

· 159
Luciana Collection (USA; China). 21st century.

· 160
St Andrew's Abbey (Valyermo, California, US), 1990s.

· 161
Bris, ca. 1996. Probably refers to firm founded by José Gregorio Hernández in Mérida, Venezuela.

· 162
Anonymous (Cuba), 21st century.

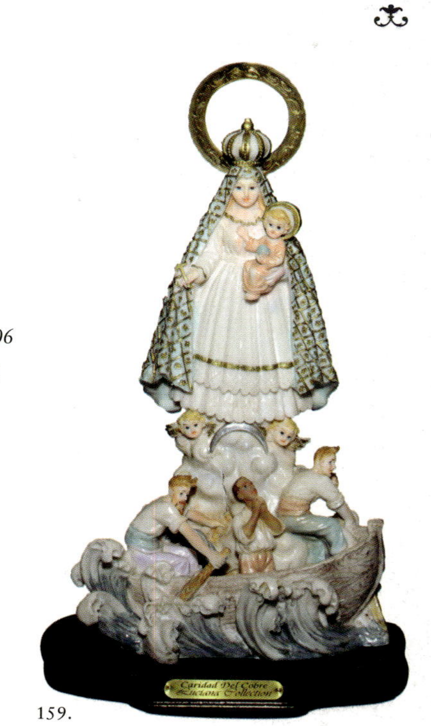

159.

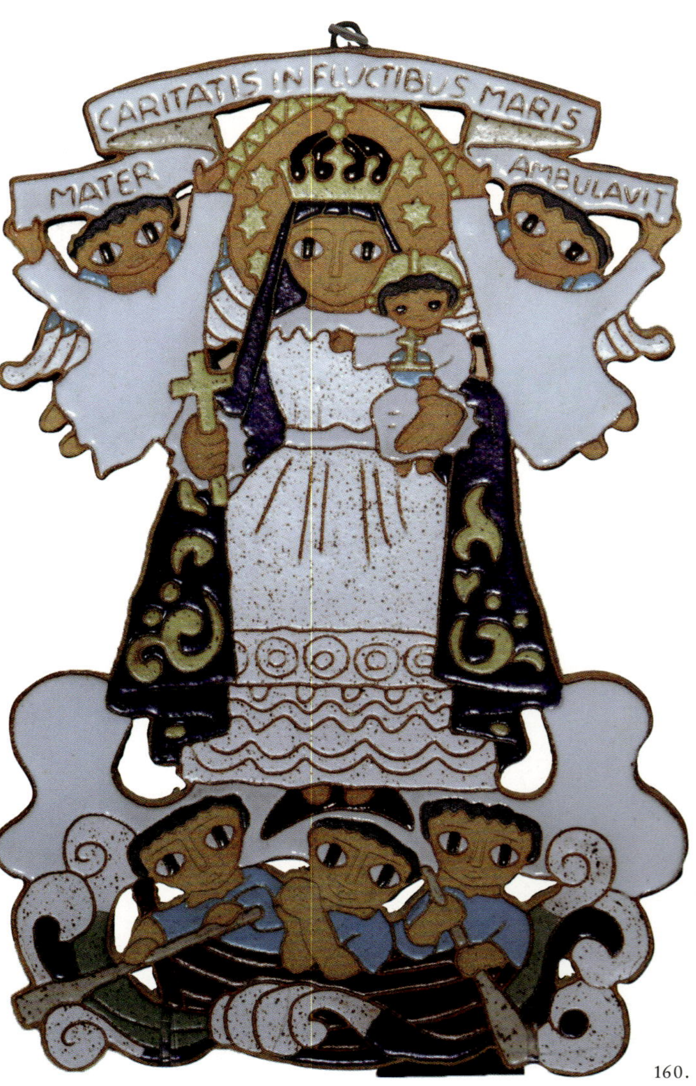

160.

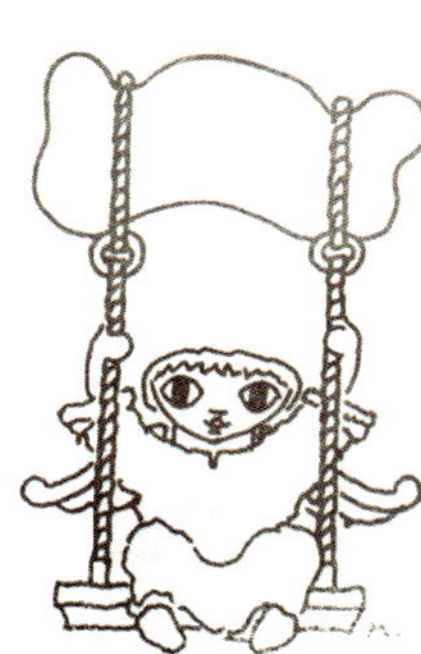

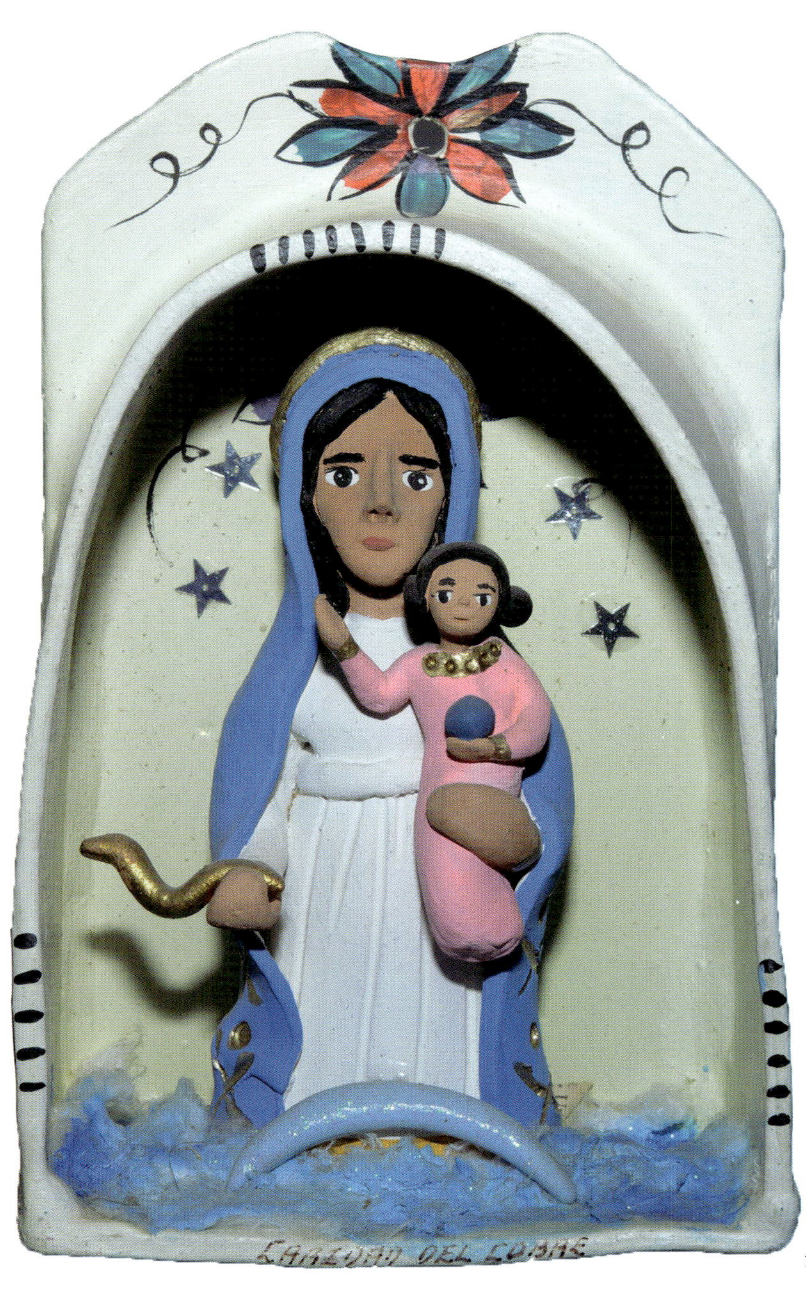

161.

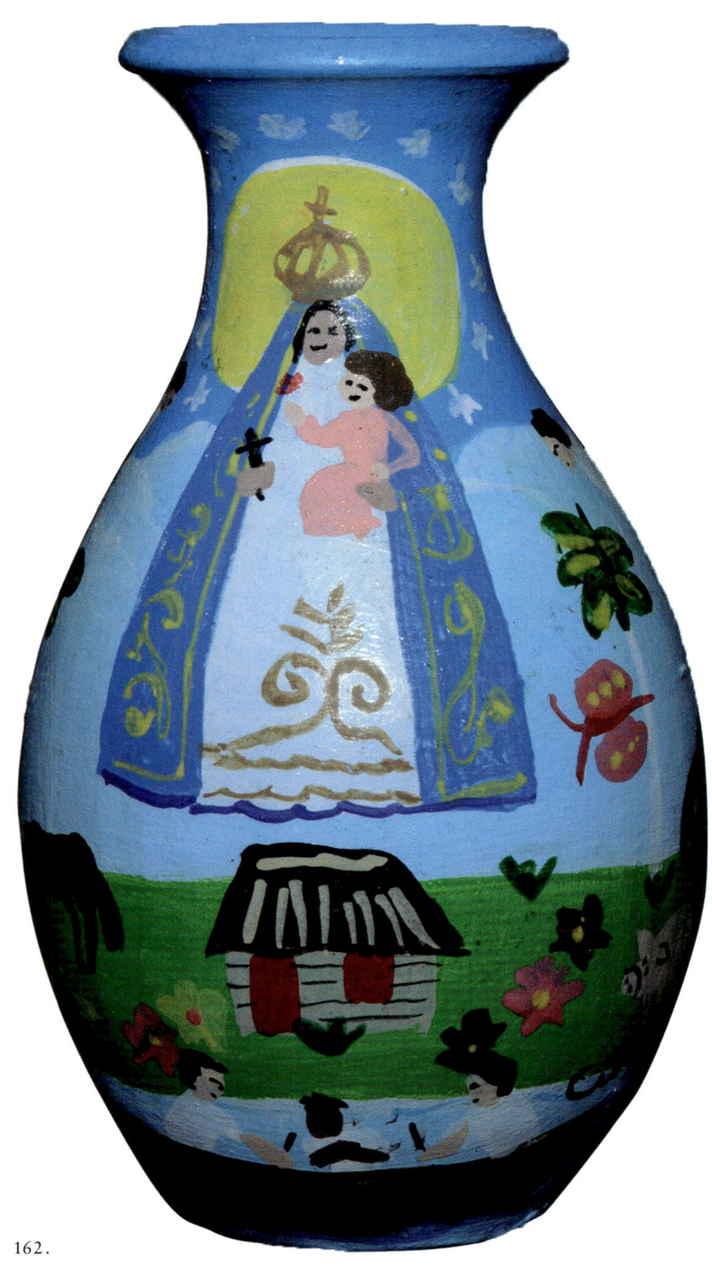

162.

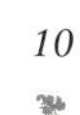

GUANTANAMO

Guantanamo Bay and surrounding areas in that Southeastern part of Cuba were occupied by the American invading forces in June 1898 and the U.S. has been present there ever since. By the terms of a bilateral treaty, there is no timetable requiring an eventual U.S. departure. "Gitmo" is, simultaneously, a part of Cuba in the U.S. and vice versa. A U.S. naval base for over a century, it has housed and hosted thousands of American troops.

To satisfy the needs of servicemen who want to keep a memento of their stay in foreign territory, many Guantanamo souvenirs are sold in the base, which returning officers bring back to the mainland after their tour of duty. Items include decorative plates, mugs, pitchers, bells (Fig. 163), as well as a large attractive piece made by Katry (Fig. 164). The shape of the island is a frequent source of inspiration.

· 163

Unmarked (US), 1960s-1990s.

· 164

Katry. Guantanamo Bay.

Unmarked (US), 20--.

· 165

Surprise in souvenir Capitol cup.

Unmarked (Japan?), 1940s.

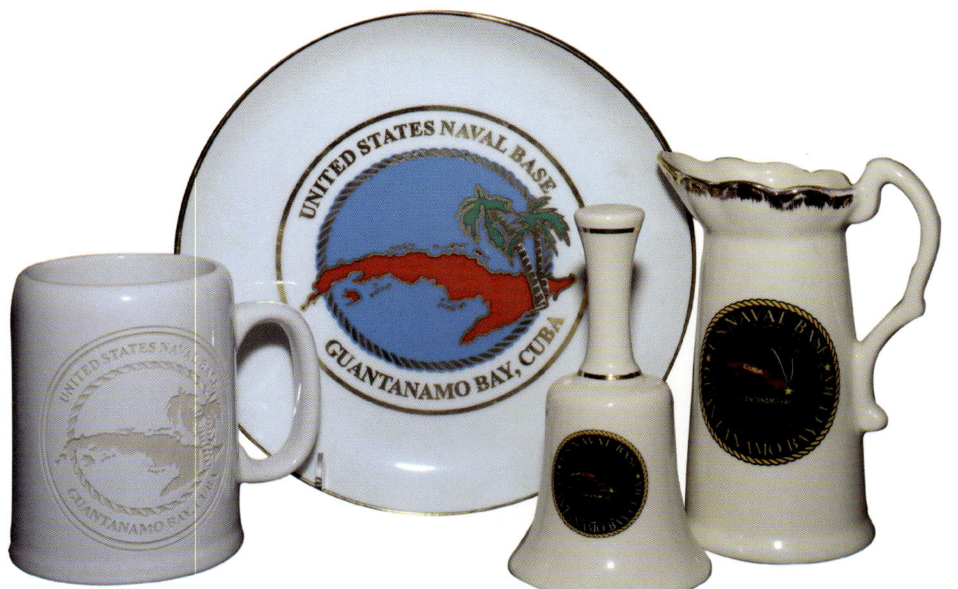

163.

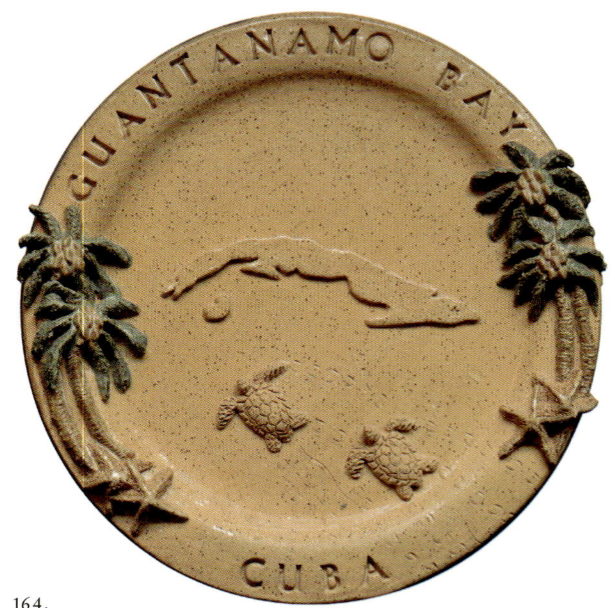

164.

Souvenirs

Tourists love souvenirs. Such items will remind them of the far-away places visited and of the wonderful memories of their trip once they are back home. With the passing of time, they will look with nostalgia at their past and those exotic lands will come alive again.

Cuban souvenirs come in many shapes and forms. Some are in silver (engraved spoons), or cloth (handkerchiefs, knits, napkins, tablecloths, T-shirts), or paper (post cards), or liquid (rum), or metal (key chains). A large number of them, of course, are made in ceramics: cups and saucers, pitchers and glasses, various plates, tiles, ornaments, etc. One curious ordinary-looking cup and saucer set goes on to reveal nude women in its transparent bottom (Fig. 165). Live and see.

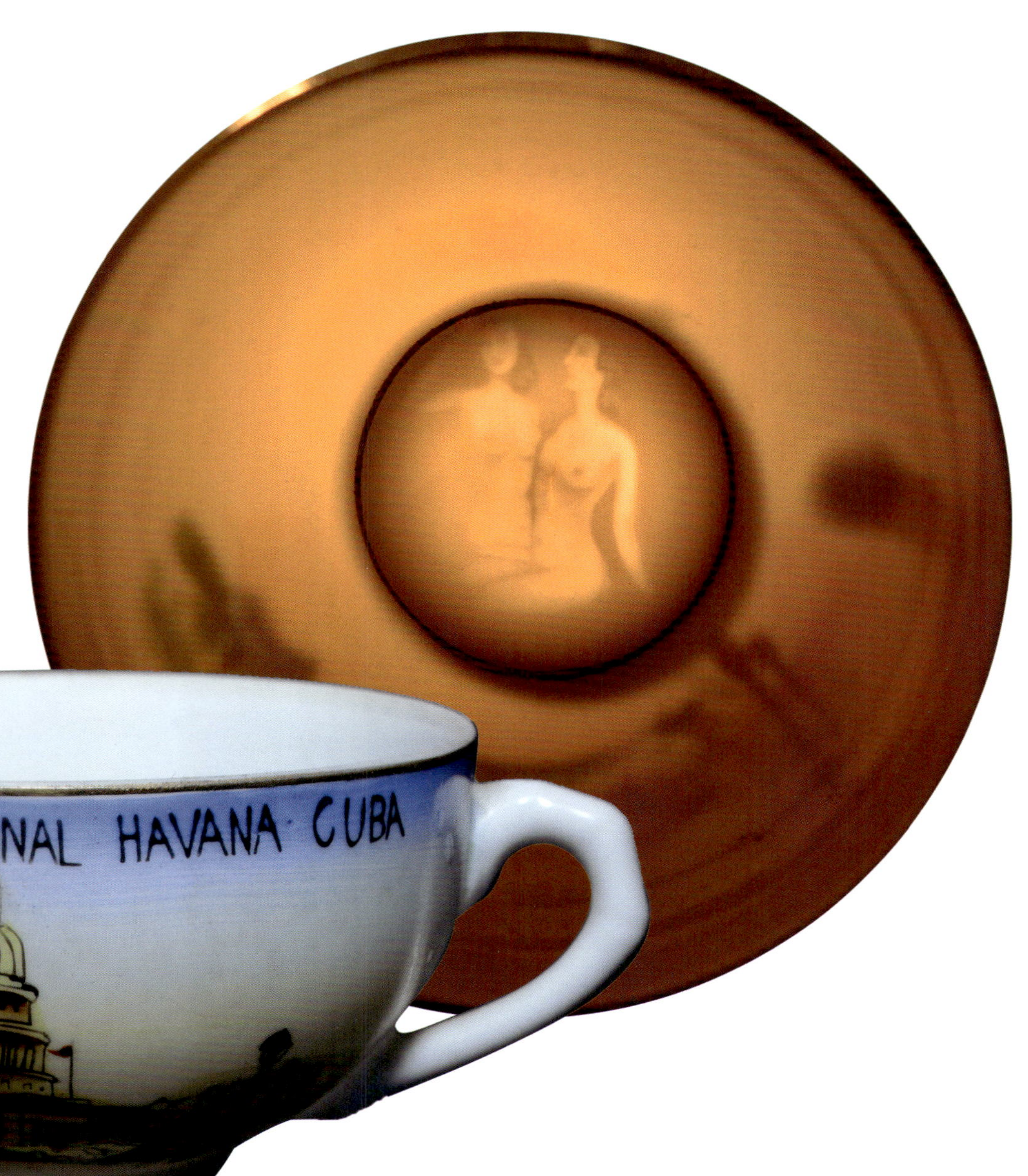

165.

It is important to note that the pieces which have been made over time for the tourist market are most often found outside of the island, wherever each tourist calls home. Among the more representative pieces of this tourist trade are views of Cuba's coat of arms (Fig. 166), Havana's Capitol (Fig. 167), Havana's Cathedral (Fig. 168), Havana's Central Park (Fig. 169), Havana's Hotel Nacional (Fig. 170), Havana's *Maine* Monument (Fig. 171), Havana's Morro Castle (Figs. 172 and 175), Havana's Prado promenade (Fig. 173), Music and dance scenes (Fig. 174), Palm trees (Fig. 176), Pastimes such as bullfights (Fig. 177) and cock fights (Fig. 178, left tile), street vendors (Fig. 178, right tile) and other genre scenes.

Nowadays, tourist shops around Old Havana and in the San José Warehouse, are full of ceramic pieces hand-painted with Havana views, including the Bodeguita del Medio restaurant, colonial buildings and the colorful *almendrones:* cars from the 1940s and 1950s which surprise visitors with relics of a by-gone era.

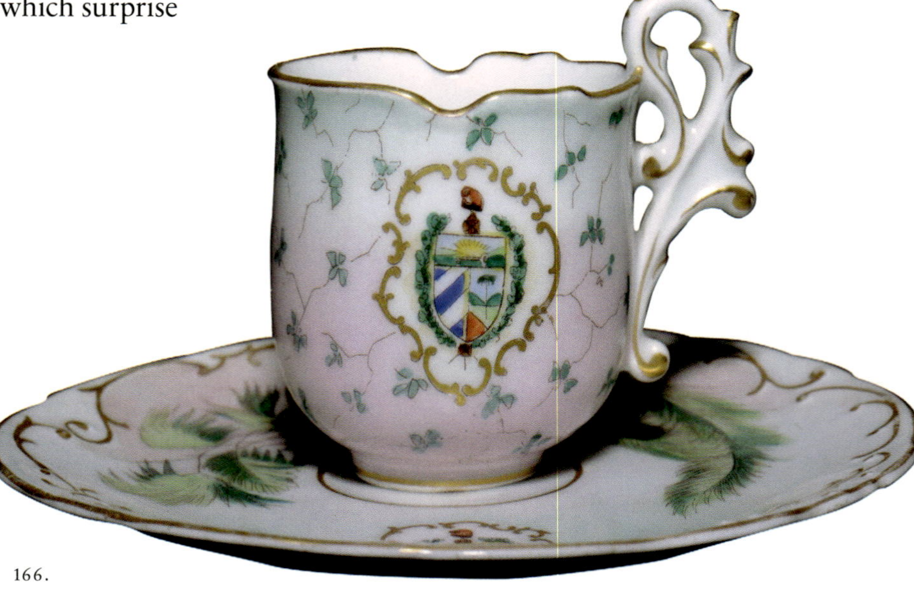

166.

· 166
Cuba's coat of arms.
Unmarked (UK?), 1930s?

· 167
Havana's Capitol.
Chikaramachi (Nagoya, Japan), 1950s.

· 168
Havana's Cathedral.
Unmarked (US?), 1950s.

· 169
Havana's Morro Castle.
Unmarked (US?), 1950s.

· 170
Havana's Hotel Nacional.
Chikaramachi (Nagoya, Japan), 1950s.

· 171
Havana's Maine Monument.
Unmarked (Japan), 1950s.

· 172
Gédé. Havana's Central Park.
George Dreyfus (Paris, France), 1940s.

· 173
Gédé. Havana's Prado promenade.
George Dreyfus (Paris, France), 1940s.

· 174
Left plate: Daniel. Hand painted.
Unmarked, 1940s?
Right plate: Andrés Segura Solé.
William Adams & Co.
(Sttafordshire, UK), 1950s.

· 175
Havana's Morro Castle. López y Sánchez (Havana, Cuba), 1950s.

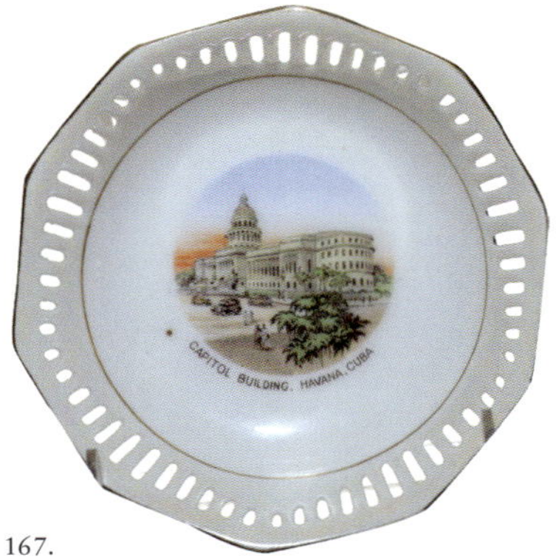

168.

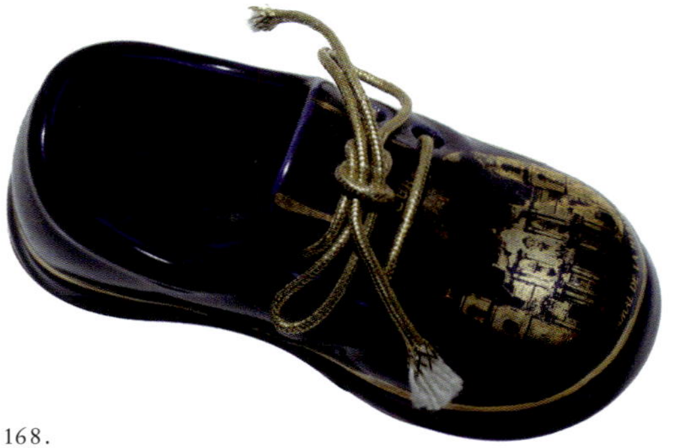

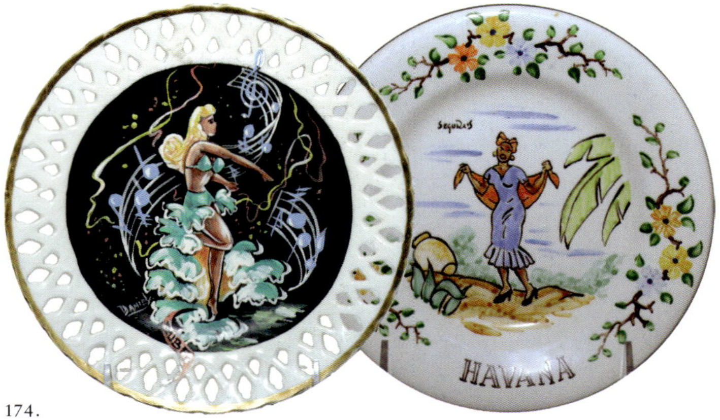

167.

174.

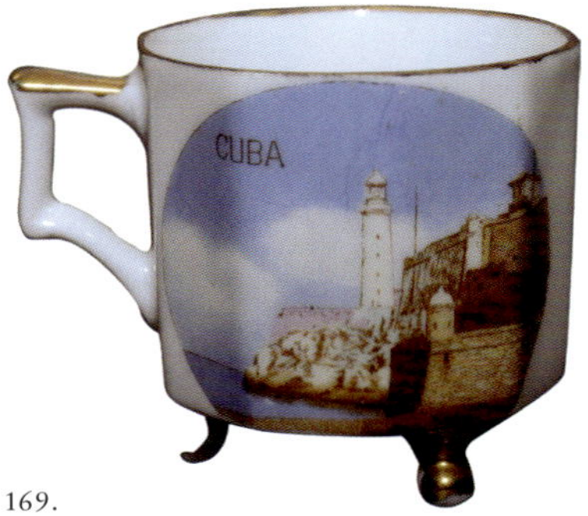

169.

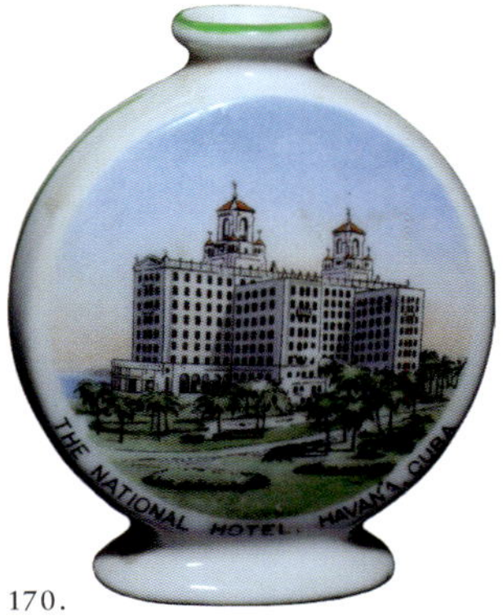

170.

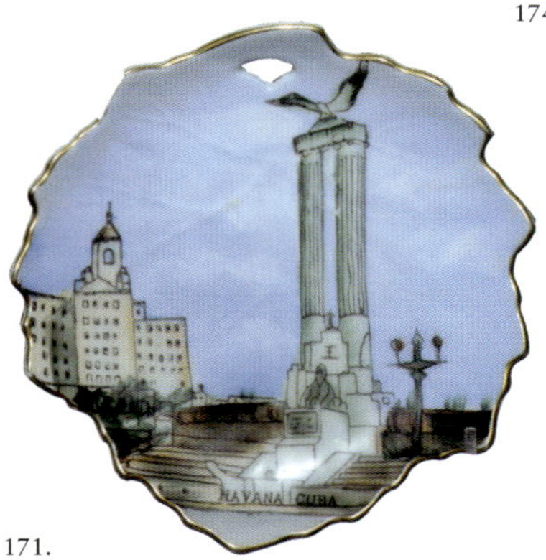

171.

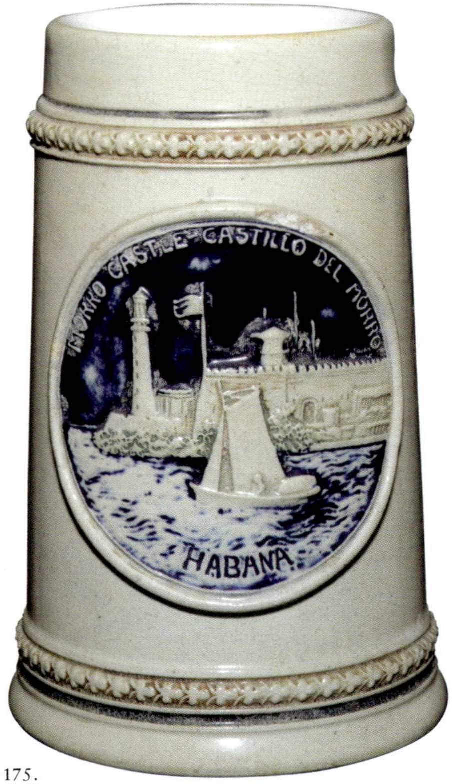

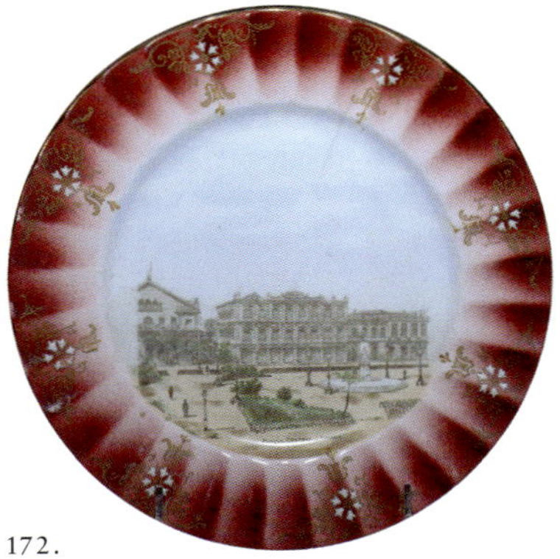

172.

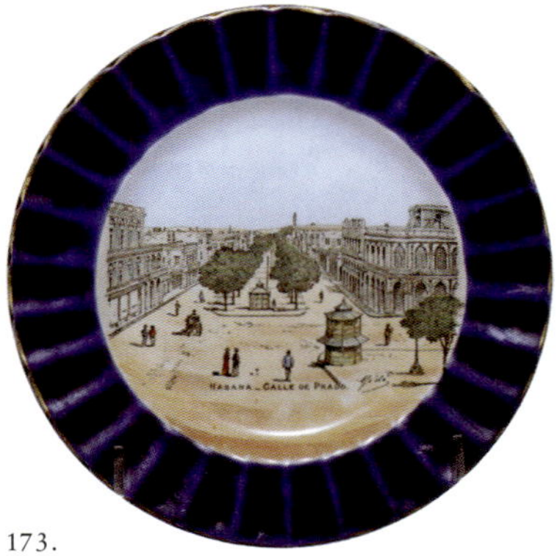

173.

175.

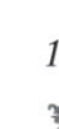

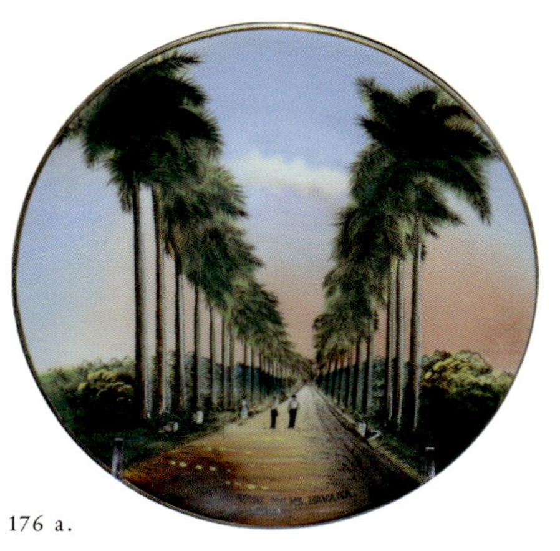

176 a.

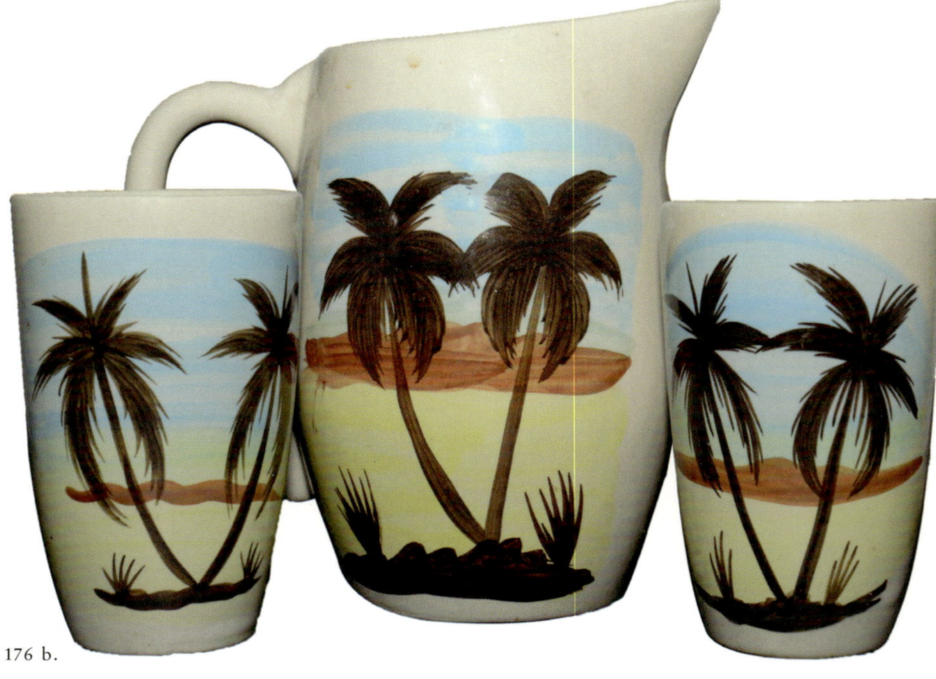

176 b.

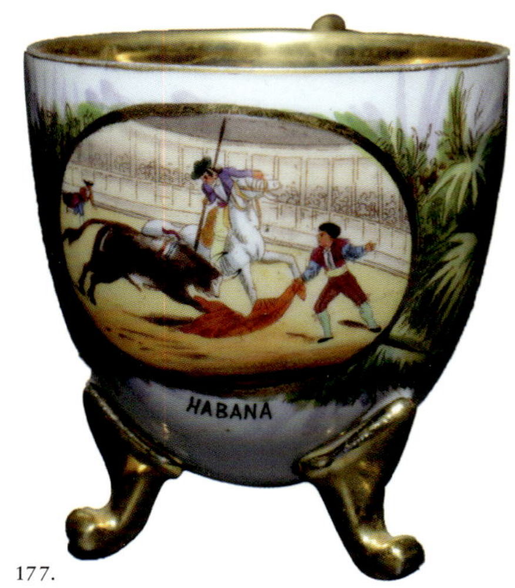

177.

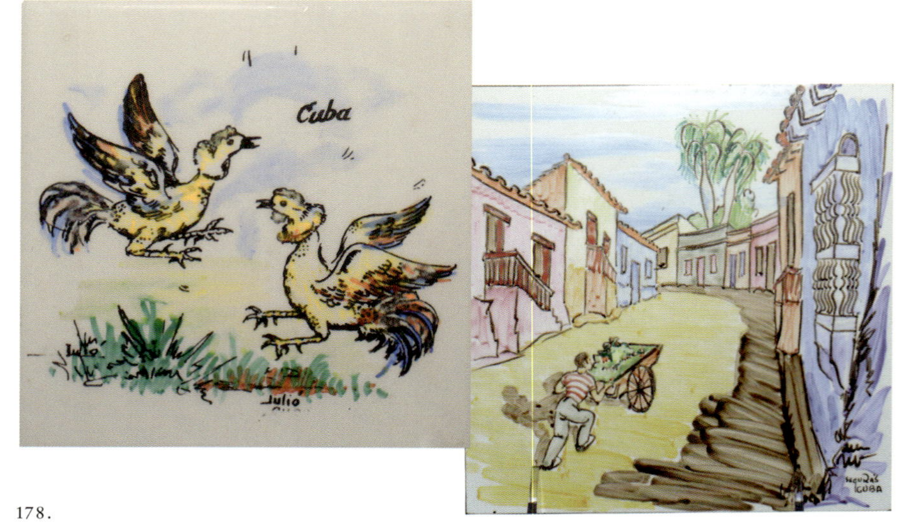

178.

· 176 a

Plate: Avenue of Royal palms. Tirschenreuth (Bavaria, Germany), 1940s.

· 176 b

Vases and jar: Palm trees. Unmarked (Isle of Pines?), 1950s-60s.

· 177

Bull fight. Unmarked (UK?), 1890s?

· 178

Left: Julio Pérez Medina. Cock fight. Unmarked, 1950s; right: Andrés Segura Solé. Street vendors. Unmarked, 1950s.

· 179 a

Typical bohío / country hut. Unmarked (Spain), 1920s?

· 179 b

Typical bohío / country hut. Unmarked (US?), 1940s?

· 180

Hills surrounding Trinidad. Unmarked, 2000s.

· 181

Pedro Castillo. Scene from Camagüey. Unmarked, 1949.

Leaving Havana behind, we also find the typical *bohío*/ country hut (Fig. 179a-179b), the hills of Trinidad (Fig. 180) and a rural scene from Camagüey (Fig. 181), already mentioned. A latticed bowl depicts a couple of flamingos in a pond, courtesy of CNE China (Japan).

A few of the pieces in this section are signed: Pedro Castillo (Fig. 181), Daniel (Fig. 174, left plate), Géde (Fig. 173), Julio Pérez Medina and Andrés Segura Solé (Fig. 178).

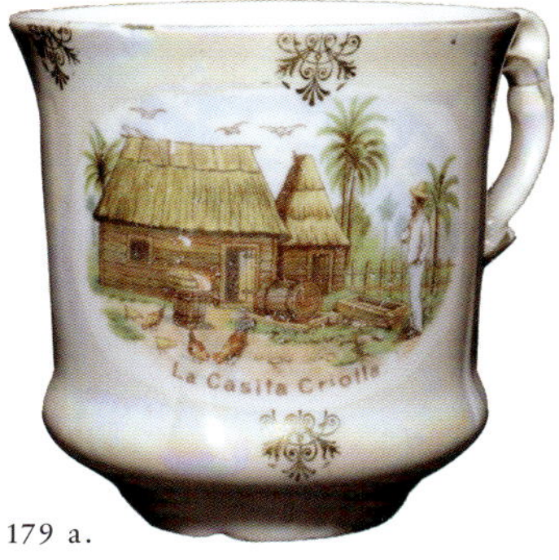

179 a.

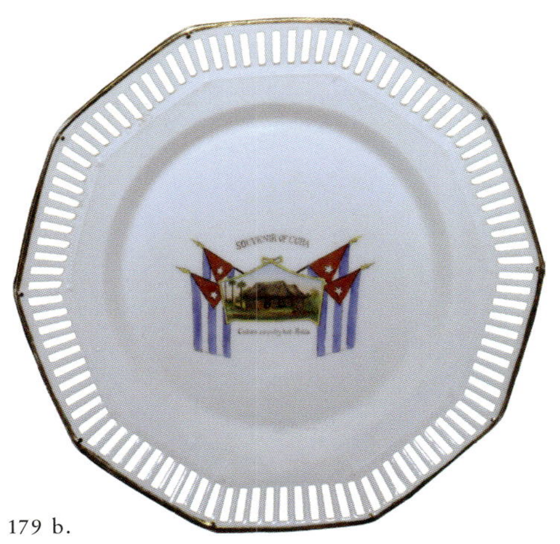

179 b.

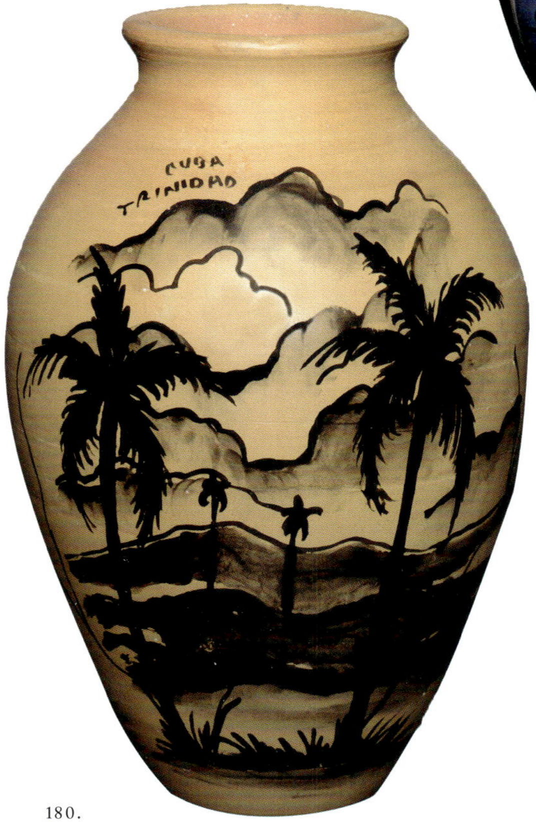

180.

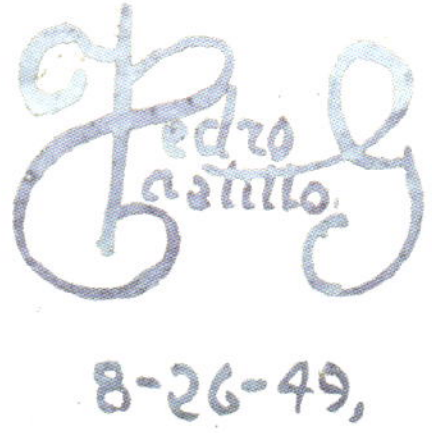

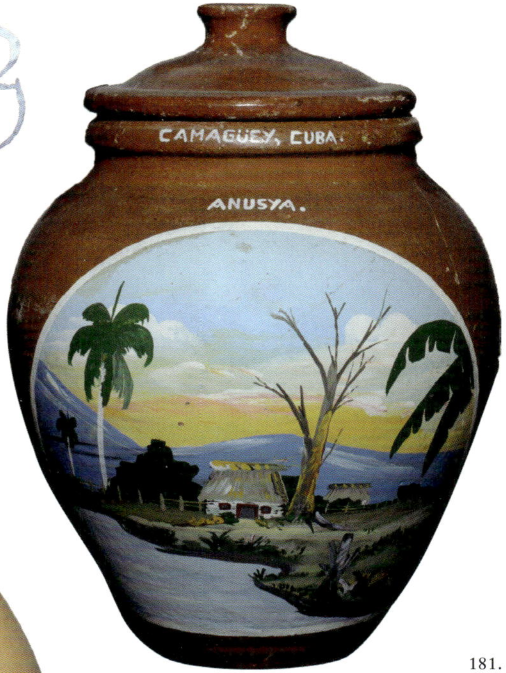

181.

Miscellaneous

Countless other Cuba-themed ceramic items have been produced. A short discussion of some of the images and motifs displayed follow in the next paragraphs.

It is important to underscore that, in addition to pieces made for all kinds of customers who follow Cuba with a sense of fascination, there is also a particular Cuban-American market for some of these pieces. Catering to the sense of identity—as well as to feelings of displacement and nostalgia—of the Cuban exile community in the US, several ceramic pieces depicting provincial coat of arms, landscapes and other reminders of the native land are often found in US local markets.[49]

Map of the Island

The map of Cuba is usually present in many ceramic pieces The earliest one I have located, dated from around 1804, is a creamware Liverpool pitcher. It shows the image of George Washington, and the map of Cuba bordering the map of the East Coast of the United States (we are such close neighbors that sometimes it is inevitable that our island appears in a US map).

I first saw one copy being displayed in the New York Metropolitan Museum. In February 2018 another copy was being offered on ebay and the asking price was US $3,800.00. Others have sold for over $15,000. There are a few such jars, each of them slightly different. Some are attributed to the Herculaneum pottery (Toxteth, Liverpool), others to Wedgood (Stafforshire).[50] Fortunately for the collector on a stringent budget, the Mottahedeh firm (Cranbury, New Jersey) has made a reproduction, probably in Portugal, of one of those pitchers.

Another early rendition of Cuba's map appeared in a 19th century English plate made for La Cafetera, Almacenes Gamba in Havana, mentioned earlier. More recently, we have been able to admire one of the earliest Cuban maps made in Portugal at the beginning of the 16th century (as part of the so-called Cantino planisphere) reproduced in a Lisbon vase in 1994 (Fig. 182). Many centuries after Cantino, Cuban artist Elsa Biaggi shared with us her vision of the island (Fig. 183). As would be expected, other Cuban maps have appeared elsewhere.

---

49. The Sentir Cubano store on Miami's 8th street SW is a good place to find a variety of mugs, tiles, plates and other Cuba-themed ceramic trinkets. Ebay is not a bad place either.

50. For illustrations see Ada Walker Camehl, *op. cit.*, p. 2 and Paul Atterbery, *op. cit.*, p. 238.

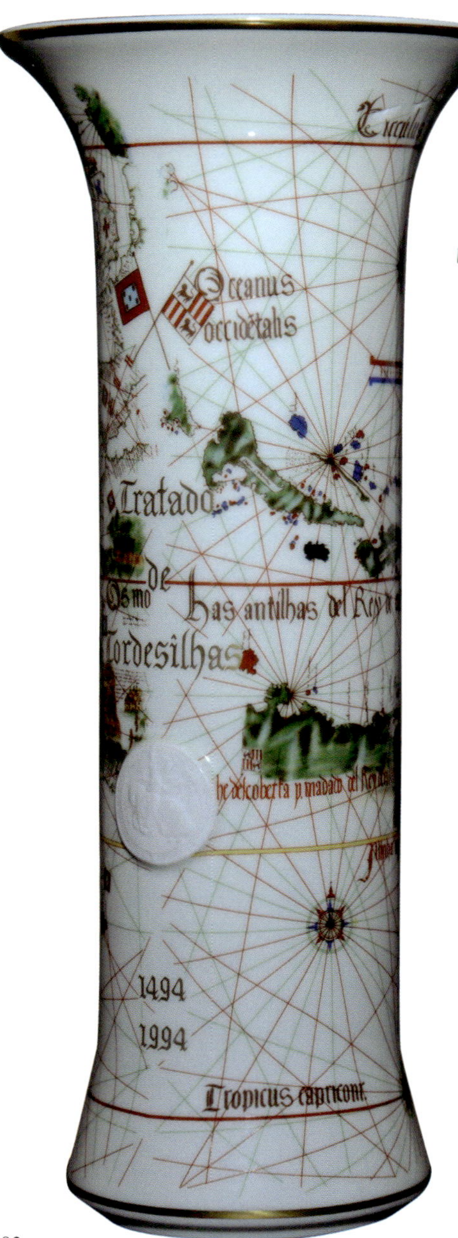

182.

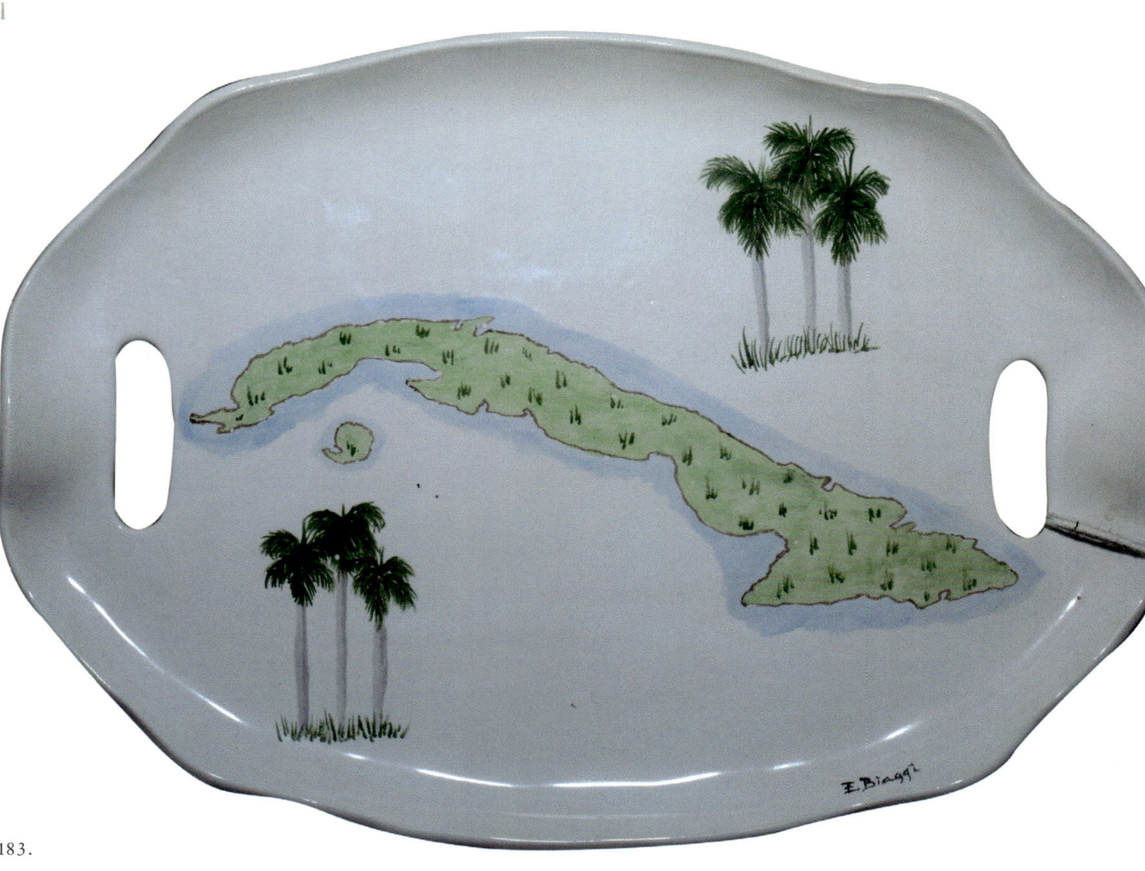

183.

· 182
Cuba in 16th century Cantino map.
Vista Alegre (Portugal), 1994.

· 183
Elsa Biaggi. Unmarked (US?), 2000s.

Coat of Arms

Cuba's coat of arms is another frequent visitor to the ceramic world. Three pieces merit special attention. An unmarked large plate with a fleur-de-lis pattern surrounding the central image (Fig. 184). The seller told me that it had been offered to her grandfather by the Cuban Government in the earlier years of the 20th century. Some decades later, a blue and white plate was produced by the famous Pickman / La Cartuja factory in Seville around 1930s (Fig. 185) and, most probably also from Seville, an unmarked framed item assembled out of four separate tiles (Fig. 186). More recently, a plate (probably as part of a set with the individual Cuban provincial shields) has been produced by the Bidasoa group in San Sebastián, Spain.

Italy has not been absent from our story. Our Coat of arms looks splendid in a plate from the Capodimonte factory, near Naples, Italy (my friend Silvia B. owns a copy). And, while travelling through the town of Deruta (Perugia), Italy, in 2014, my classmate Eduardo Azcárate found a ceramic portrayal of the Cuban Coat of arms at the Grazia Maioliche Artistiche establishment. Our shield shows up also in ashtrays and plates. Most specially, as we saw earlier, it is prominently displayed in the presidential china of the 1920s and 1950s (Fig. 6 and 7).

---

[51] Liborio symbolizes the average Cuban. This endearing and enduring character was created around 1900 by Cuban artist Ricardo de la Torriente (1869-1934). According to several experts, this piece was made by Schafer & Vater Porcelain Factory in Volkstedt Rudolstad, Thuringa, Germany.

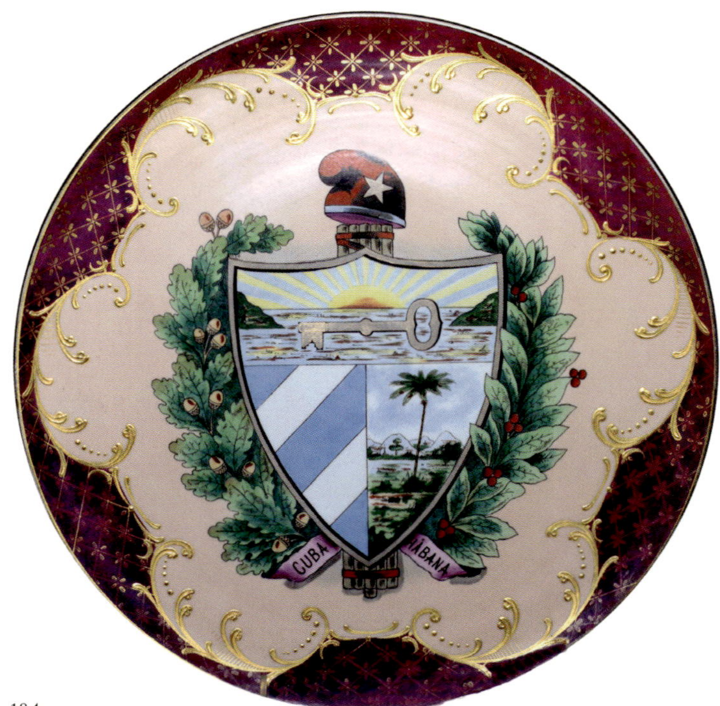

184.

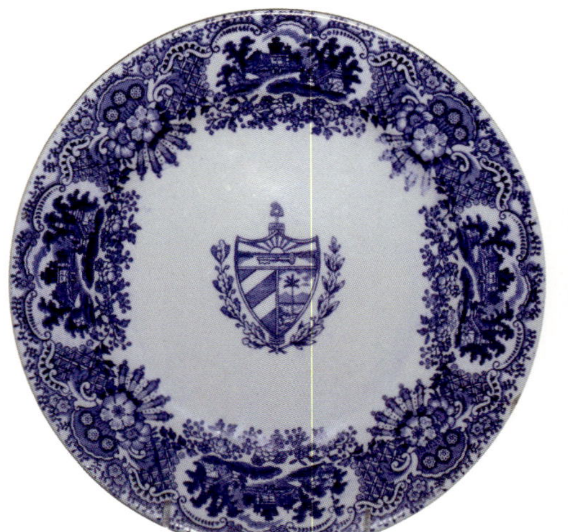
185.

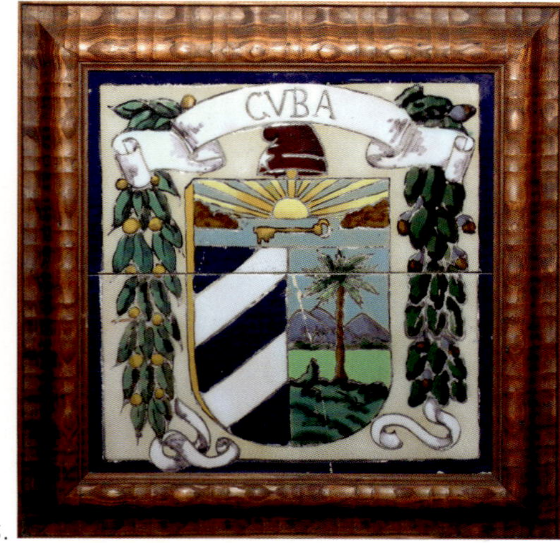

186.

The Flag

Two patriotic items displaying the Cuban flag stand out: The popular Liborio character,[51] perhaps as a match holder (Fig. 187) and the Cuban Republic itself (Fig. 188), which also bears the Cuban shield. There is also a ceramic jar with the Cuban flags of Carlos Manuel de Céspedes (1819-1874) and Narciso López (1797-1851) side by side, which is kept at the Bacardí Museum in Santiago de Cuba (I believe it belonged to Francisco Vicente Aguilera (1821-1877). The Cuban flag, together with the flags of the other Allied countries in World War II was featured in a commemorative plate by Knowles, Taylor & Knowles (East Liverpool, Ohio, US).

· 184
Cuban Coat of Arms.
Unmarked, 1900s.

· 185
Cuban Coat of Arms.
Pickman (Seville, Spain), 1930s.

· 186
Cuban Coat of Arms.
Unmarked (Seville, Spain), 1940s?

· 187
Liborio waving flag. Unmarked, but probably Schafer & Vater (Rudolstad, Thuringa, Germany), 1940s?

· 188
Cuban Republic.
Unmarked, (Occupied Japan), 1940s.

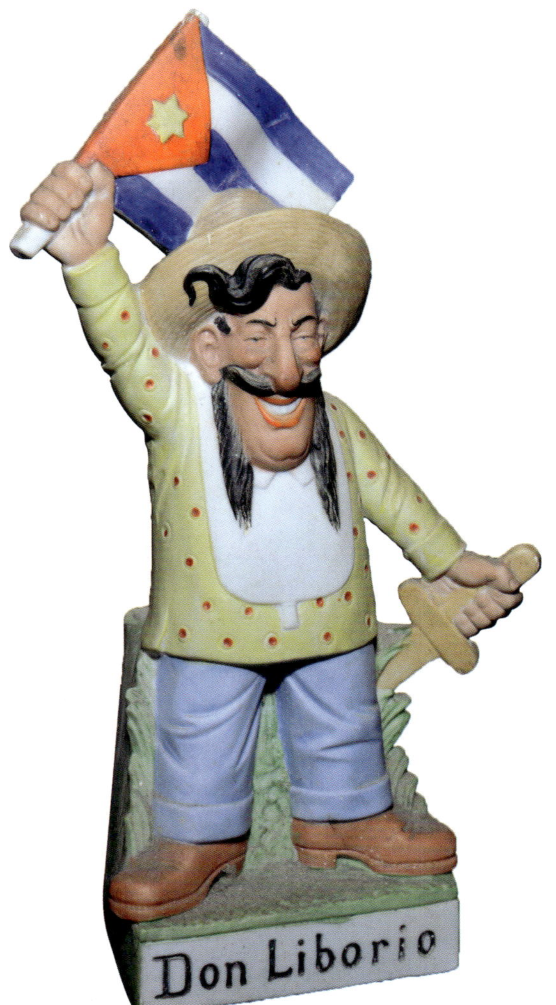

187.

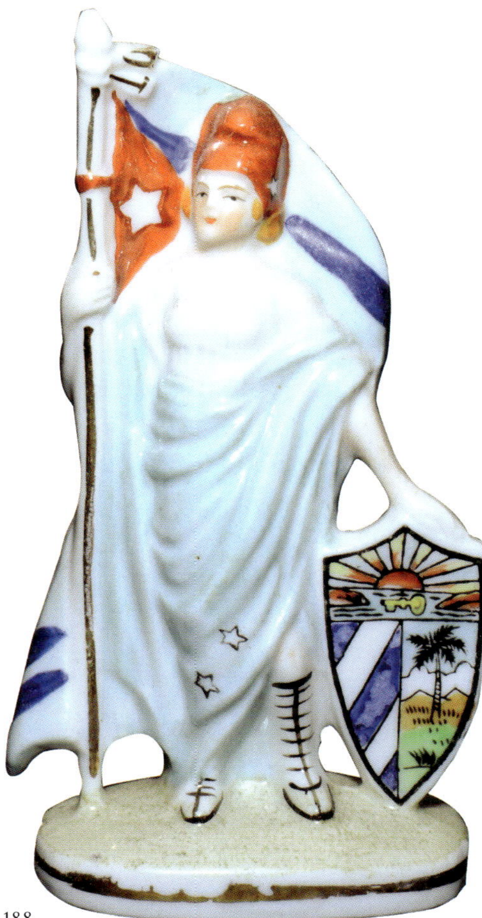

188.

Flora and Fauna

We should begin by recalling the many pre-Columbian ceramic pieces which have been unearthed and which provide the earliest depictions of our animals. They can be admired in Cuban museums as well as in the illustrated books on the subject.[52]

To the best of my knowledge, not much was done on this subject during the colonial period.[53] But, in recent times, our fauna and flora has not gone unnoticed by ceramists. Cuba's lily can be seen in an unmarked cup, while the Cuban flamingo, used by Audubon to paint his well-known *American* flamingo, has been portrayed in plates and mugs (Fig. 189).[54] The tiny Cuban emerald hummingbird (Fig. 190) and Caibarien's crab (Fig. 192) have also been preserved in ceramic, while the extinct Cuban macaw has been brought back to life thanks to the "Vanished Species Collection" by Aldon accessories, the artists at Compton & Woodhouse (England, 1997) and also in the work of Siddhia Hutchinson (Fig. 191). Contemporary mugs depict several Cuban butterflies (as portrayed in postage stamps) as well as Cuba's ferocious crocodile, now made friendlier as the smiling handle on a coffee mug (Fig. 193).

The reader should also be aware that the March, 2018 catalog of the California-based Williams Sonoma company displays their new "Havana Garden" dinnerware set featuring various Cuban birds. The catalog adds: "Inspired by the lush landscapes and vibrant flavors of Cuba, our latest collection brings the island vibes home". The vibes of Cuba on the contemporary American table!

---

52. See Ramón Dacal Moure, *Historiografía arqueológica de Cuba*. México, D.F., Centro Nacional de Conservación, Restauración y Museología, 2005, pp. 63-69; Caridad Rodríguez Cullel, "Catálogo gráfico de los diseños decorativos en la cerámica taína de Cuba", en Modesto Amado Martínez Castillo (ed.), *Cuba Arqueológica*. Santiago de Cuba, Editorial Oriente, 1978, pp. 179-224; Irving Rouse, *Archeology of the Maniabón hills, Cuba*. New Haven, Yale University Press, 1942, plate 4: Ernesto E Tabío, *et. al. Prehistoria de Cuba.* La Habana, Academia de Ciencias de Cuba, 1966, plate XIV, p. 269; Roberto Valcárcel Rojas, *Archaeology of Early Colonial Interaction at El Chorro de Maíta, Cuba*. Gainesville, Fla. University Press of Florida, 2016, Fig. 73, p. 213.

53. Around 1815, the prestigious Nymphenburg, Germany, porcelain factory issued a 22-plate service reproducing parrots designed by Jacques Barraband (sold at Sotheby's Zurich sale on June 1, 1994). I have not been able to confirm whether the Cuban parrots from that series were incorporated into this magnificent porcelain set. See Emilio Cueto, *Illustrating Cuba's flora and fauna.* Miami, Fla. Historical museum of Southern Florida, 2002, Fig. 80, p. 60.

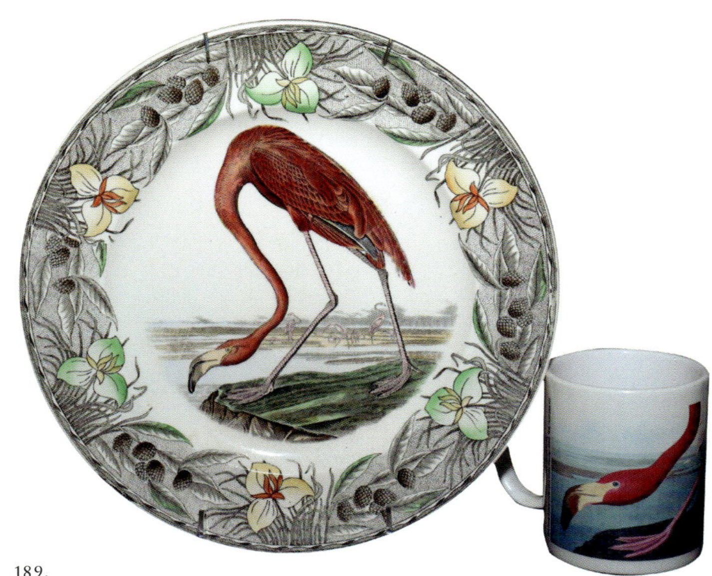

189.

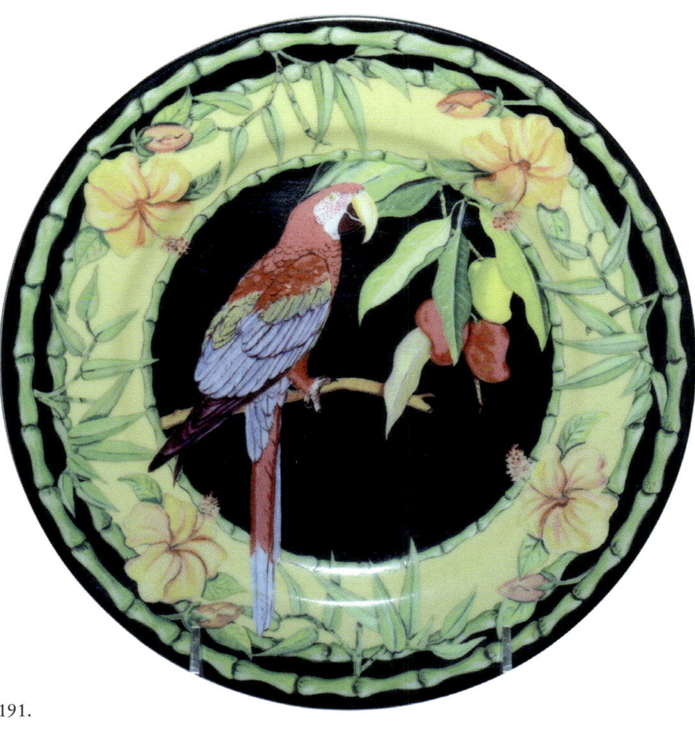

191.

· 189
John James Audubon. "The Birds of America". Adams (UK), 1940s; Unmarked, undated mug.

· 190
Cuban emerald hummingbird. Bronson Collectibles (China), 1996.

· 191
Siddhia Hutchinson. Cuban macaw (guacamayo). Andrea by Sadek (Japan), ca. 1984.

· 192
Caibarien's crab. American Gift Corporation (Miami, Florida, US), 2000s.

· 193
Unmarked, 21st century.

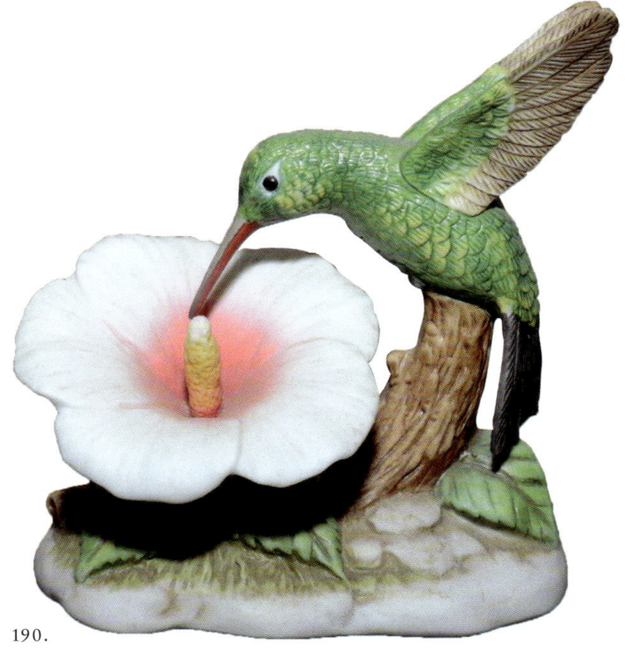

190.

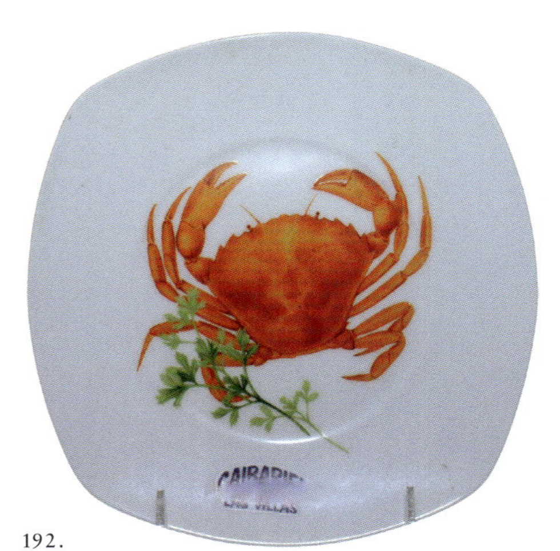

192.

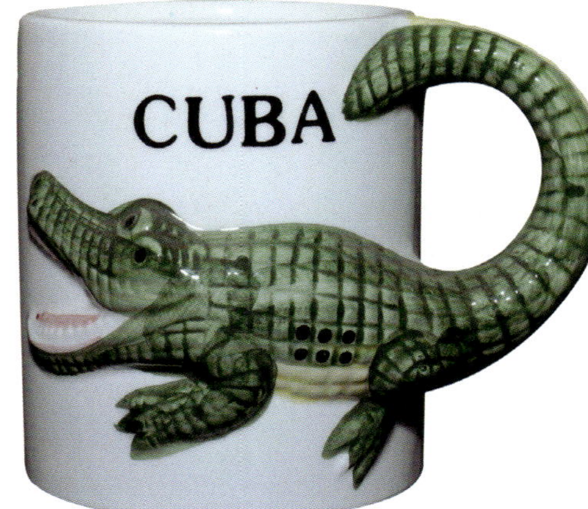

193.

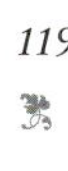

Historic figures

Other items include images of Cuban politicians such as Eduardo Chibás (1907-1951, Fig. 194), Ché Guevara (1928-1967, Fig. 195) and Fidel Castro (1926-2016) himself (I remember seeing a large piece made in Eastern Europe kept at the Birán home of the Castro family in Holguín province). Colonial Captain General Arsenio Martinez Campos (1831-1900) has also made his appearance in an 1878 Adams plate, most probably for the Spanish market (Fig. 196).

Some years ago, my friend Amauri Gutiérrez offered me a 1953 José Martí (1853-1895) plate made in the US (Fig. 197) and ceramists in the Island of Youth also decorated some jars with the image of our national hero.[55] Martí has also appeared in ashtrays from Cuban Crafters Cigars and in figurines.

More recently, in Santiago de Cuba, I picked up a hand-painted piece with the image of our great romantic poet José María Heredia (1803-1839, Fig. 198). Crossing over to the US, Cuban-American Desi Arnaz (1917-1986) travels to California with his wife and "I Love Lucy" friends in designs by Preston Willingham (Fig. 199) and Jim Kritz.

Visiting Santiago de Cuba, in the kitchen of Diego Velázquez' old home I saw in January 1999 (and then I did not see it again) a large multicolored water jar with the bust and name of Francisco Frías, fourth *Conde de Pozos Dulces* (1809-1877).

On the return trip, at the Pharmaceutical Museum in Matanzas, I checked a beautiful blue urn, a wedding gift, with the portraits of the owner, Frenchman Ernesto Triolet (?-1900) and his first wife María Justa de Figueroa. It is proudly displayed on the counter of the former pharmacy, founded in 1882.[56]

· 194
Eduardo Chibás. Unmarked. 1950s.

· 195
Che Guevara and Santa Clara Battle. Colditz Porcelain. (Colditz, German Democratic Republic), 1983.

· 196
Arsenio Martínez Campos. Adams (Staffordshire, UK), July 18, 1878.

· 197
José Martí. Vernon Kilns (Vernon, California, US), 1953.

· 198
José María Heredia. Unmarked (Cuba), 2010s.

· 199
Preston Willingham. Desi Arnaz driving to California. "I Love Lucy" Cookie jar. Vandor (Salt Lake City, Utah, US), 1996.

---

54. See Emilio Cueto, *Illustrating Cuba's flora and fauna, op. cit.*, pp. 38, 45-97.

55. See Antonio Núñez Jiménez, *Cuba: cultura, estado y revolución*. México, D.F., Presencia Latinoamericana, 1984, p. 274.

56. It has been featured in Vladia Rubio, "Sombras del farol de la guardia", *Bohemia*, June 19, 2009, p. 9, and can be seen online at Pinterest.com, www.cubawhatson.com, www.shutterstock.com, and encompasstours.com

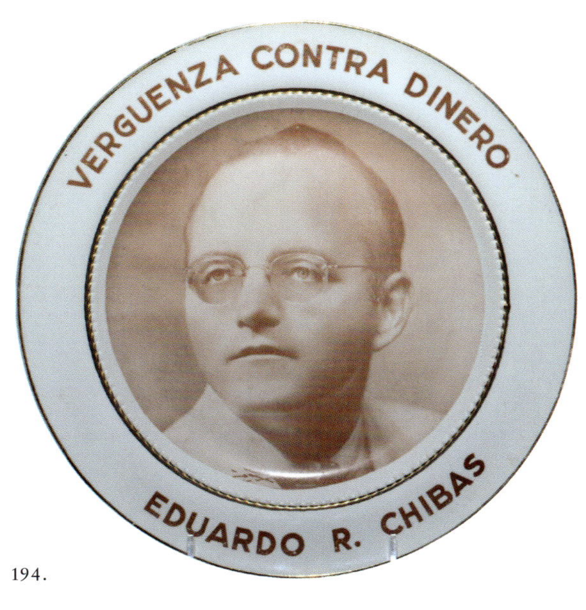

194.

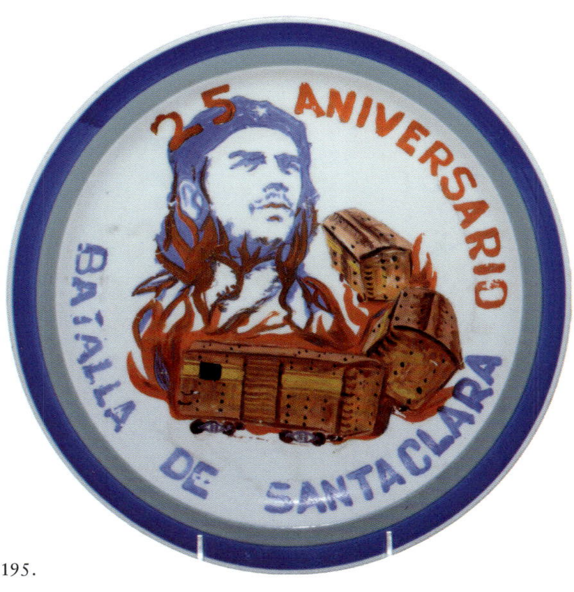

195.

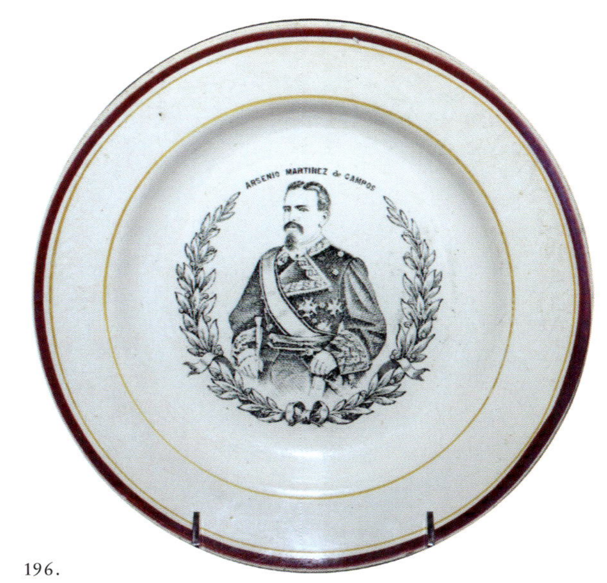

196.

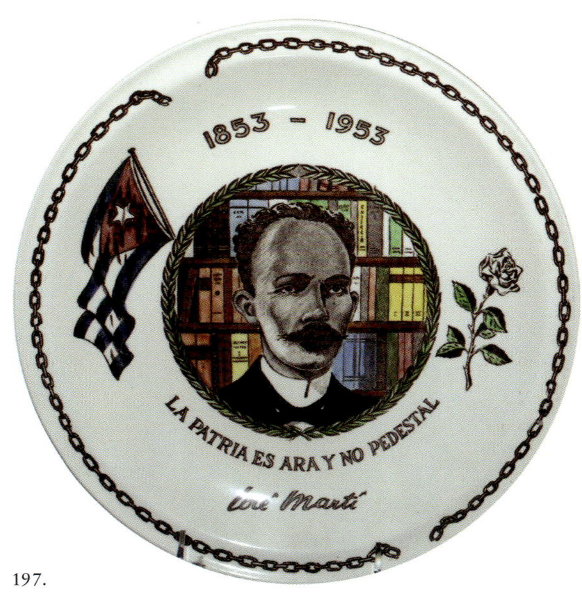

197.

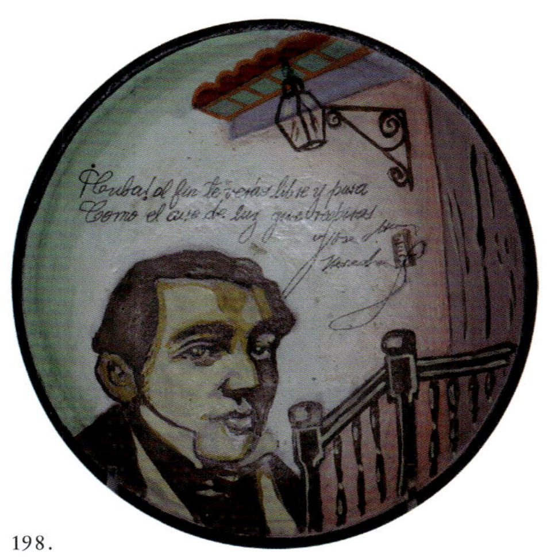

198.

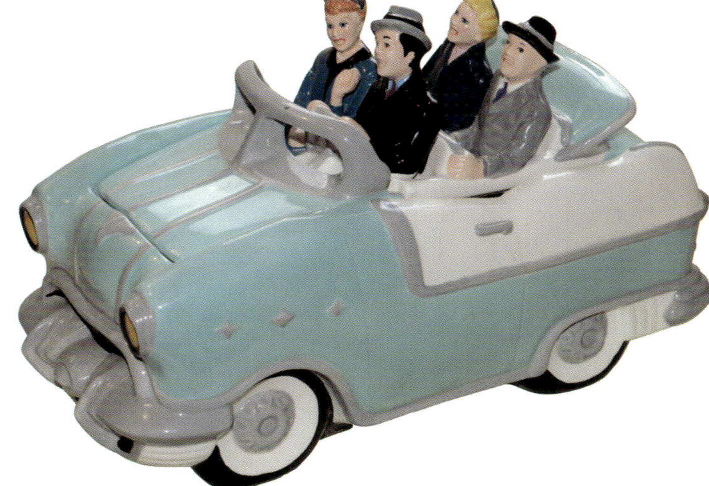

199.

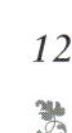

City Views

During the 1940s (?), the German Bauscher firm illustrated some spectacular magenta-rimmed plates with views of The *Maine* monument and the Fountain from the Casino Nacional (Figs. 200 and 201). In the late 20th century, the Office of the Historian of Havana ordered a set of pieces for its Habana collection from the Pickman factory in Seville illustrating Havana's Captain General's Palace (Fig. 202). At around the same time, on this side of the Straits of Florida, *The Miami Herald* store issued a series of plates with views of Havana and Santiago (Fig. 203). The Pinero potters at Talavera (Spain) have also produced colorful pieces displaying the Capitol and the Morro Castle.

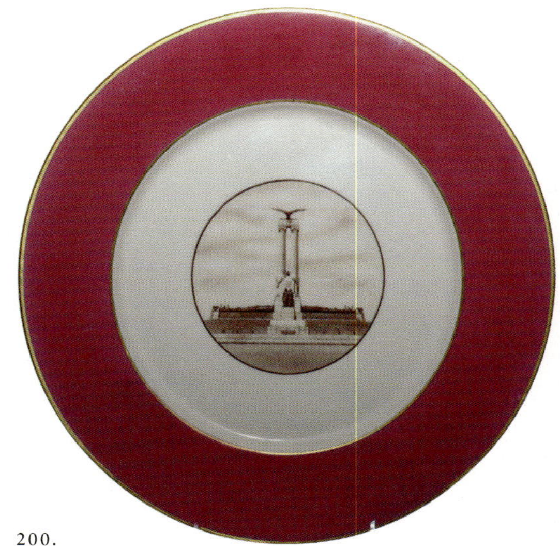

200.

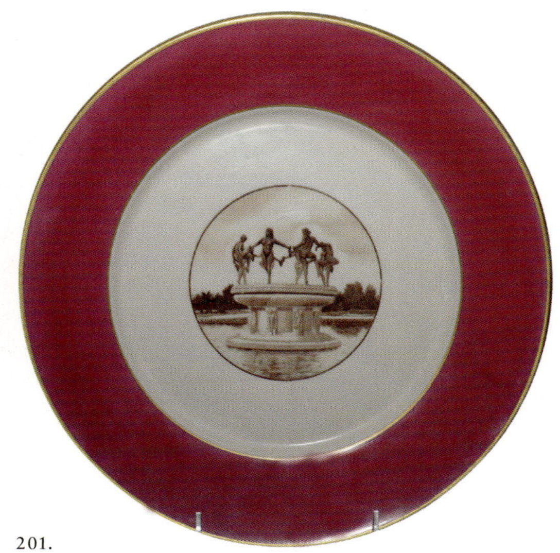

201.

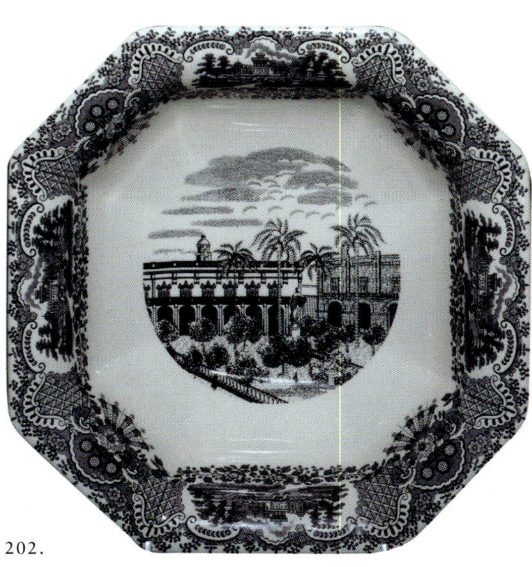

202.

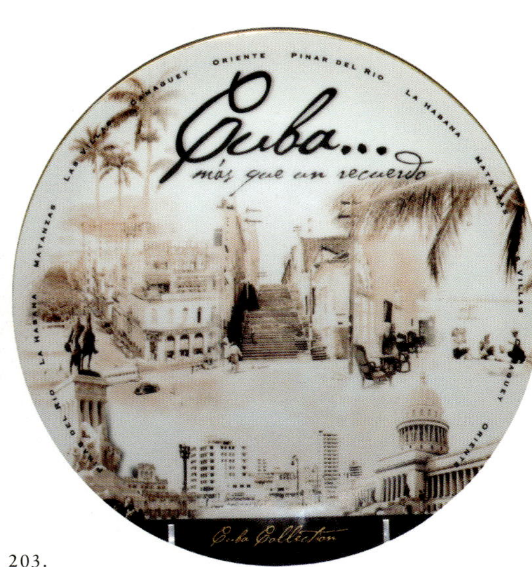

203.

· 200
Maine Monument. Bauscher (Weiden, Germany), 1940s?

· 201
Fountain from Casino Nacional. Bauscher (Weiden, Germany), 1940s?

· 202
Havana's Palace of the Captain General. Pickman (Seville, Spain), 2000s.

· 203
Havana and Santiago views. Cuba Collection. *Miami Herald* Store (Miami, Florida, US), 2000s?

· 204
Havana planters. Creil et Montreux (Seine-et-Marne, France), 1850-60s?

· 205
Frédéric Mialhe. 19th century sugar mill. Sureda (Spain), 1990s?

Genre scenes and other pieces

Among of the earliest Cuban genre views transferred onto ceramics that I know of are the two sets of tiles embedded in the walls around the courtyard of the Casa de la Obra Pía in Old Havana. Both panels, *Vista de la Plaza Vieja o Mercado principal de La Habana* and *Vista del Paseo de Paula, en la Habana* reproduce views by Garneray, discussed in an earlier section.[57] The tiles were made in Valencia around 1825, as a special-order item from the owners of the Obrapía 160 home (subsequently transferred next door to its present location).[58]

An interesting 19th century French plate portrays a couple of wealthy Havana planters (Fig. 204) while, a century later, various Spanish Sureda plates reproduce scenes by the ubiquitous Mialhe (Fig. 205), a Cuban ceramist gives us a contemporary rendition of Cuba's zapateo dance by Basque artist Victor Patricio de Landaluze (1827/28/30-1889, Fig. 206) and American potters try their hands at a more modern Cuban dance scene (Fig. 207). A "Latin Dances" plates set by Fields Marketplace allows you to have dessert over cha cha cha, mambo and salsa displays.

204.

205.

---

57. The panels have been reproduced in Roger Arrazcaceta Delgado, "La cerámica de aplicación arquitectónica de la época colonial en La Habana". *Gabinete de Arqueología* (La Habana), 6, 2009, Figs. 31-32, p. 211. They can also be seen online at www.rantapallo.fi.

58. See Inocencio V Pérez Guillén, *Las azulejerías de la Habana: cerámica arquitectónica española en América*. Valencia, Universidad de Valencia, 2004, p. 291.

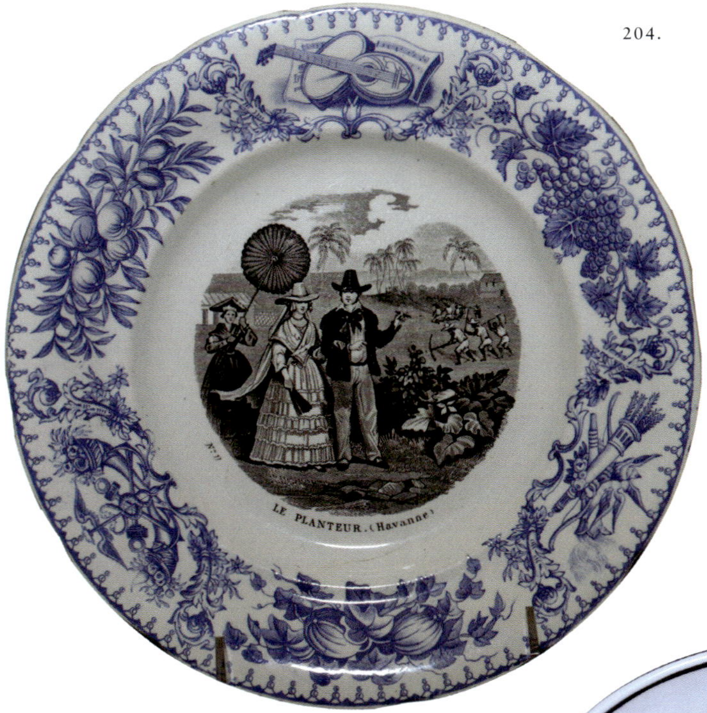

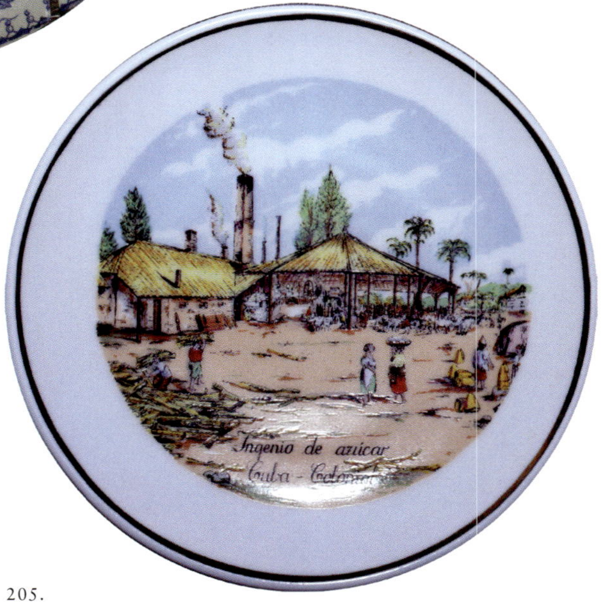

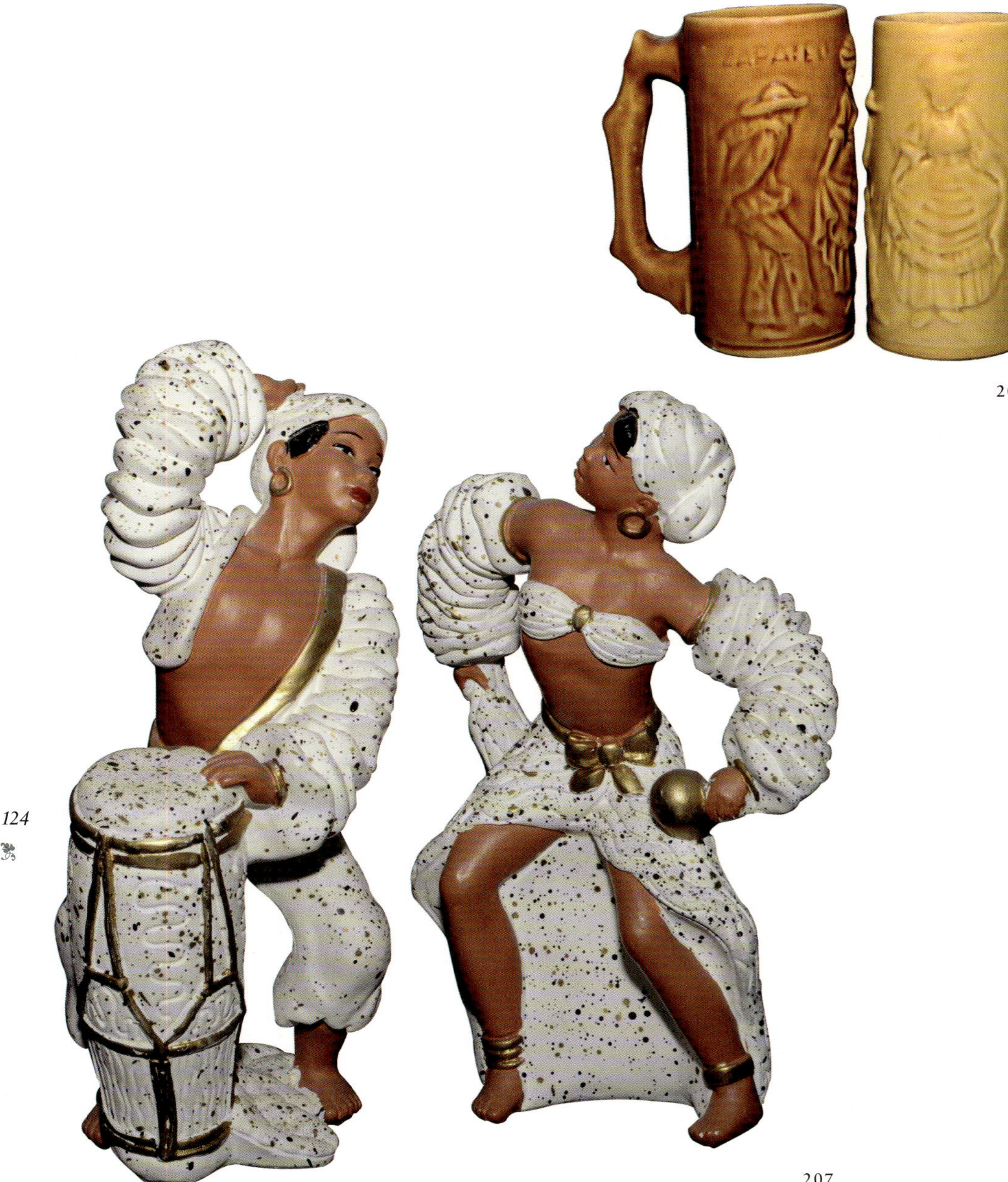

206.

207.

In 1974, R. Delfín transferred into a set of 40 tiles a splendid scene of the King's Day parade in Havana, as drafted by German artist Adolf Hoeffler (1825-1898).[59] The proud owner is my friend Adolfo Jiménez, in Miami. Other items include Soviet and Cuban pioneers hand in hand (Fig. 208), dancers from Cuba's National ballet (Fig. 209) and a Havana harbor view issued by Fred Olsen's cruise to Havana (Fig. 210), carrying tourists who certainly saw the crowded "camello" bus inching its way through Havana streets (Fig. 211).

Needless to say, there are countless other pieces. Among those not illustrated in this book the reader should know about a Cuban float in the Veiled Prophet parade in St Louis Missouri in 1951, by Vernon Kilns; a 1914 "Love cup" hand painted by Gertrude Forgett on a blank Limoges vase with Cuban scenes; a 2002 witty genre scene by Cuban ceramist Iglesias portraying several female neighbors gossiping; mugs with Cuban stamps displaying coffee (Gallo design, Villeroy & Bosch, Germany) and air mail themes (China), or even advertising the Havana Night's Club Show in Las Vegas. I have also seen a "Cuban Holiday" mug by Balfour Ceramic in Attleboro, Massachusetts.

---

59. The original image can be seen in *La Ilustración Española y Americana* (Madrid), 25 de diciembre de 1869, p. 12.

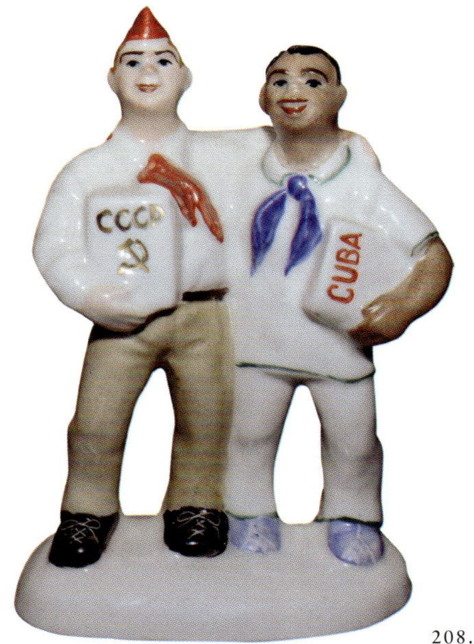

208.

· 206
Víctor Patricio de Landaluze. Unmarked (Cuba), 1980s?
· 207
Popular dancers. Unmarked (US?), 1950s.
· 208
Soviet and Cuban pioneers. Unmarked (USSR/Ukraine?), ca. 1970s.
· 209
Cuba's National ballet. Fábrica II Congreso (Isle of Pines/Youth, Cuba), 1980s.
· 210
Fred Olsen cruise to Havana. Porsgrund (Norway), 2001.
· 211
"Camello" bus. Unmarked (Cuba), 2010s.

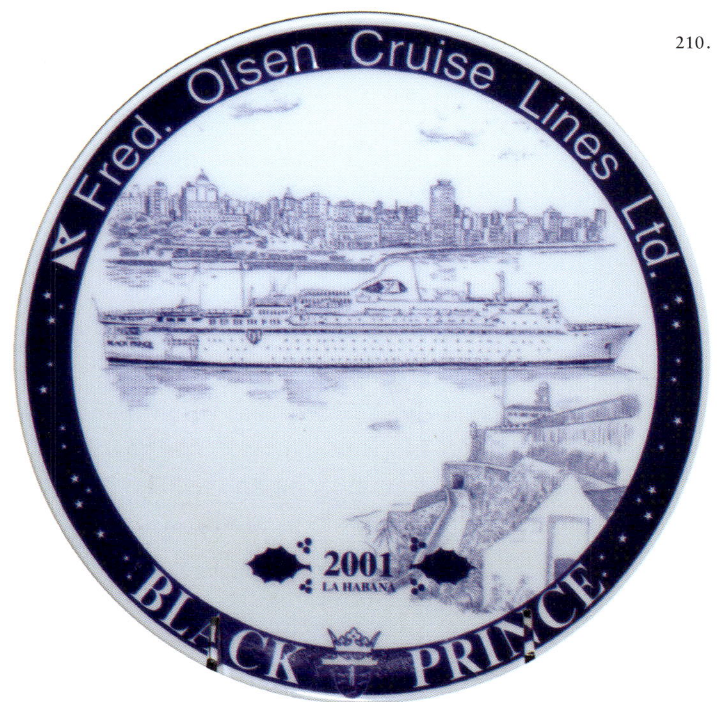

210.

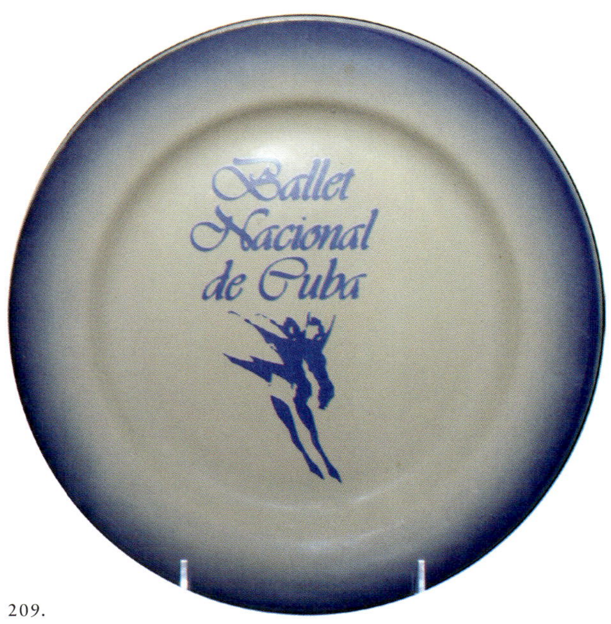

209.

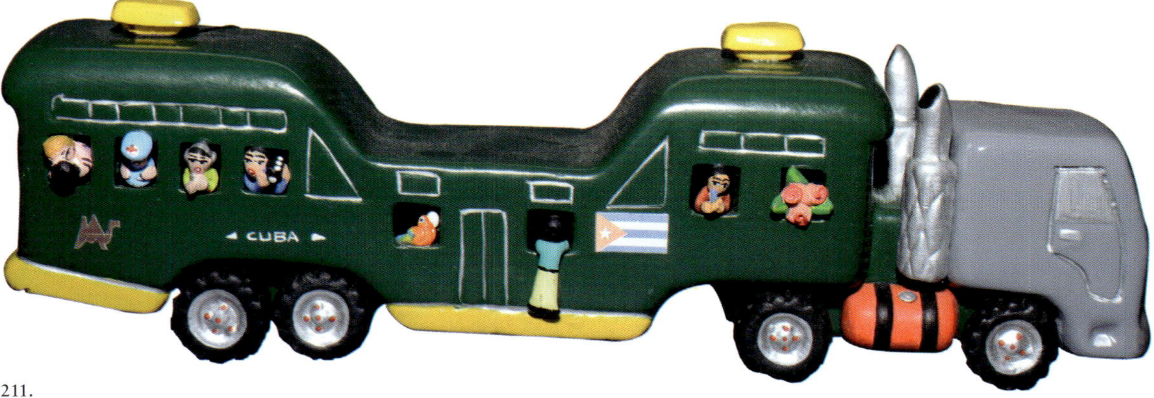

211.

The list continues: a Cuban chef carrying salt and pepper shakers; a trinket displaying the logo of the XI World Youth Festival celebrated in Havana in 1978 made in the Zsolnay Porcelánmanufaktúra in Hungary; a ship named "Habana" made by the San Claudio firm in Asturias (illustrated at p. 133); bongo players by Sampson (Japan, Fig. 213); and (Chicago, US; Spain); as well as a piano player from Cuba (Fig. 212); a Havana balm jar (Chard, US); or a set of decorative plates by HausenWare, made in China for the Sonoma, California firm. Not to be forgotten is a covered "Havane" vase done by GMF in the quaint village of Moustiers-Ste-Marie in southeastern France, or the Madame Alexander porcelain Cuba doll (US).

The well-known Ceramic Arts Studio in Madison, Wisconsin, has issued a figurine of a woman carrying fruit on her head. She is Carmen, often referred to as a Cuban character designed by Betty Harrington, but, as I see it, her looks and demeanor point more in the direction of Mesoamerica than the Antilles.

Recently, I have seen on ebay a "Recuerdos de Cuba" series produced by Guillón Atelier (Buenos Aires, Argentina) illustrating Havana's Catherdral and Capitol, José Martí's birthplace, the former Asturian Social Center, etc. The sky is the limit.

We should also mention that some ceramic pieces can be found in Havana's buildings or public spaces. A large mural by Isavel Gimeno and Aniceto Mario is to be admired in Old Havana, across from the Paula Church, and another Havana view can be seen on Prado street. In the corridors of Cuba's Ministry of foreign affairs I once saw two Mialhe views (Havana's cathedral and Cojímar) transferred to decorative tiles. Surely, many more have escaped my attention.

Two Cuban works merit special mention: a delicate saxophpone displaying the bell tower of Camagüey's cathedral, by Jaime A. López García (Fig. 219) and a miniature landscape inside a Fabergé-like egg made in Bauta, Artemisa Province, by Rael Rodríguez Capote (Fig. 220). St Petersburg and Bauta. So far… and yet so close!

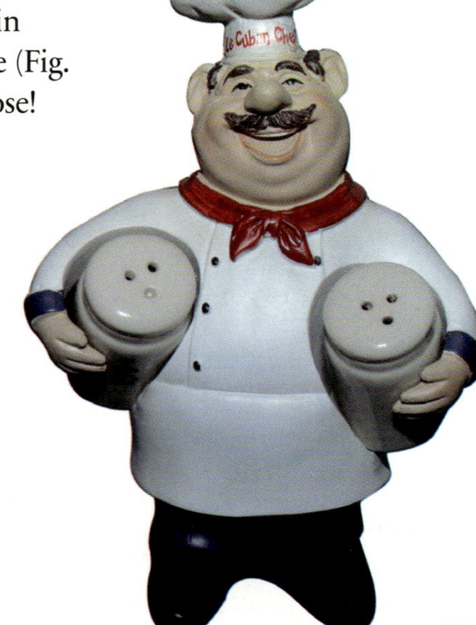

214.

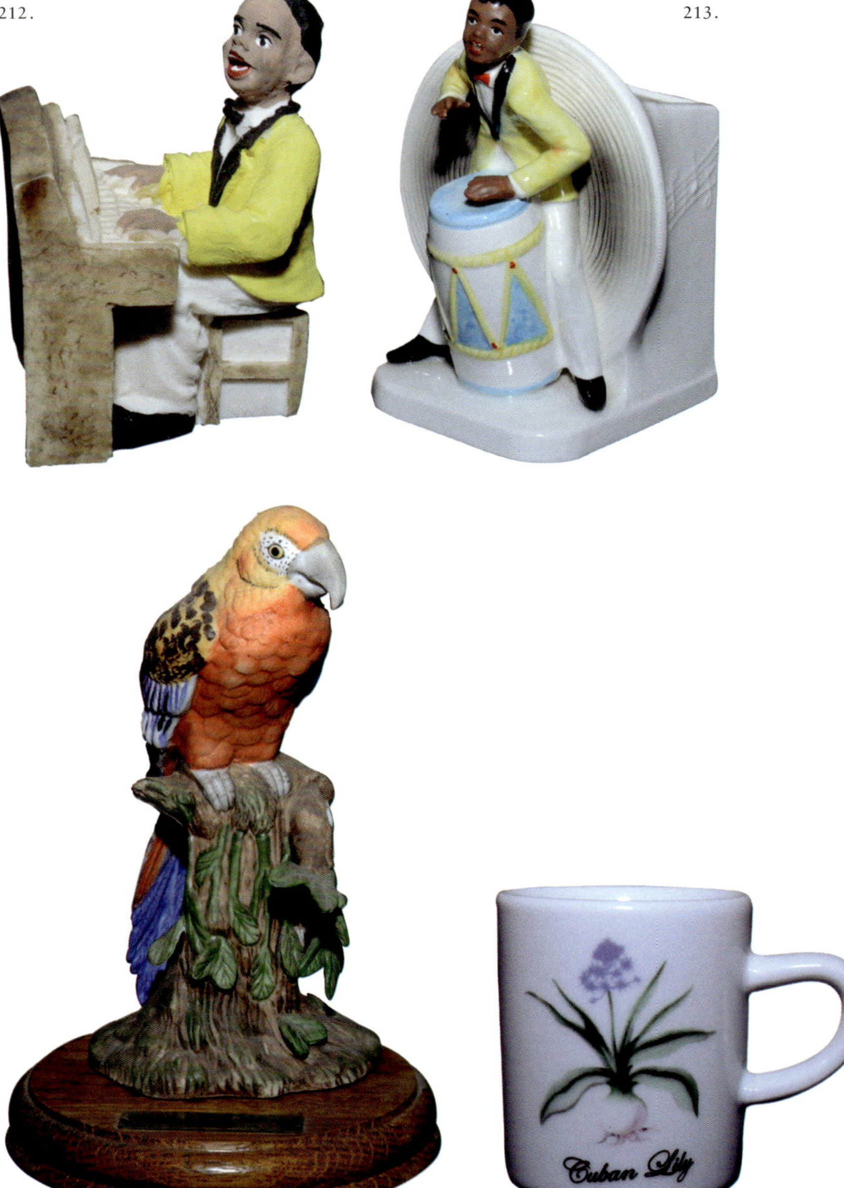
212.

213.

215.

216.

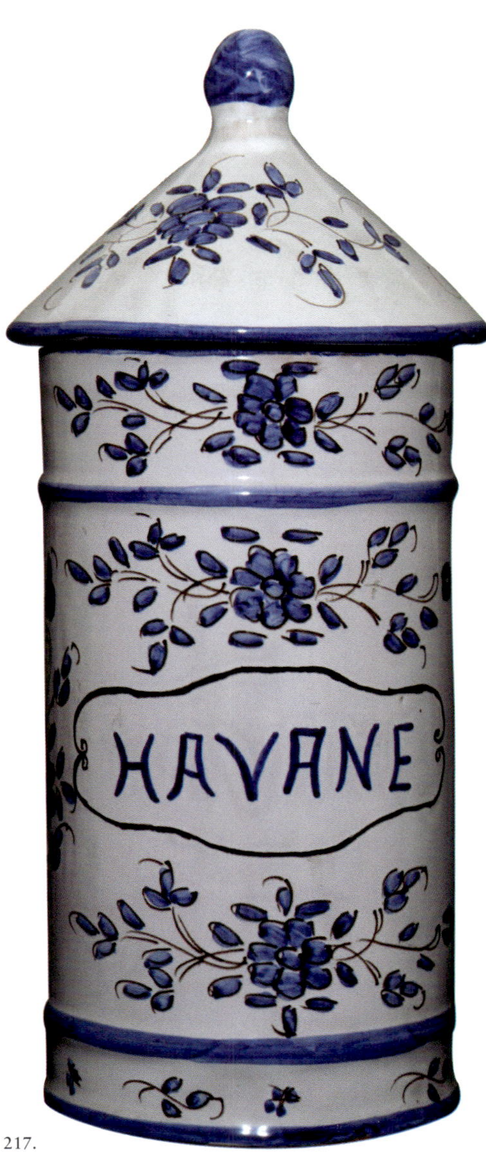

217.

· 212

Cuba. Unmarked. ca. 2008.

· 213

Sampson import, Japan, 1964.

· 214

Le Cuban Chef. US?, ca. 2010.

· 215

Cuban Red Macaw,
Aldon Accesories (US), 1990s.

· 216

Cuban Lily. Unmarked. 20th century.

· 217

Havane, GMF, Moustiers-Ste. Marie, (France), 21st century.

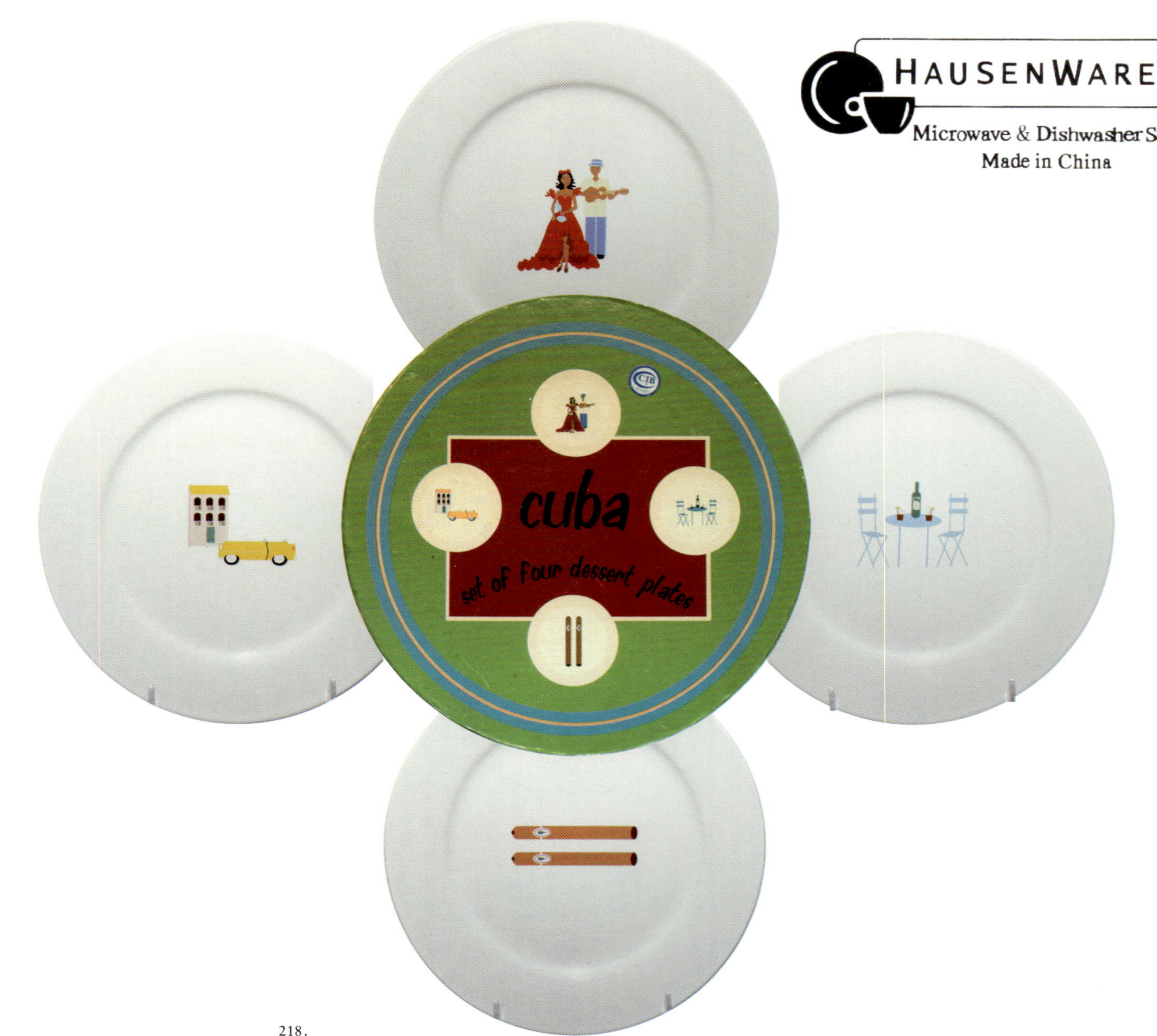

218.

· 218

Hausen Ware, (China), 21st century.

· 219

Jaime A. López García. Saxophpone displaying bell tower of Camagüey's cathedral (Cuba), 2014.

· 220

Rael Rodríguez Capote. Landscape inside a Fabergé egg (Cuba), 2016.

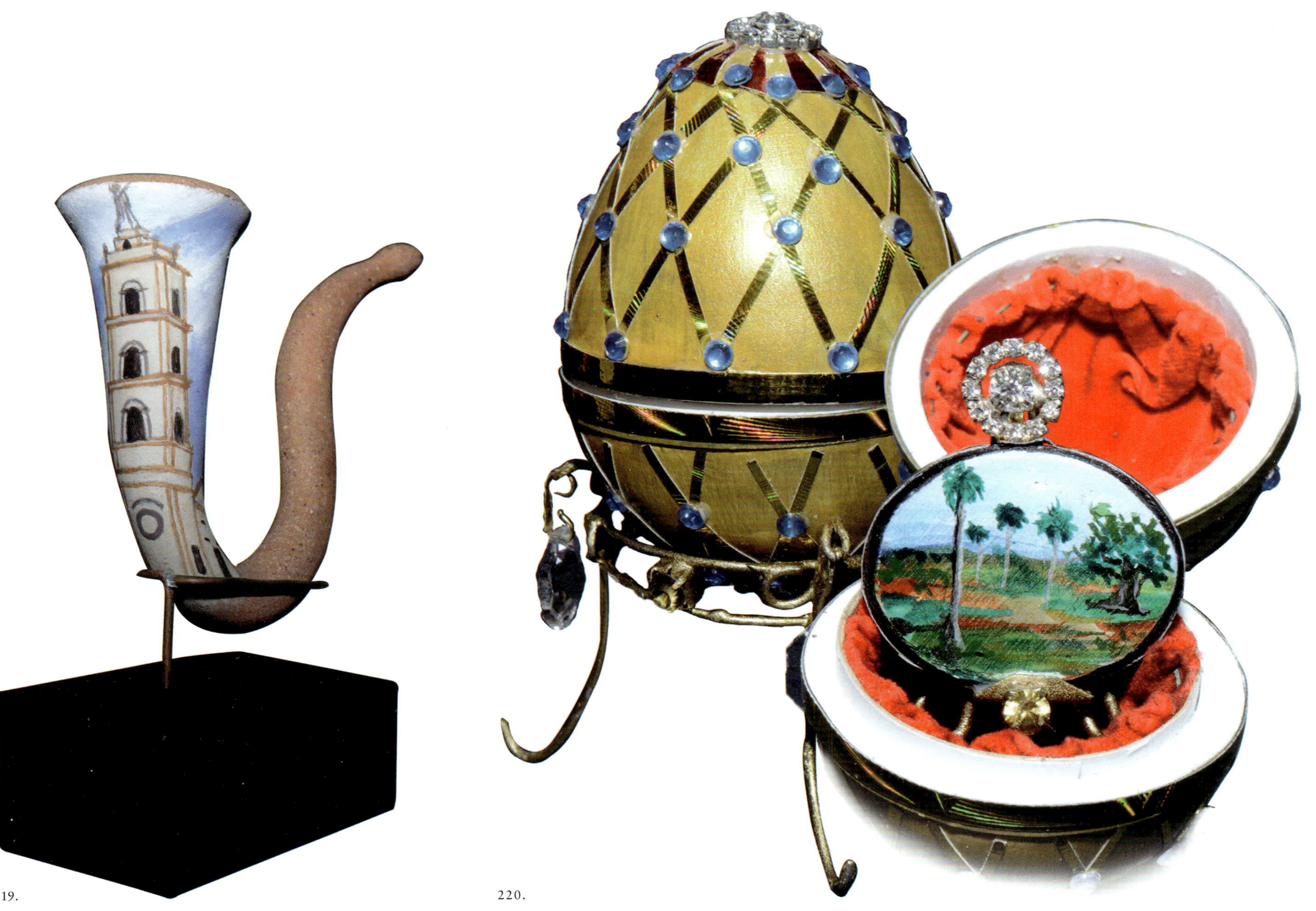

219.

220.

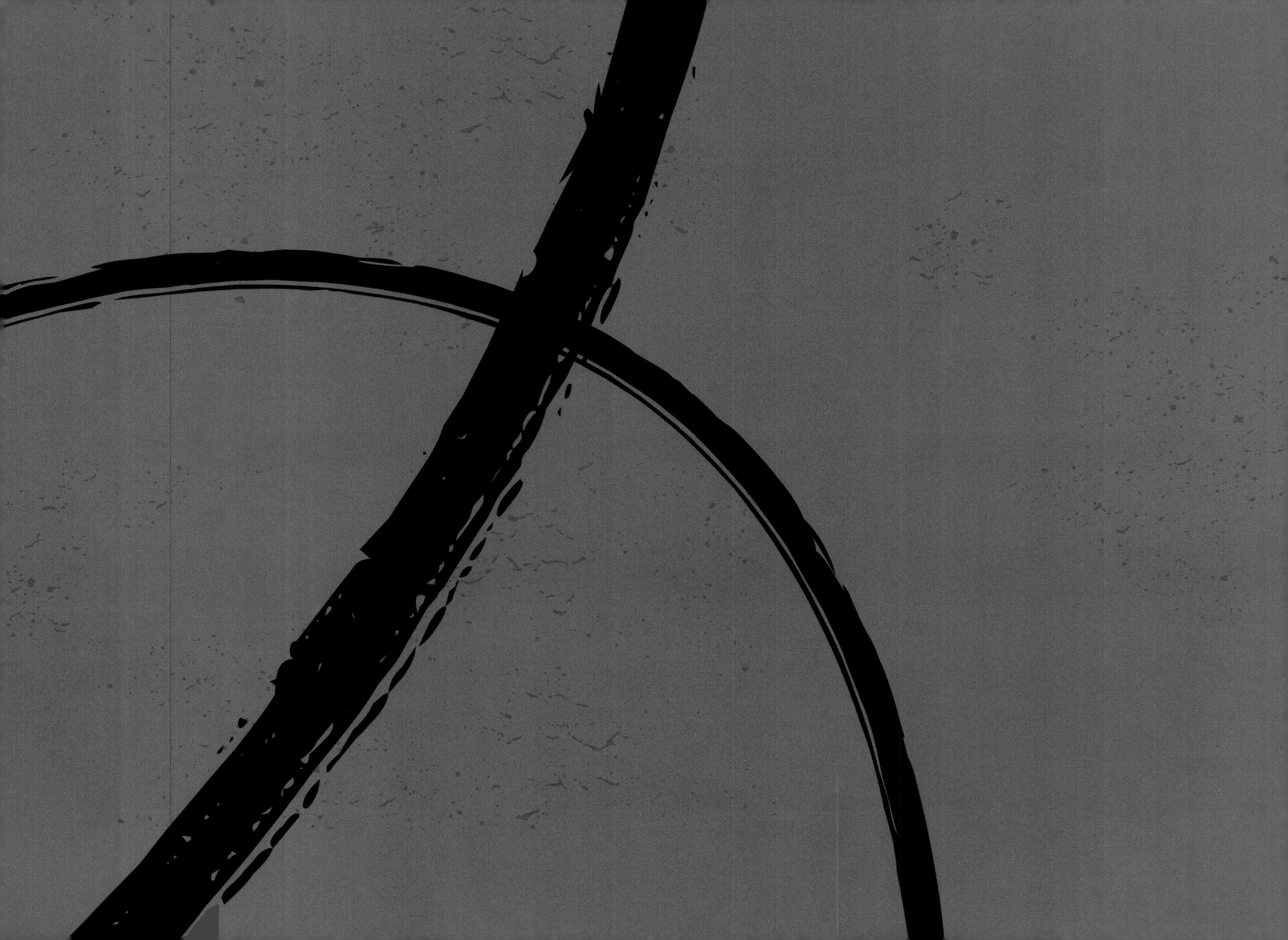

Cuba

CUBA SELLS

In the 1980s I met an antique dealer at the famed Portobello market in London who told me she had a Cuba porcelain piece in her shop. Intrigued, I travelled to her store in the town of Bath only to be disappointed: she presented me with an 1840s black pitcher depicting a Chinese view (Fig. 221). Why on earth would this oriental-looking object be named "Cuba"?

Not to disappoint her, I did purchase the puzzling piece. Only much later I realized that this was part of a much wider context: "Cuba" sells (and buys).[60] And manufacturers, fully aware of this quaint phenomenon, are not shy to take advantage of it. I have been collecting these kinds of pieces ever since and my observations on this phenomenon are based on a study of my own collection as well as the result of many hours looking at images in antique catalogs, auction houses and the internet.

In spite of its relatively small size and population, Cuba has left a mark in the world much larger than one would suspect. The island's location, its benign climate and the charm of its inhabitants have attracted tourists from all over, who, in turn, write books and blogs about their pleasant (or not quite) experiences in the country. Cuba's music (from Ernesto Lecuona's *danzas* to the *Buena Vista Social Club* phenomenon) and dances, both popular (bolero, danzón, rumba, conga, cha cha cha, mambo, pachanga) and classic (*Ballet de Cuba*, Alicia Alonso, Loipa Araujo, Charín Suárez, Jorge Esquivel, Carlos Acosta), have captured the world's imagination and respect.

Moreover, the success of its athletes has resulted in a steady presence of gifted players in US (and foreign) teams, a trove of Olympic medals and millions of followers among the general public. And Cuban art has many international followers, if we are to believe the countless exhibitions, books and auction records at Sotheby's and Christie's.

Finally, there is Cuba's geopolitical status and presence in the world stage (1762 seizure by the British, Spanish American War of 1898, Bay of Pigs invasion in 1961, October 1962 missile crisis, successful literacy campaign, preeminence in the Non-Aligned Movement, armed intervention in African wars, medical solidarity brigades throughout the Third World, the first black, latin, astronaut, human rights record, the US embargo, the Mariel boat lift and other *balsero* crises, the long-ruling Castro dynasty). They all have kept the island in the headlines for well over half a century.

As a result of this (over)exposure, Cuba has become a place to be reckoned with. And one which mostly evokes positive vibes. So much so, that manufacturers of all kinds of wares are prone to name their products with the name of "Cuba", "Cuban", "Cubana", "Qban", "Havana" or "Habana", fully aware that such name will attract the attention of buyers. Cuba as a brand all of its own because Cuba sells. Indeed. One can say with confidence that the world of ceramics has for a long time turned its attention to Cuba.

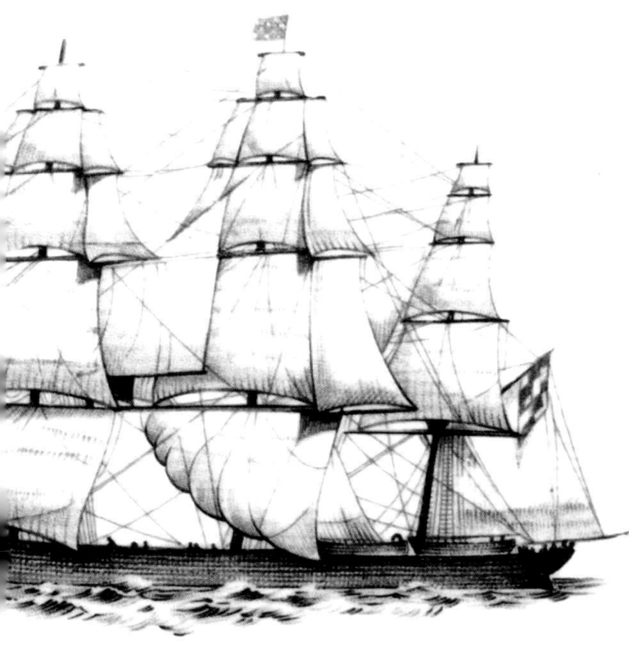

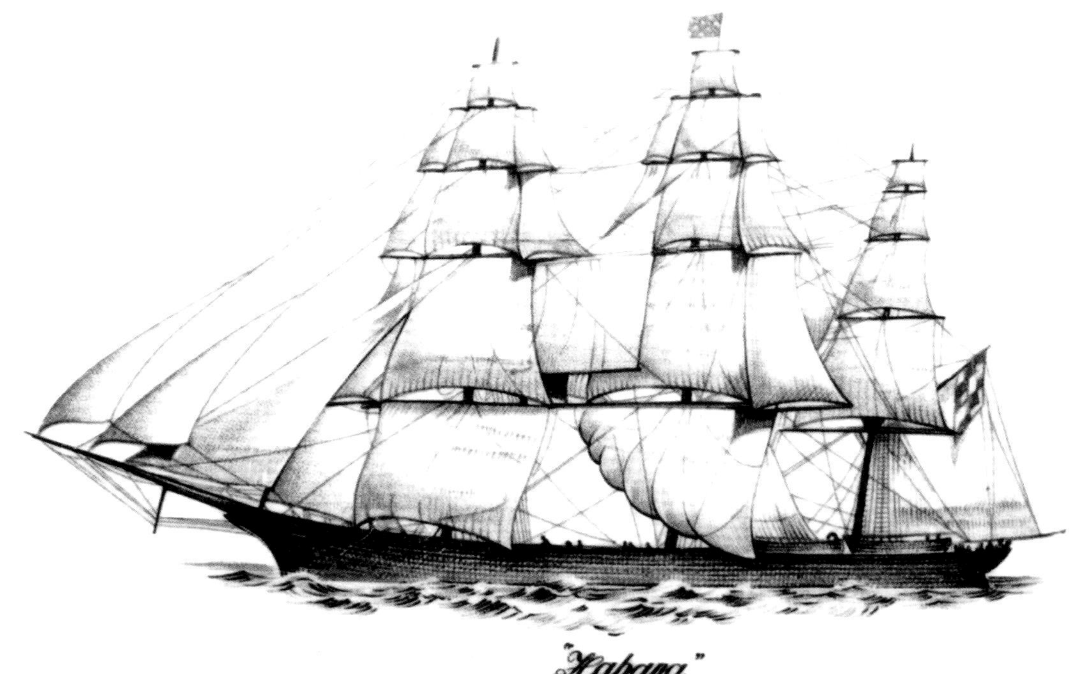

[60] According to W. Turner, writing around 1907, this Cuba pattern "would be used mostly on earthenware plate for the Cuban trade, which was extensive at Swansea a half a century or more ago". The original copper plate, kept at the Royal Institute at Swansea, indicates also the name of the Havana agent: Acacio Velez y Co., Cuba. "Swansea fayence", in Ethel Deane (ed.), *The Collector*. London, Horace Cox, pp. 122-124.

Most of these pseudo Cuban ceramic and porcelain pieces, named after Cuba, Havana (or derivatives thereof) for no apparent reason other than a good sales pitch, consist of coffee, tea and dinnerware sets. The vast majority of them —25 in my collection alone— are from England (Figs. 221, 222, 223, 224, 225, 226, 227, 228, 229, 230, 231, 232, 233, 234, 235, 236, 237, 238, 239, 240).

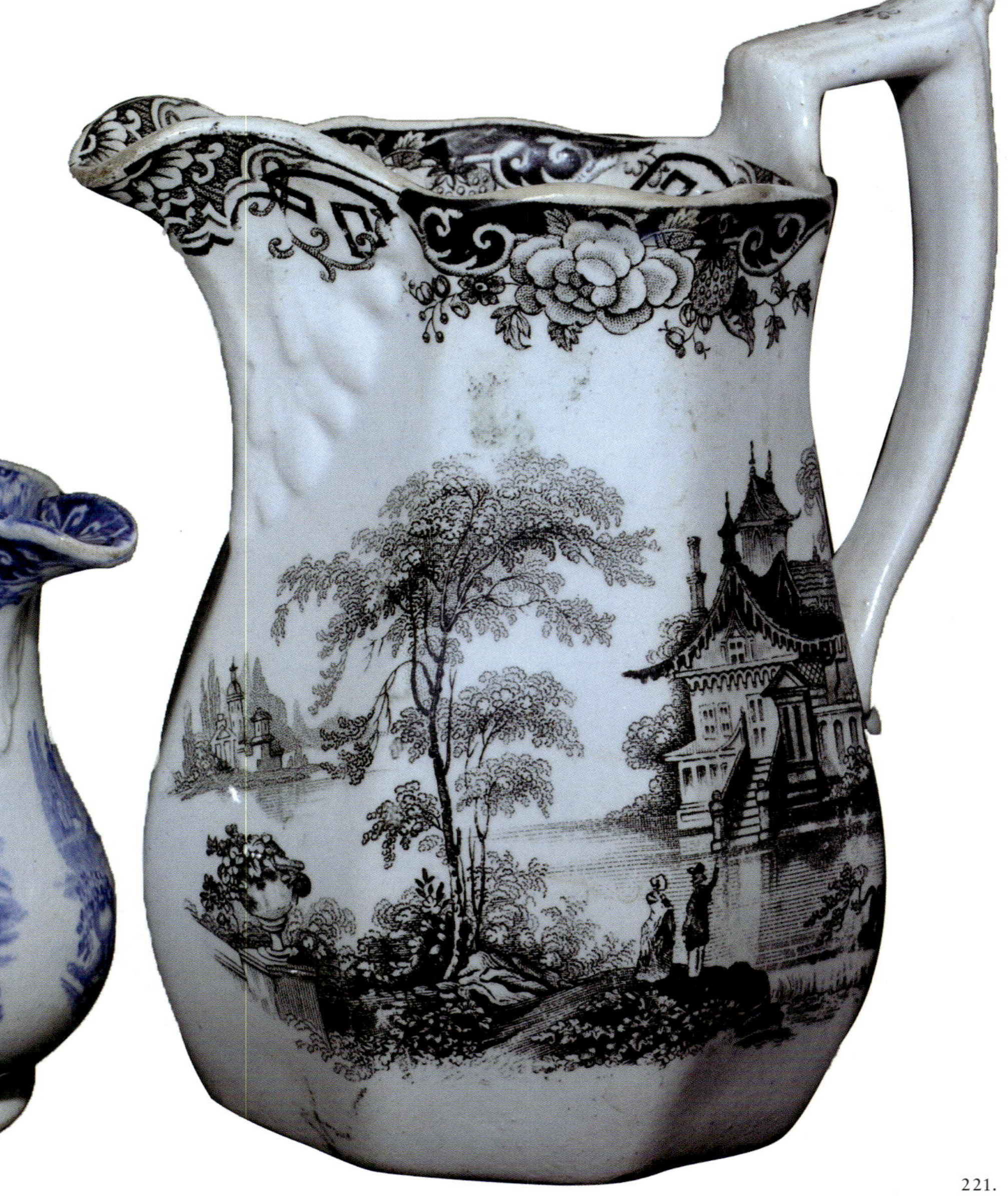

221.

· 221
"Cuba". Dillwyn & Co. (Swansea, Glamorganshire, Wales, UK), ca. 1847.
· 222
Jessie Taite. "Cuban Fantasy". Midwinter Modern (Staffordshire, UK), 1967.
· 223
Clarice Cliff. "Havana". A. J. Wilkinson (Newport, Burslem, UK), 20th century.
· 224
"Havana". Johnson Brothers (Hanley, Staffordshire, UK), 21st century.
· 225
"Cuba". BCM Nelson Ware (Hanley, Staffordshire, UK), 20th century.

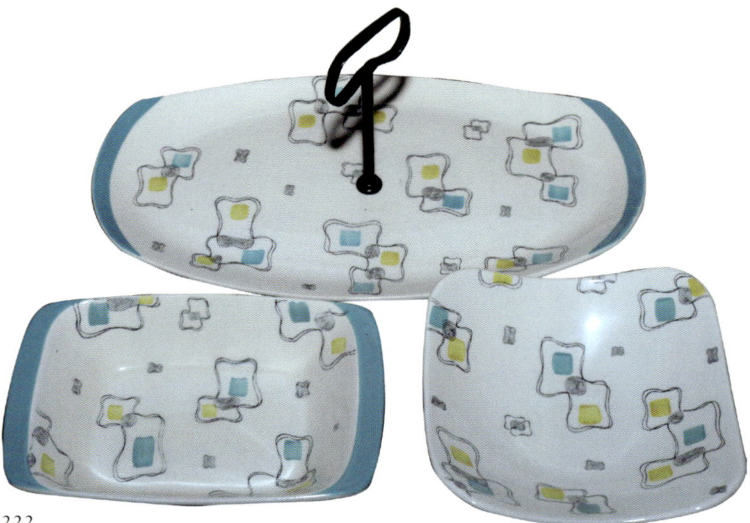

222.

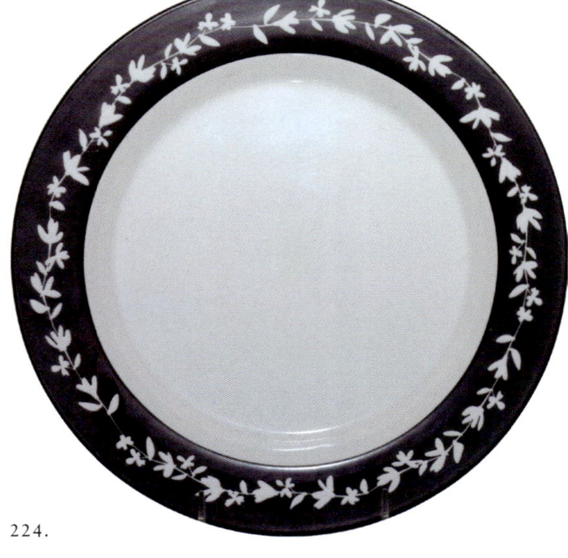

224.

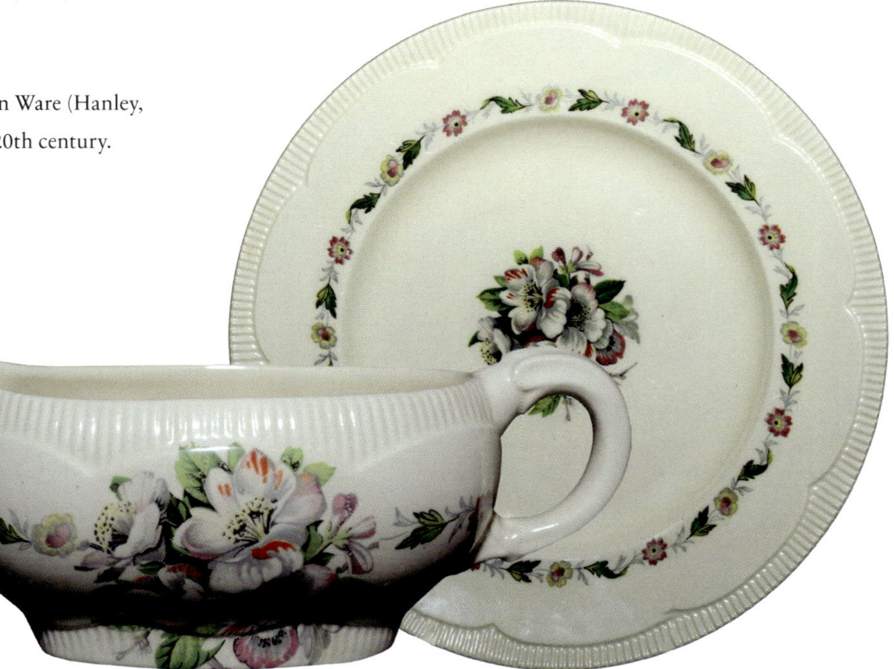

223.

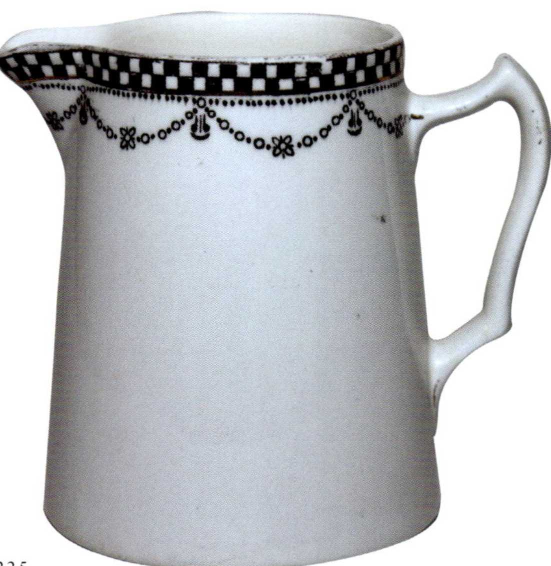

225.

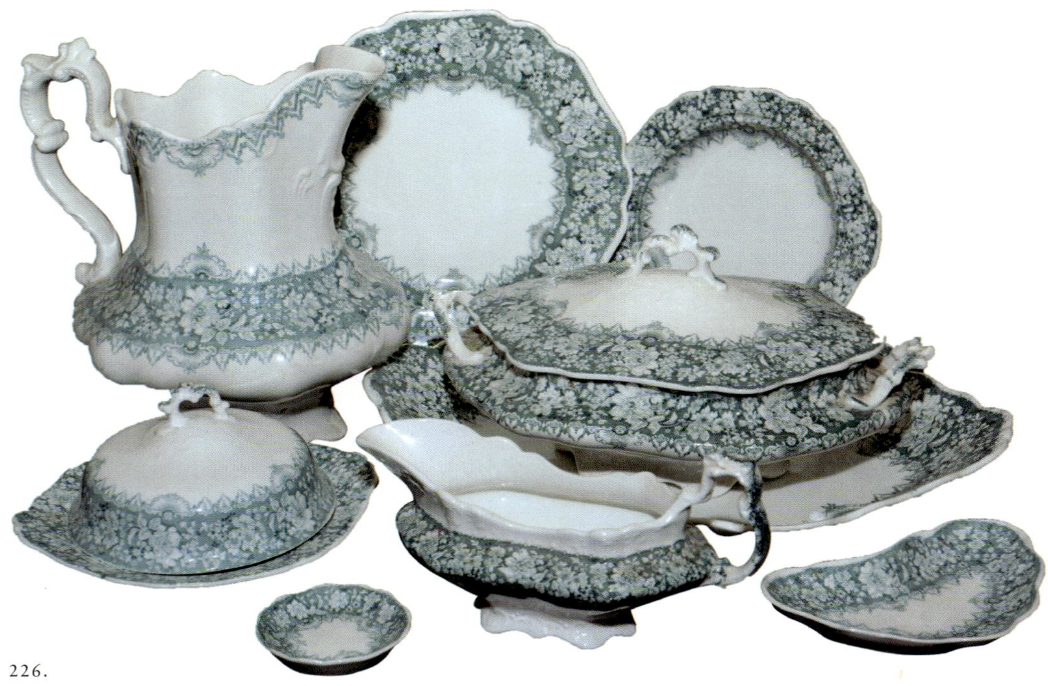
226.

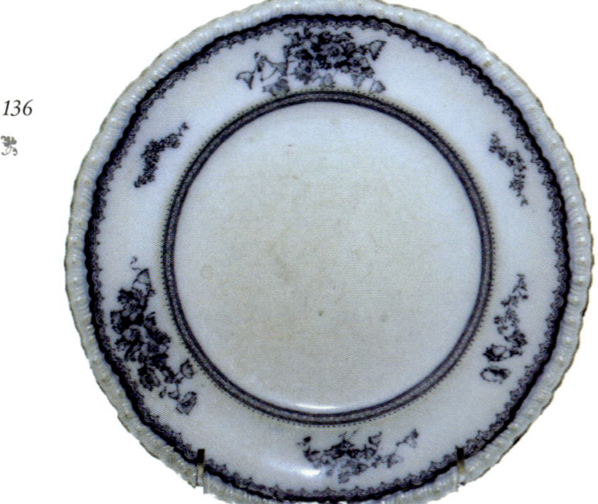
227.

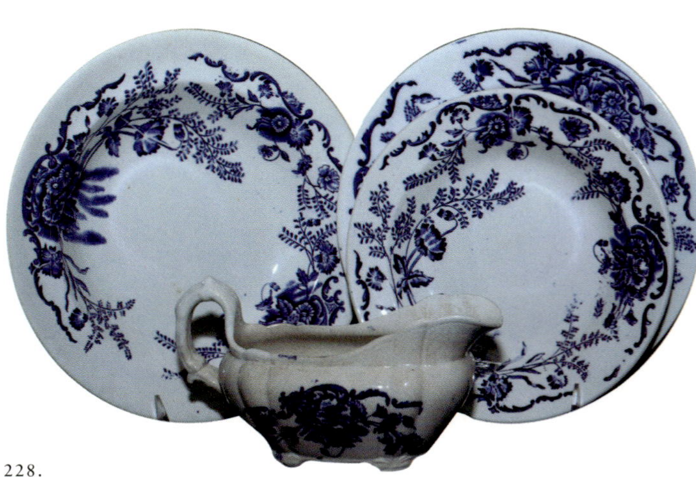
228.

· 226
"Havana". Johnson Brothers (Hanley, Staffordshire, UK), 20th century.

· 227
"Cuba". Bridgwood & Son (Longton, Staffordshire, UK), 20th century.

· 228
"Cuba". William A. Adderley (Longton, Staffordshire, UK), 20th century.

· 229
"Cuba". Royal Grafton (Staffordshire, UK), 20th century.

· 230
"Cuba". Spode Copeland (Stoke-on-Trent, Staffordshire, UK), 20th century.

· 231
"The Havana" Grindley (Tunstall, Staffordshire, UK), 21st century.

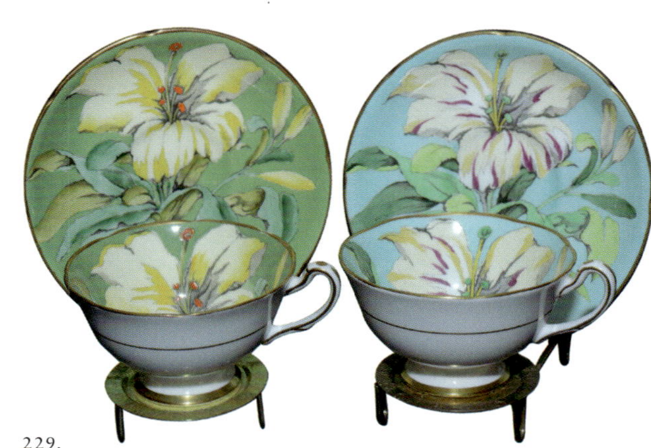

229.

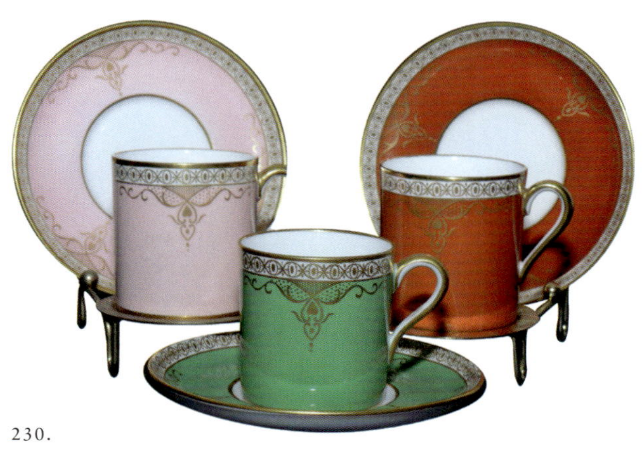

230.

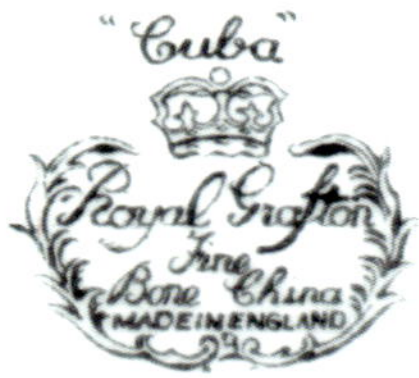

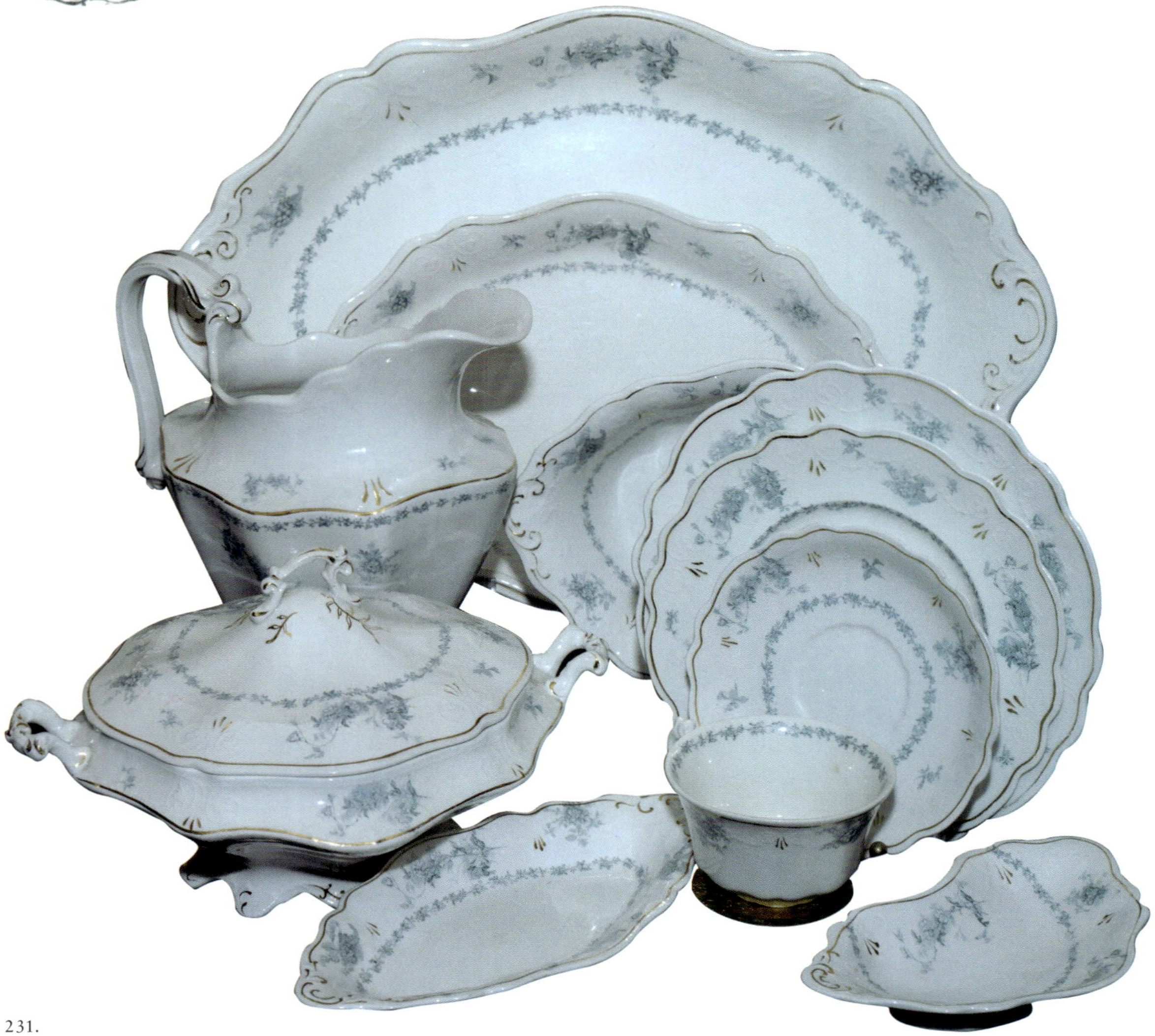

231.

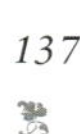

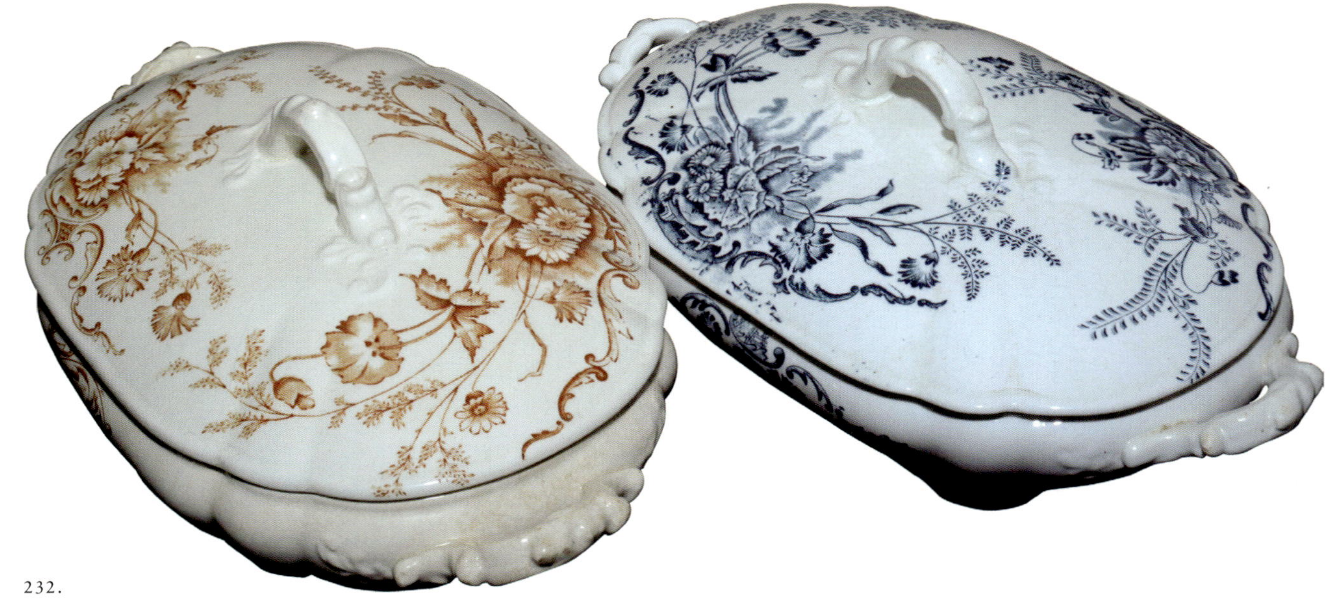

232.

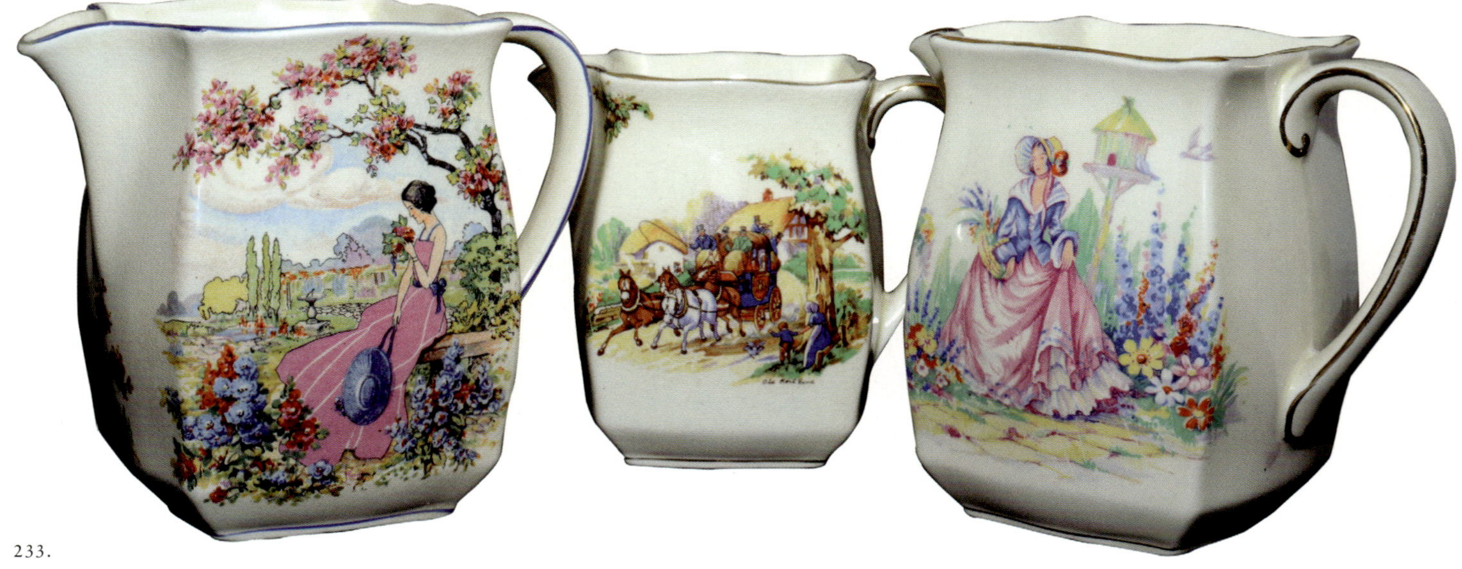

233.

· 232
"Cuba". Pountney (Bristol, UK), 20th century.

· 233
"Cuban No. 2" and "Cuban No. 3". Falcon Ware (Longton, UK), 20th century.

· 234
"Cuba". Grindley (Tunstall, Staffordshire, UK), 20th century.

· 235
"Cuba". Miniature Toby Jug. Royal Doulton? (Stoke-on-Trent, Staffordshire, UK), 20th century.

· 236
"Cuba". Adams Etruscan Ware (Staffordshire, UK). 20th century

· 237
"Cuba". Marked No. 324238 (UK). 20th century.

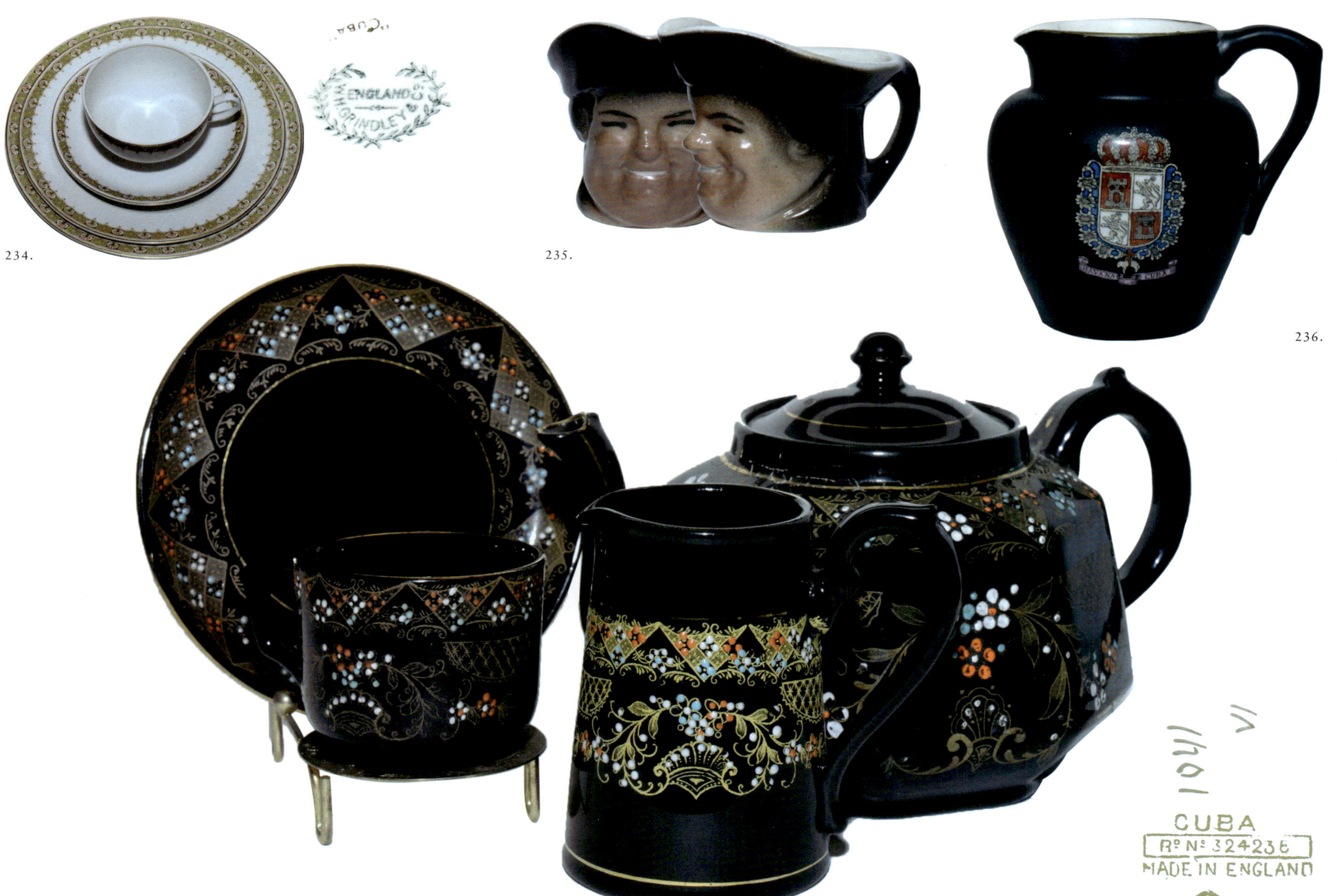

234.

235.

236.

237.

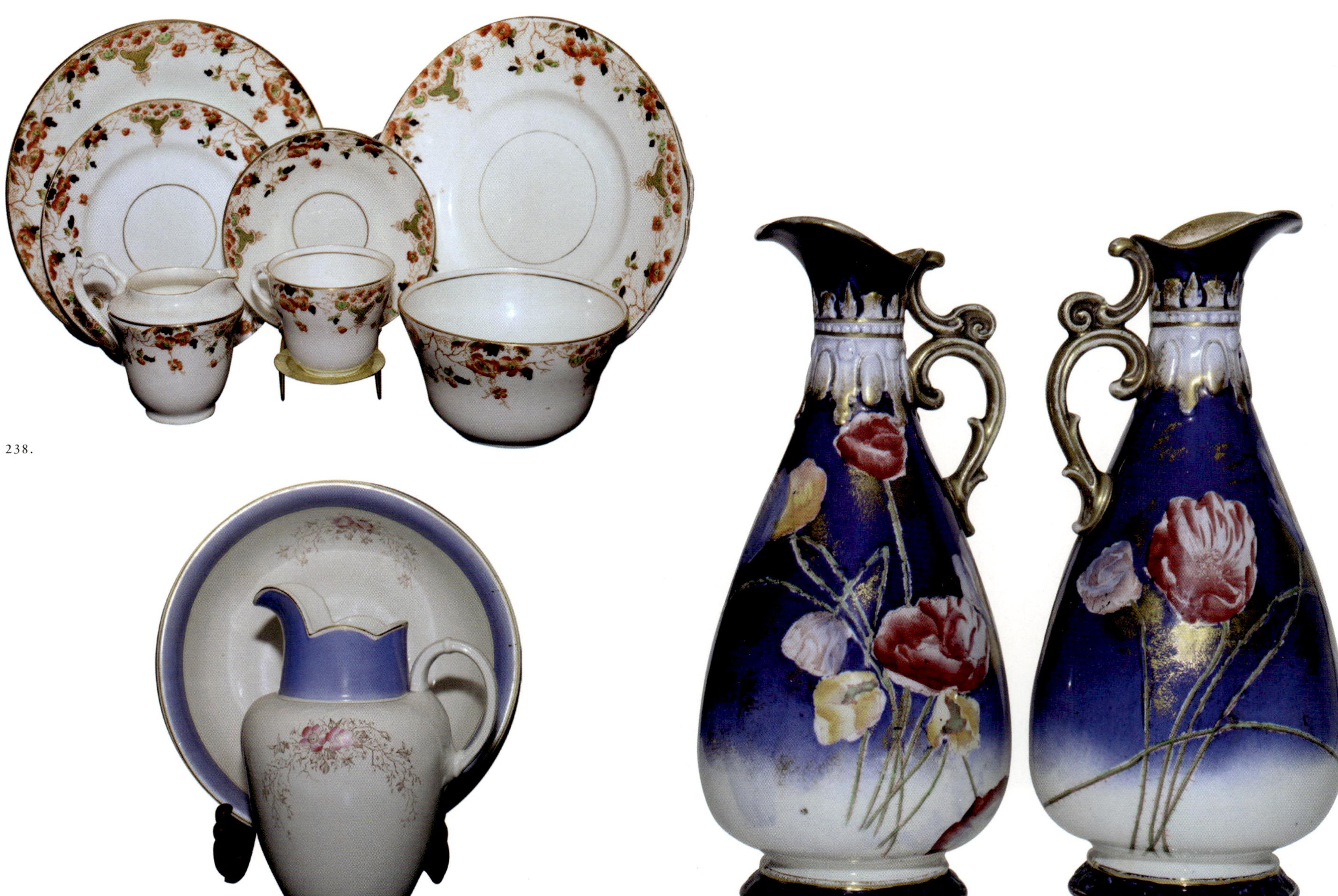

238.

239.

240.

Other countries represented are Belgium (Fig. 242), China (Figs. 243, 241), France (Figs. 244, 245, 246), Germany (Figs. 247, 248, 249), Japan (Figs. 251, 252), Sweden (Figs. 253, 254), and the US (Figs. 255, 258, 256, 257, 262, 259, 263). In addition, there are many unmarked pieces of unknown origin (Figs. 260, 261).

One particular dish merits special attention: a beautiful German Rosenthal porcelain piece stamped "Paris-Viena-Habana" (Fig. 248). Need more be said?

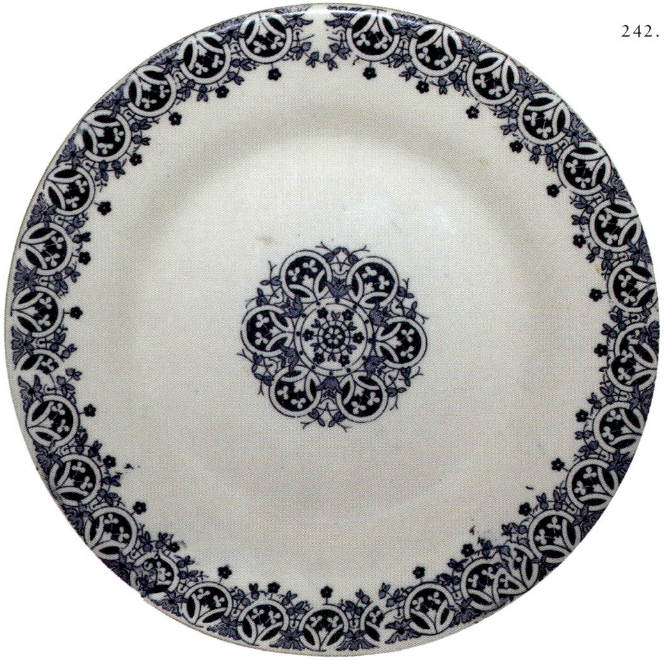

· 238
"Cuba". Clifton China, Wildblood, Heath & Sons (Longton, Staffordshire, UK), 20th century.

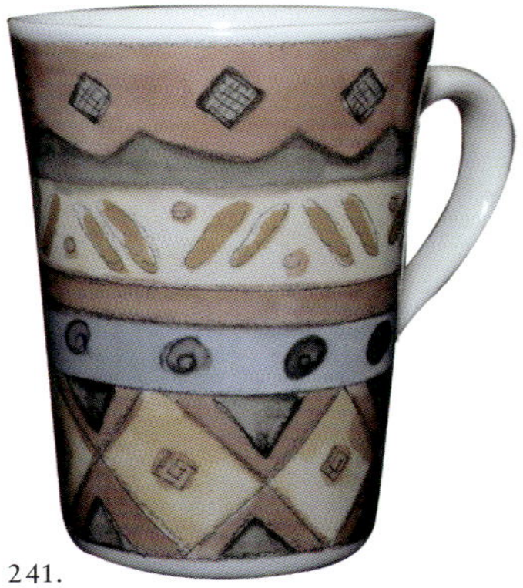

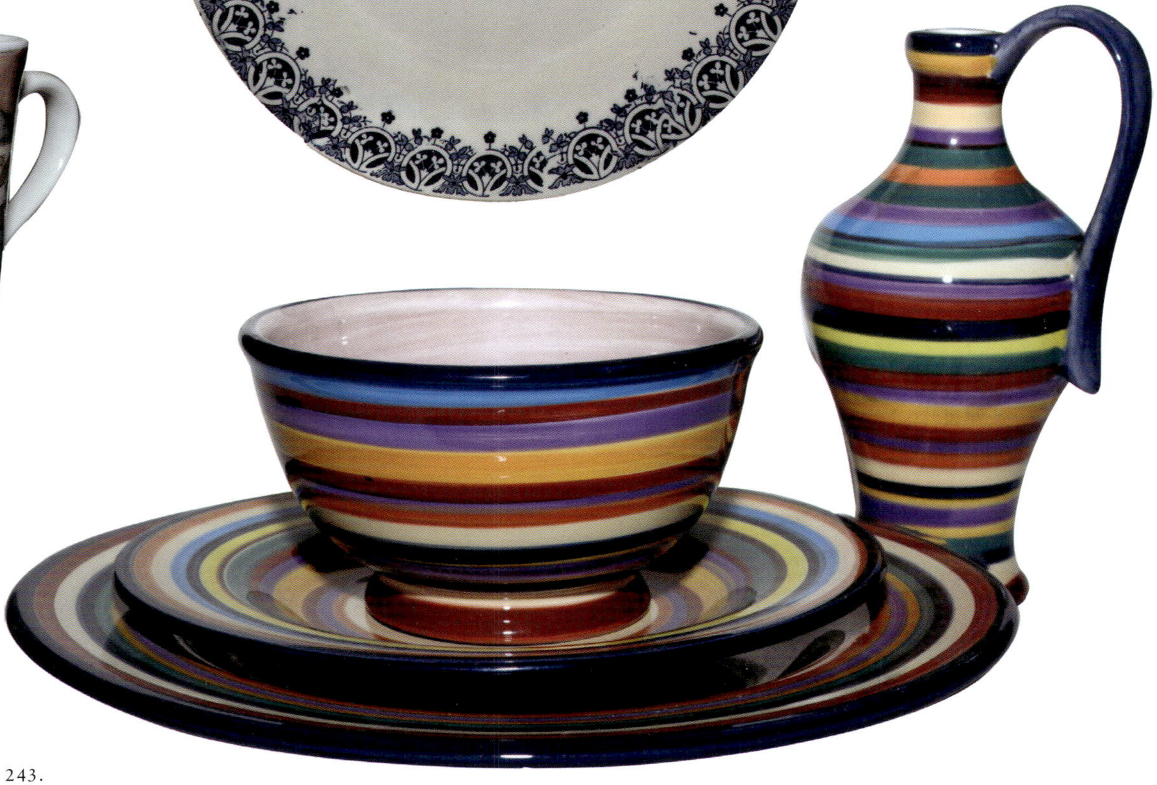

· 239
"Havana". Stanley (Middleport, Burslem, UK), 20th century.

· 240
"Cuban blue". Edge Malkin (Burslem, Staffordshire, UK), 20th century.

· 241
Sue Zipkin. "Café Cubana". Sango (China), 21st century.

· 242
"Cuba". Porcelane Opaque de Gien (Gien, Belgium), 20th century.

· 243
"Havana". Tabletops Unlimited (Carson, California; China), 21st century.

242.

241.

243.

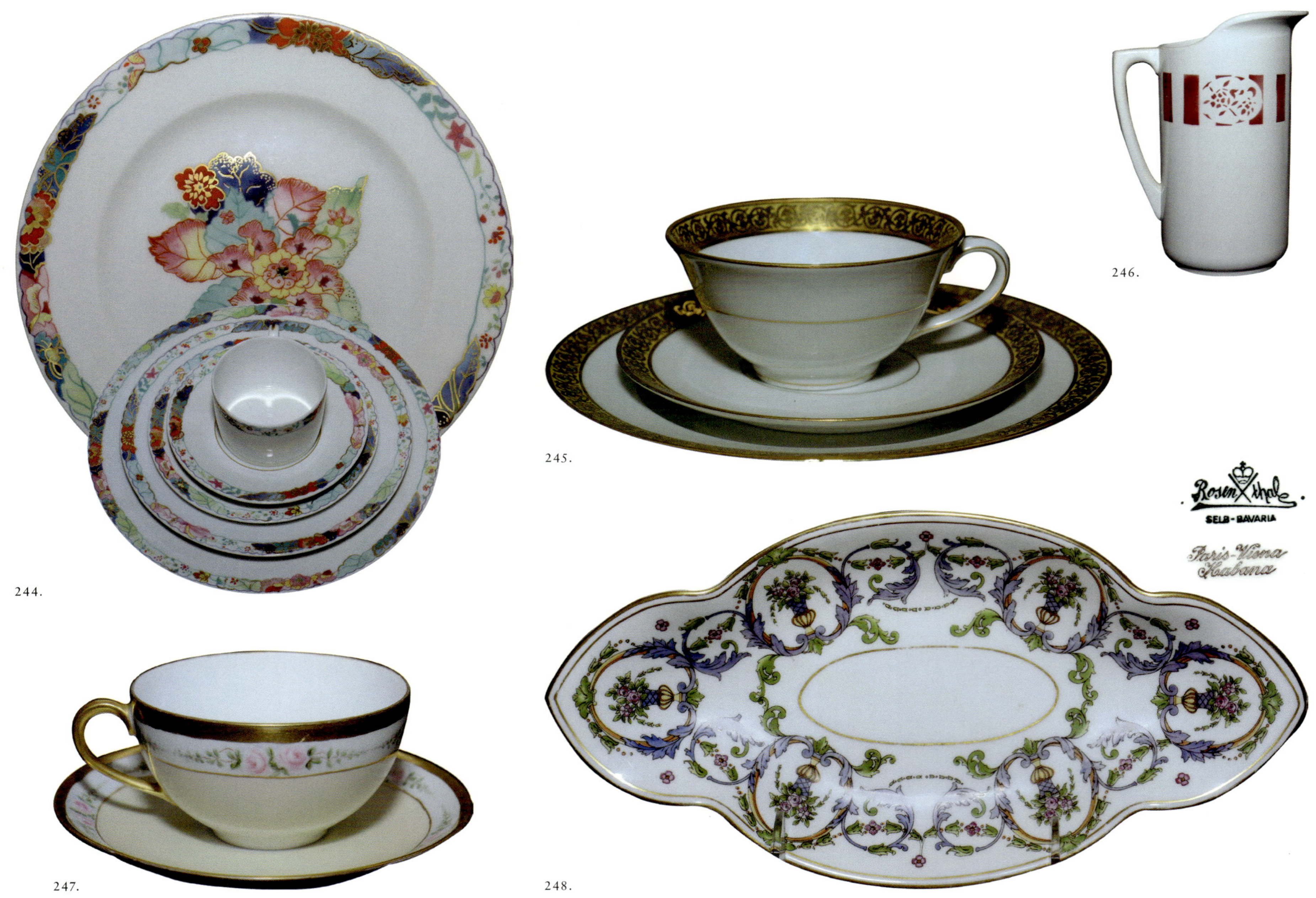

244.

245.

246.

247.

248.

· 244
“Havana”. Ancienne Manufacture Royale (Limoges, France), 20th century.
· 245
“Havana”. Charles Field Haviland (Limoges, France), 20th century.
· 246
“Cuba”. Faiencerie de Castres (Castres, France), 20th century.
· 247
“Havana”. Thomas Sevres (Marktredwitz, Bavaria, Germany), 20th century.
· 248
“Paris-Viena-Habana” (Rosenthal, Bavaria, Germany), 20th century.
· 249
“Havana”. Thomas Sevres (Marktredwitz, Bavaria, Germany), Hand painted (Akron, Ohio, US). 20th century.
· 250
“Havana”. Noritake Younger Image (Japan), 21st century.
· 251
“Havana”. Noritake (Japan), ca. 1912.
· 252
“Havana”. Sasaki Aerobleu (Japan), 21st century.
· 253
“Cuba”. Rörstrand (Kungsholmen, Stockholm, Sweden). 20th century.
· 254
“Cuba”. Upsala-Ekeby. Gefle (Ekeby, Sweden), post 1960s.

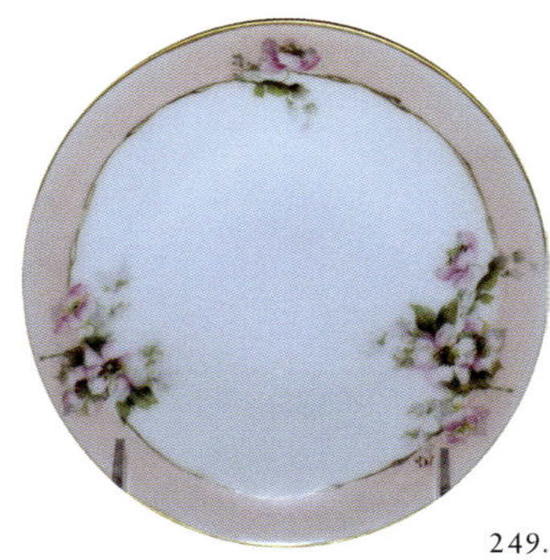
249.

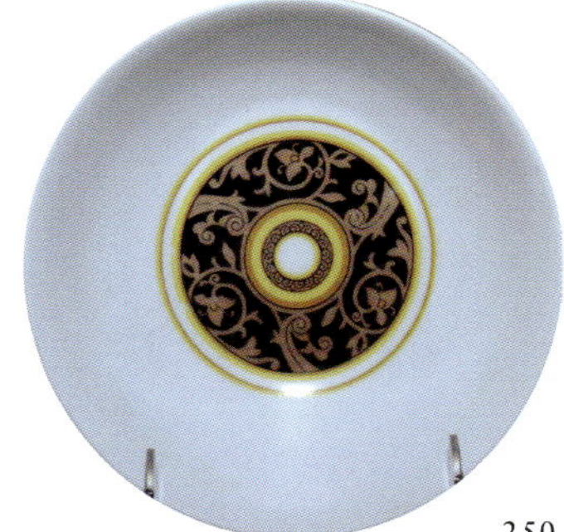
250.

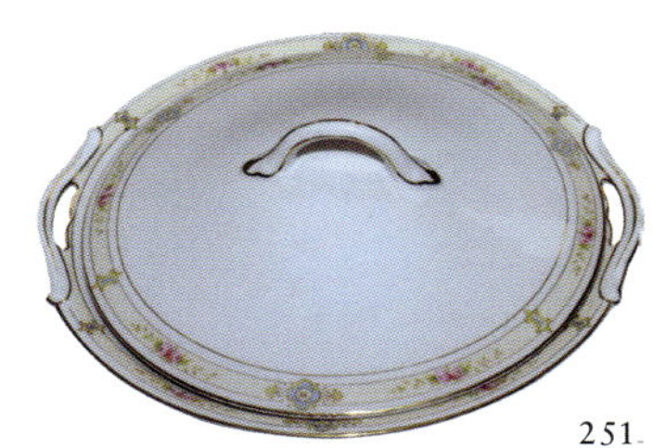
251.

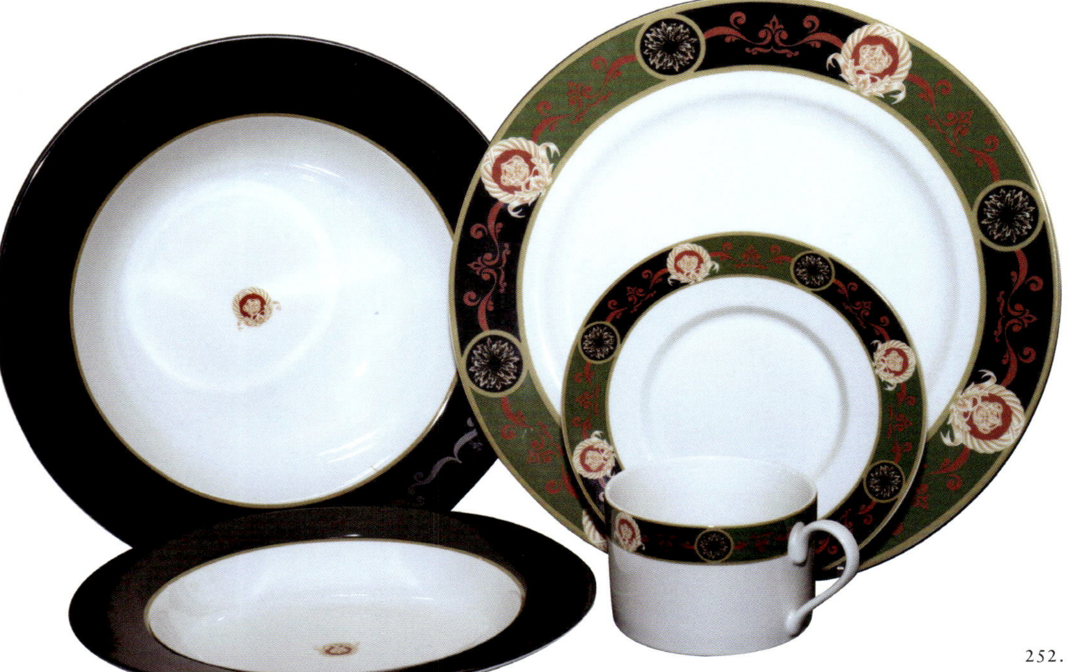
252.

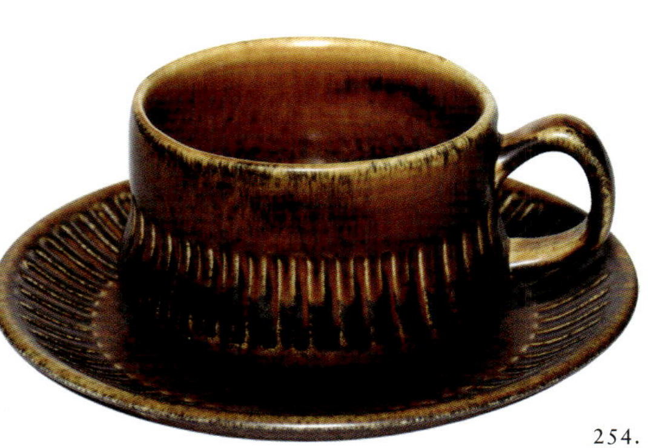
254.

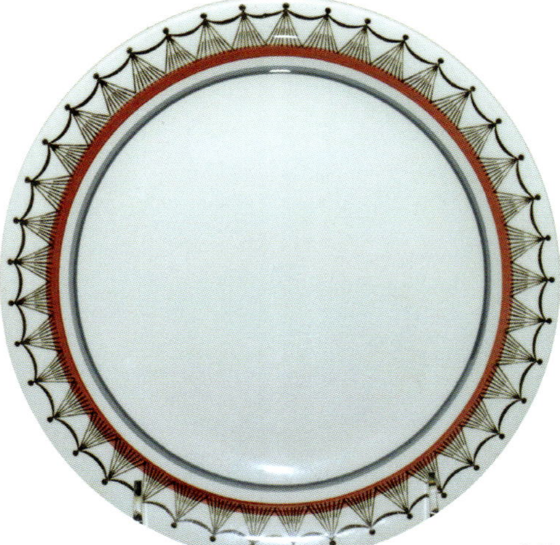
253.

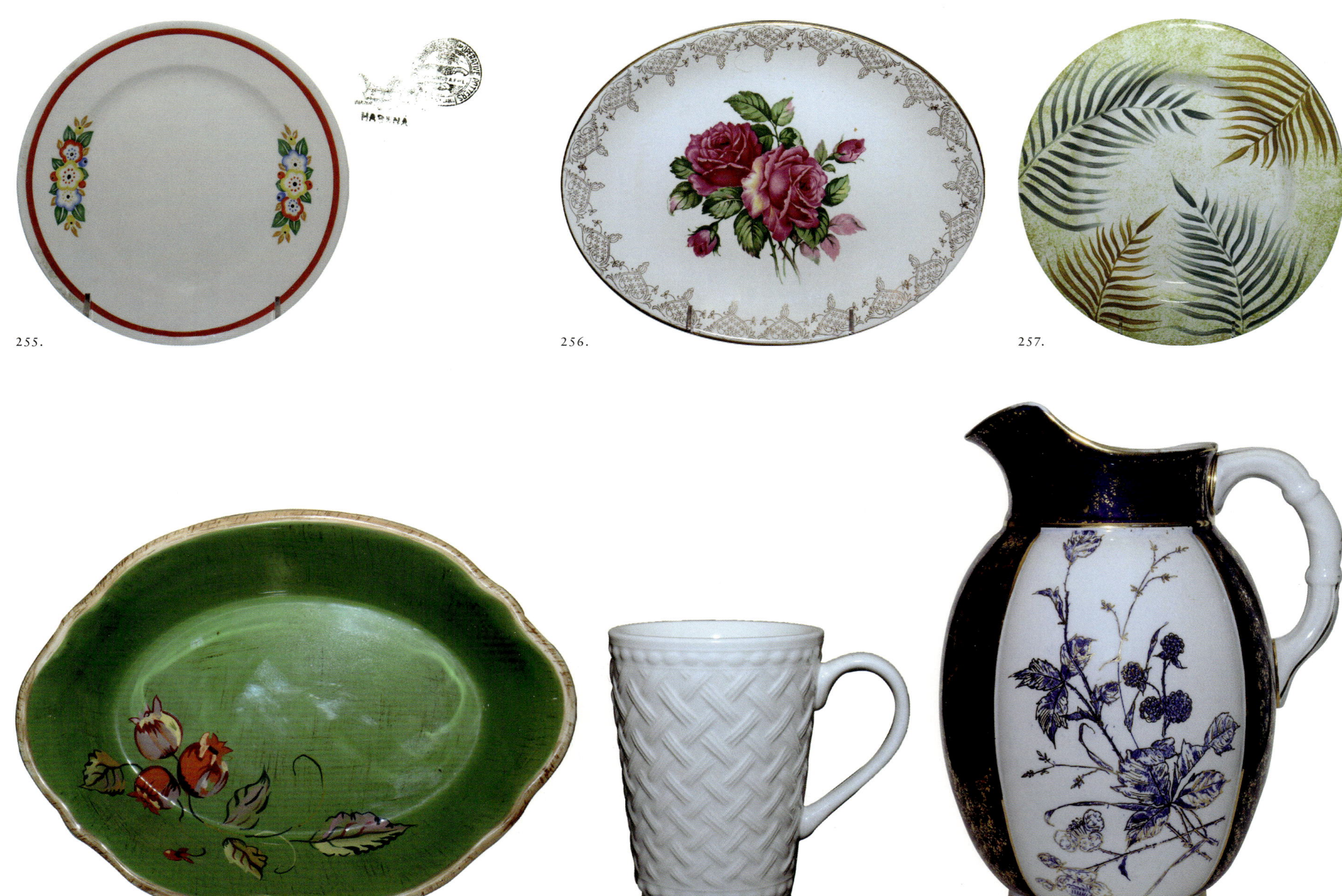

255.

256.

257.

258.

259.

260.

· 255
"Habana". Royal / National Brotherhood (Sebring, Ohio, US), 20th century.

· 256
"Cuban Rose". Royal Shelton (US?), 20th century.

· 257
"Havana". Home Essentials (Jersey City, New Jersey, US), 21st century.

· 258
"Havana". Zrike (Oakland, California, US), 21st century.

· 259
"Havanna Weave". Ten Strawberry street (Denver, Colorado, US), 21st century.

· 260
"Havana". Unmarked (US?), 20th century.

· 261
"Havana". Unmarked (US?), 20th century.

· 262
"Qban Royal". The Royal China (Sebring, Ohio, US), 20th century.

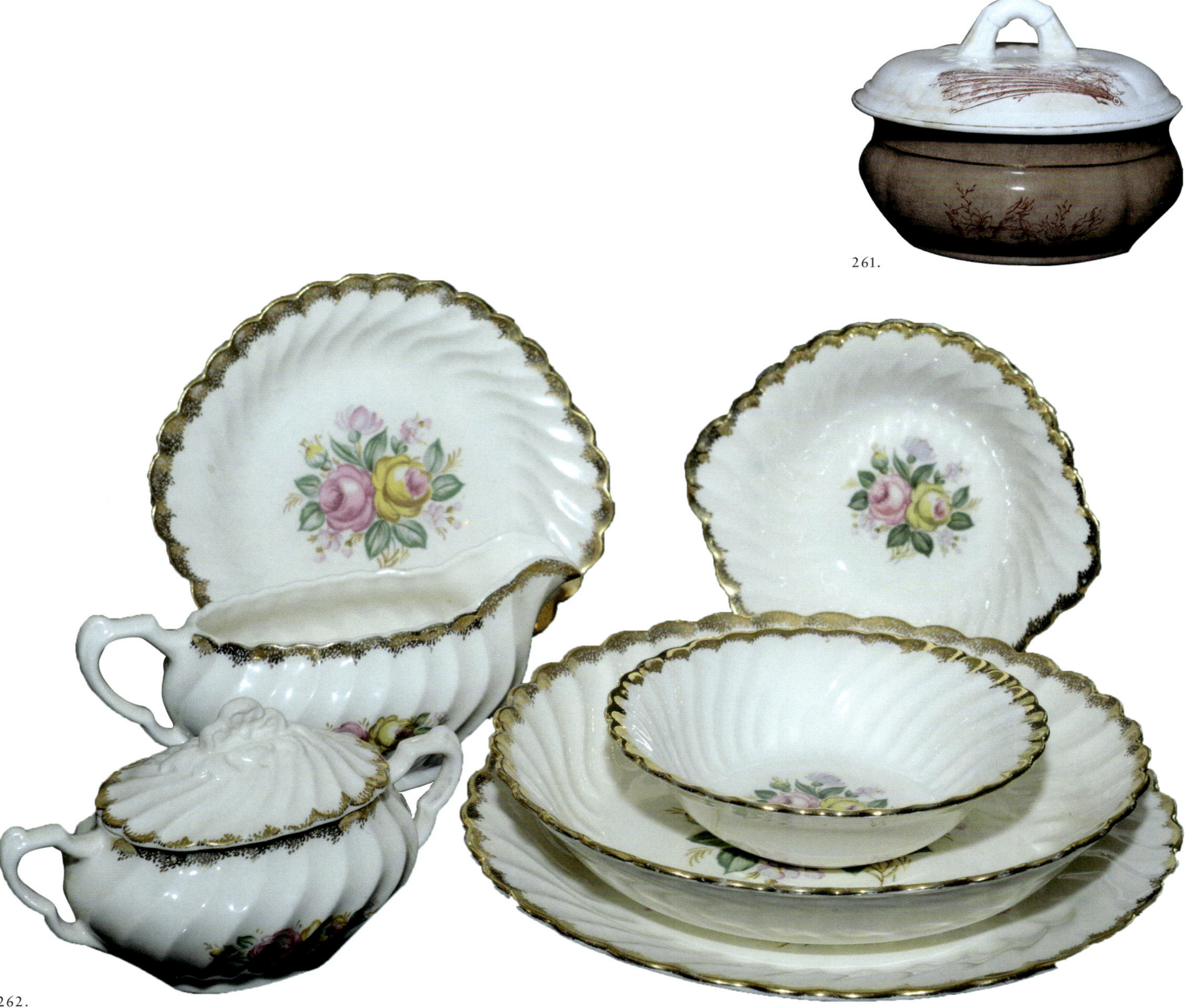

261.

262.

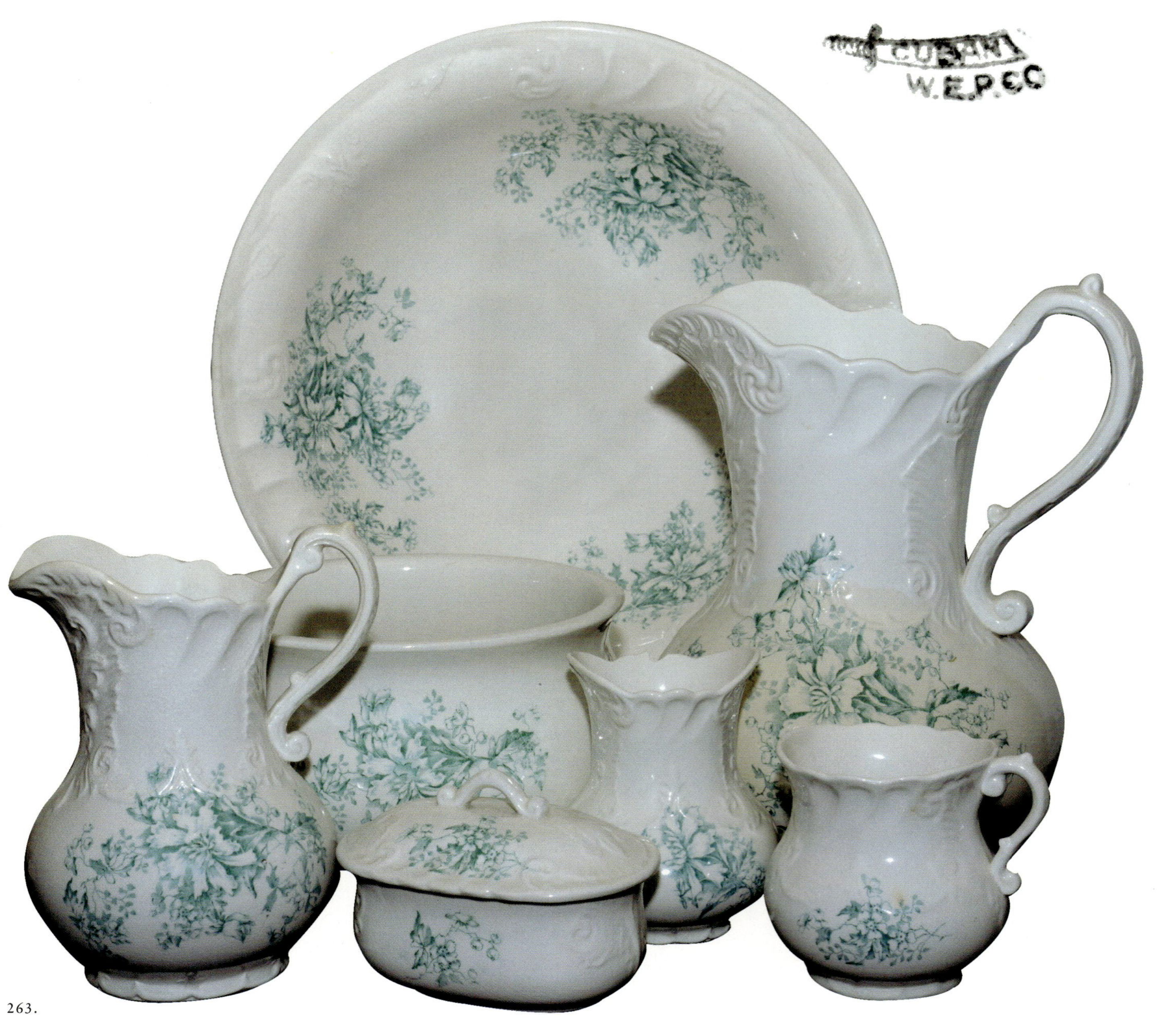

263.

· 263
"Cuban". West End Pottery Co. (East Liverpool, Ohio, US), 20th century.
· 264
"Cuba". George Jones (Stoke-on-Trent, Staffordshire, UK), 1873.

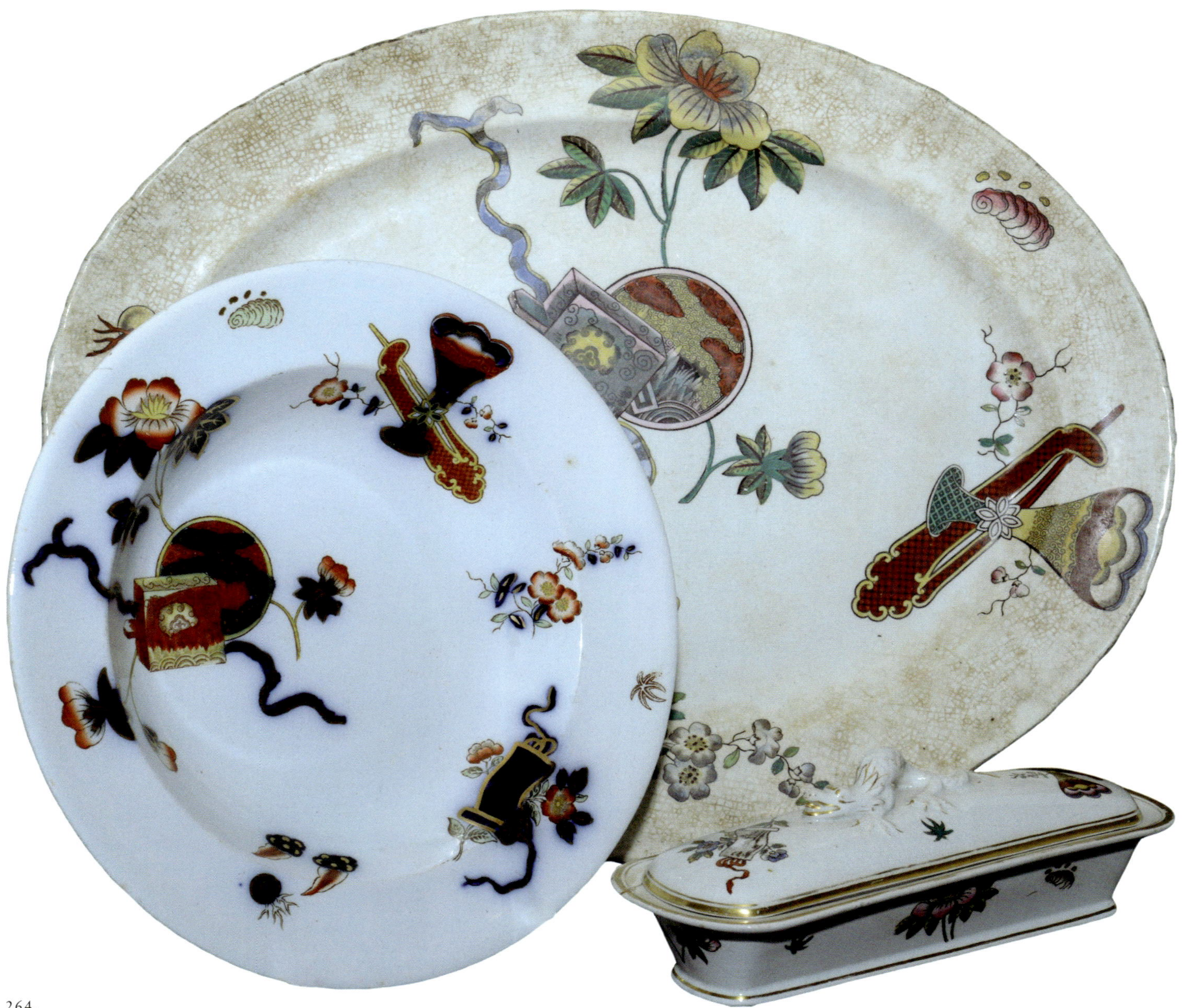

264.

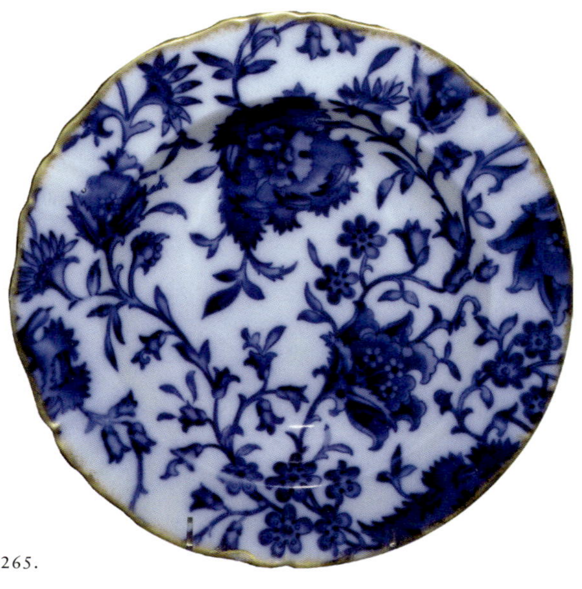

265.

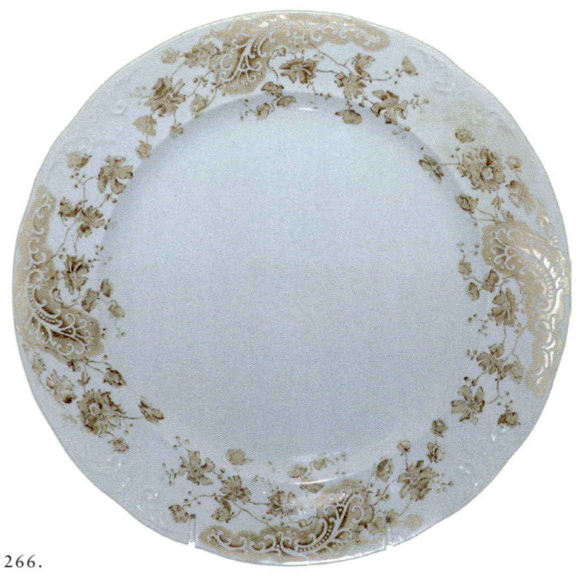

266.

· 265
"Cuba". William A. Adderley (Longton, Staffordshire, UK), 20th century.

· 266
"Havana". John Tams Crown Pottery (Seacombe, Liverpool, UK), 20th century.

· 267
"Havana Garden". Williams Sonoma, (US), 2018.

· 268
"Cuba". Wedgwood & Co., (UK), 20th century.

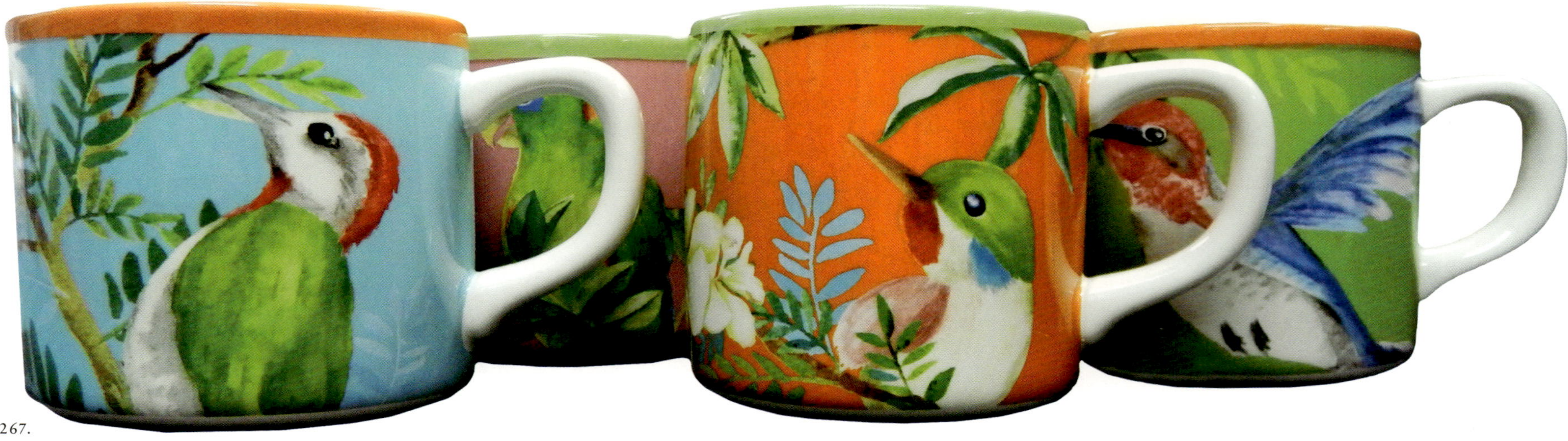

267.

Which brings me to a few final paragraphs by way of conclusion. For over 250 years Cuba-themed ceramics of all kinds have been used for many purposes and in many countries. A Dutch smoker would purchase the coveted snuff from a Havana-labeled jar in a Gouda tobacco shop. A London family would pick up the soap in the bathroom while admiring a Cuban peasant dance, the same image which would much later greet a visitor to a Dutch ceramics Exhibit at the main Amsterdam Museum. Galician soup would be served on a tureen depicting Havana's Customs House. Cuba's poultry seller would peek out of a dish in Utrecht or Liverpool. A French lady would admire a Cuban couple in a plate adorning her mantelpiece. A Portuguese scholar could examine one of Cuba's earliest maps in a Lisbon vase.

For his part, a baseball fan would have coffee in a demitasse announcing his favorite Cuban team, another one would drink it out of a cup with a Cuban flamingo disguised as an American bird, and yet a third would have his Miami *cafecito* on a mug depicting the coat of arms of a Jesuit school originally from the Old Havana and Marianao suburbs of Havana.

Many Cubans would pray before a ceramic statute of the Patron Saint of the island —or other heavenly intercessors— in a makeshift home altar. Cuban citizens could rejoice at seeing their flag, coat of arms and most popular patriots honored in commemorative plates. Americans would do likewise with respect to their military leaders during the Spanish American War.

Thousands and thousands of homes throughout the world would serve their meals in "Cuban" of "Havana" pattern dinnerware. How exotic and how exciting!

Cuba in ceramics all over the place. An island the size of Pennsylvania and half the population of Greater Mexico City. Who would have ever thought…

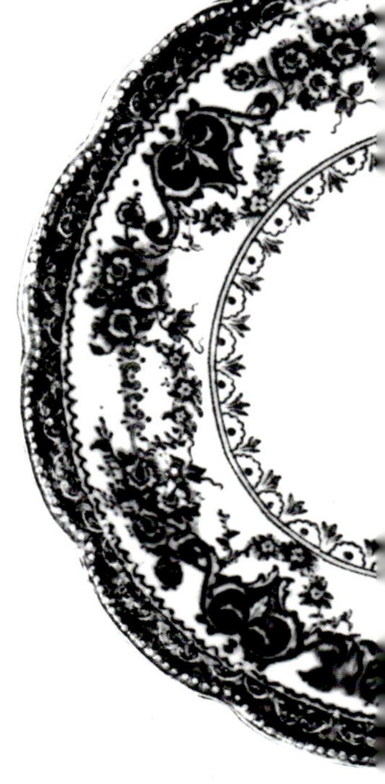

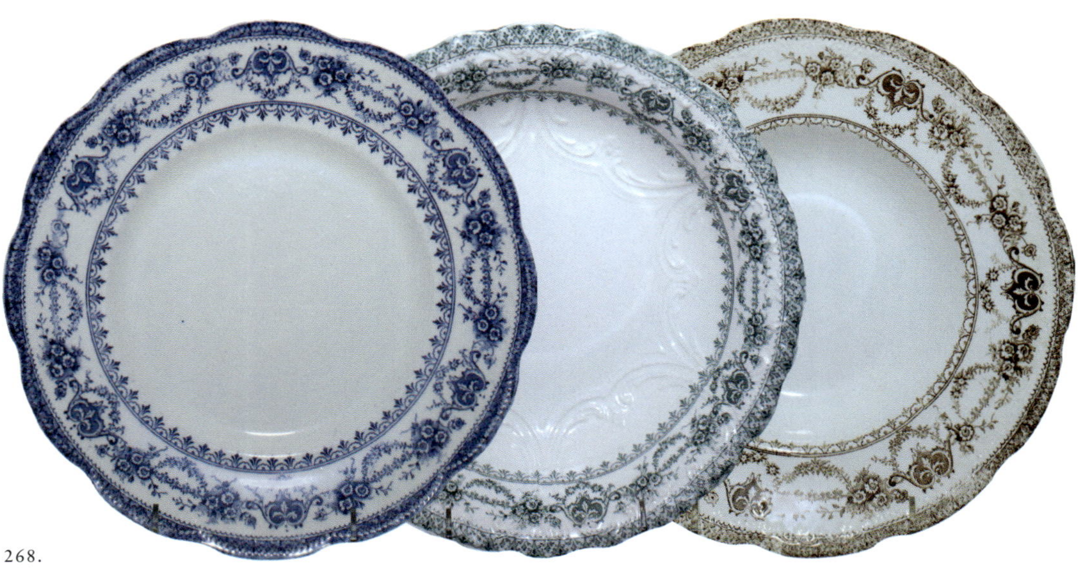

268.

Indexes

INDEXES

factories / distributors / trade names

pattern names and marks

artists

countries represented

BIBLIOGRAPHY

Alfonso López, Félix Julio. *Arqueología del béisbol cubano. Béisbol y nación en Cuba.* La Habana, Editorial Científico-Técnica, 2015, pp. 3-23.

Arrazcaceta Delgado, Roger. *La cerámica de aplicación arquitectónica de la época colonial en La Habana.* Gabinete de Arqueología (La Habana), 6, 2009, pp. 197-215.

_____. "Cerámica inglesa en la Habana colonial". *Opus Habana*, 3-4, 1999, pp. 45-49.

Atterbury, Paul. *English Pottery and Porcelain: an Historical Survey.* London, Peter Owen, 1980.

Beek, Pieter. *Céramique Maastricht.* Maastricht, Gemeente Maastricht; Heerlen Algemeen Burgerlijk Pensioenfonds (ABP), 1991.

Bello Piñeiro, Felipe. *Cerámica de Sargadelos.* La Coruña, Do Castro, 1979.

Berge, F Van Den, *et. al. Maastrichtse ceramiek uit de 19 de eeuw: Petrus Regout, Clermont & Chainaye, Guillaume Lambert & Cie, N.A.* Bosch, Maatschappij tot de vervaardiging van fijn aardewerk 'Société Céramique'. Lochem, De Tijdstroom, 1976.

Boagers, Marie-Rose. *Drukdecors op Maastrichts aardewerk 1850-1900: Petrus Regout, Société Céramique, Clermont & Chainaye, Guillaume Lambert, F. Regout.* Lochem, Antiek Lochem, 1992.

Boger, Louise ADE. *The dictionary of world pottery and porcelain.* New York, Scribner 1971.

Bradley, Eric. "Ceramic decorative art of the Aesthetic Movement". *Antique Trader* (US), January 19, 2012. Viewed in internet.

Bretos, Miguel. *Matanzas, The Cuba Nobody knows.* Gainsville, University of Florida Press, 2010.

Buelga, Marcos. *Vistas de ciudades en la cerámica española del siglo xix.* Oviedo, Museo de Bellas Artes de Asturias, 2005.

Camehl, Ada Walker. *The Blue-china Book.* New York, Tudor, 1948.

Cerámica inglesa en México. México, D.F., Museo Franz Mayer, The British Council, Artes de México, 1996.

Cluett, Robert. *George Jones ceramics.* Atglen, Pa., Schiffer Publishing, 1998.

Conde, Alfredo. *Azul cobalto: historia posible do marqués de Sargadelos.* Barcelona, Edhasa, 2001.

Cooper, Emmanuel. *Ten Thousand Years of Pottery.* Philadelphia, University of Pennsylvania Press, 2000.

Coysh, Arthur Wilfred. *Blue and White Transfer Ware, 1780-1840.* Newton Abbot, David & Charles, 1974.

_____. *Blue-printed Earthenware, 1800-1850.* Newton Abbot, David and Charles, 1972.

_____. *The Dictionary of Blue and White Pottery, 1780-1880.* 2 volumes, Woodbridge, Suffolk, Antique Collector's Club, 1989.

Cueto Emilio. *La Cuba pintoresca de Frédéric Mialhe.* La Habana, Biblioteca Nacional de Cuba José Martí, 2010.

_____. *Illustrating Cuba's flora and fauna.* Miami, The Historical Association of Southern Florida, 2002.

_____. "Las láminas del Paseo Pintoresco por la Isla de Cuba". *Revista de la Biblioteca Nacional de Cuba*, julio-diciembre 1990, pp. 127-40; *Paseo pintoresco por la Isla de Cuba*, Miami, Fla., Ediciones Universal, 1999, pp. XIII-XLII.

_____. *Mialhe's colonial Cuba.* Miami, The Historical Association of Southern Florida, 1994.

_____. *La Virgen de la Caridad del Cobre en el alma del pueblo cubano.* Ciudad de Guatemala, Guatemala, Ediciones Polymita, 2014.

Cushion, John P. *Pocket Book of British Ceramic Marks.* London, Faber and Faber, 1976.

Dacal Moure, Ramón. *Historiografía arqueológica de Cuba.* México, D.F., Centro Nacional de Conservación, Restauración y Museología, 2005.

Depestre Catony, Leonardo. "El Museo del Tabaco", *Correo de Cuba* (La Habana), 4º trimestre, 2002, pp. 50-51.

Diario de La Marina (La Habana), July 27, 1930.

"La Exposición de porcelana", in Carteles, December 6, 1942.

Exposición de vajillas cubanas coloniales. Habana, Museo de Artes Decorativas, 1965.
El Fígaro (La Habana), 24 de mayo de 1908.
Filgueira Valverde, José. *Sargadelos.* A Coruña, Ediciós do Castro, 1997.
Finegan, Mary J. *Johnson Brothers Dinnerware: Pattern Directory & Price Guide.* Boone, N.C., Marfine Antiques, 2003.
Furniss, David A., *et. al. Adams Ceramics: Staffordshire Potters and Pots, 1779-1998.* Atglen, Pa., Schiffer Pub., 1999.
Gaston, Mary Frank. *The Collector's Encyclopedia of Flow Blue China.* Paducah, Ky., Collector Books, 1983.
Godden, Geoffrey A. *The Handbook of British Pottery and Porcelain Marks.* London, Barrie and Jenkins, 1982.
_____. *The Illustrated Guide to Ridgway Porcelains.* London, Barrie & Jenkins, 1972.
_____. *An Introduction to English Blue & White Porcelains.* Worthing, Geoffrey Godden-Chinaman, 1974.
_____. *Ridgway Porcelains.* Woodbridge, Antique Collector's Club, 1985.
Gómez Vallejo, Teresita. *Acercamiento a la cerámica artística cubana.* La Habana. Editorial Científico-Técnica, 2010.
González Echevarría, Roberto. *The Pride of Havana: a History of Cuban Baseball.* New York, Oxford University Press, 2001; Spanish edition, *La gloria de Cuba: historia del béisbol en la isla.* Madrid, Editorial Colibrí, 2004.
González Carmenates, Yaxely. "Caracterización de la cerámica arquitectónica camagüeyana". *Antenas* (Camagüey), sep-dic, 2004, pp. 48-52.
Halliday, Rosemary. *Extraordinary British Transferware, 1780-1840.* Atglen, Pa., Schiffer Publishing Ltd, 2012.
Henrywood, Richard K. *Staffordshire Potters 1781-1900: a Comprehensive List Assembled from Contemporary Directories with Selected Marks.* Woodbridge, Antique Collector's Club, 2002.
La Historia hecha cerámica. La Cartuja de Sevilla: 1841. Sevilla, Pickman S.A., 1989.
Kowalsky, Arnold A., *et. al. Encyclopedia of Marks on American, English, and European Earthenware, Ironstone, Stoneware, 1780-1980.* Atglen, Pa., Schiffer, 1999.
Lapique, Zoila. *La memoria en las piedras.* Habana, Ediciones Boloña, 2002.
_____. *Música colonial cubana en las publicaciones periódicas: (1812-1902).* La Habana, Letras Cubanas, 1979.
Little, W. L. *Staffordshire Blue: Underglaze Blue Transfer-printed Earthenware.* London, Batsford, 1987.
Llorach Ramos, Esteban. *Ya está el café.* La Habana, Editorial Gente Nueva, 2011.
Mcnerney, Kathryn. *Blue and White Stoneware.* Paducah, Ky., Collector Books, 2000.
Mejide Pardo, Antonio. *Documentos para la historia de las Reales Fábricas de Sargadelos.* La Coruña, Do Castro, 1979.
Meulman, Hans. *Boerenbont uit Maastrichtse fabrieken: Petrus Regout, Société Céramique.* Lochem, Antiek Lochem, 2006.
Neale, Gillian. *Blue & White Pottery: a Collector's guide.* London, Millers, 2002.
Núñez Jiménez, Anotonio. *Cuba: cultura, estado y revolución.* México, D.F., Presencia Latinoamericana, 1984
_____. *Cuba: La Naturaleza y el Hombre.* Geopoética, La Habana, 1983.
Olives Orrit, Juan. *Introducción a la loza de Sargadelos: la joya de las antigüedades de Galicia.* La Coruña, J. Olives, 2009.
Page, Bob, *et. al. Johnson Brothers, Classic English Dinnerware.* Greensboro, N.C., Page/Frederiksen Publications, 2003.
Paseo pintoresco por la Isla de Cuba. Habana, Imprenta de Soler y Comp., 1841; Miami, Fla., Ediciones Universal, 1999.
Pérez Gullén, Inocencio V. *Las azulejerías de la Habana cerámica arquitectónica española en América.* Valencia. Universidad de Valencia 2004.
Quiroga Figueroa, María. *A louza de Sargadelos.* Lugo, Deputación Provincial de Lugo, Servicio de Publicaciones, D.L. 2003.
Regout, Joseph. *Sphinx-Céramique.* Maastricht, Sphinx-Céramique, 1959.
Retrospectiva de la cerámica cubana: exposición. Habana, Museo de Artes Decorativas, 1978.
Roberts, Gaye Blake. *True Blue: Transfer Printed Earthenware.* East Hagbourne, Friends of Blue, 1998.
Rodríguez Cullel, Caridad. *Catálogo gráfico de los diseños decorativos en la cerámica taína de Cuba,* in Modesto Amado Martínez Castillo (ed.), Cuba Arqueológica. Santiago de Cuba, Editorial Oriente, 1978.
Rouse, Irving. *Archeology of the Maniabón Hills,*

Cuba. New Haven, Yale University Press, 1942.

Sánchez Cantón, F. J. *La loza de Sargadelos: apuntes histórico-artísticos.* Madrid, Publicaciones de la Escuela de Artes y Oficios Artísticos de Madrid, 1945.

Sánchez de Fuentes y Peláez, Eugenio. *Cuba monumental, estatuaria y epigráfica.* La Habana, Academia Nacional de Artes y Letras de La Habana, 1917.

Sarabia, Nydia. "Vajillas coloniales cubanas". *Romances* (La Habana), octubre de 1965, pp. 22-25.

Snyder, Jeffrey B. *Flow Blue: a Collector's Guide to Patterns, History, and Values.* Atglen, Pa., Schiffer Pub., 2004.

_____. *Romantic Staffordshire Ceramics.* Atglen, Pa., Schiffer Pub., 1997.

Soto Sagarra, Luis De. "El tesoro artístico nacional. La colección Osuna-Varela Zequeira", in *Carteles,* August 31, 1947.

Suárez Menéndez, Roberto. *Las reales fábricas de Sargadelos y Trubia: competencia, rivalidad y apoyo.* A Coruña, Ediciós do Castro, 2001.

Tabío Enresto E., *et. al. Prehistoria de Cuba.* La Habana, Academia de Ciencias de Cuba, 1966.

Trujillo, Carmen. "Vajillas coloniales", in *Opus Habana* (La Habana), No. 4, 1998, pp. 58-61.

Turner, W. "Swansea fayence", in *Ethel Deane* (ed.), The Collector. London, Horace Cox, 1907, pp. 117-125.

Valcárcel Rojas, Robert. *Archaeology of Early Colonial Interaction at El Chorro de Maíta, Cuba.* Gainesville, University Press of Florida, 2016.

Vercauteren, J. B. M. *Céramique Maastricht.* Rotterdam, Uitgeverij 010, 1996.

Vilar Checa, Eloisa. *El Marqués de Sargadelos y su obra.* La Coruña, Ediciones del Castro, 1970.

Williams, Petra, *et. al. Staffordshire.* Jeffersontown, Ky., Fountain House East, 1978.

_____. *Staffordshire II, Romantic Transfer Patterns.* Jeffersontown, Ky., Fountain House East, 1986, p. 231

_____. *Staffordshire III, Romantic Transfer Patterns.* Jeffersontown, Ky.,Fountain House East, 1988.

Williams-Wood, Cyril. *English Transfer-printed Pottery and Porcelain: a History of Over-glaze Printing.* London, Boston, Faber and Faber, 1981.

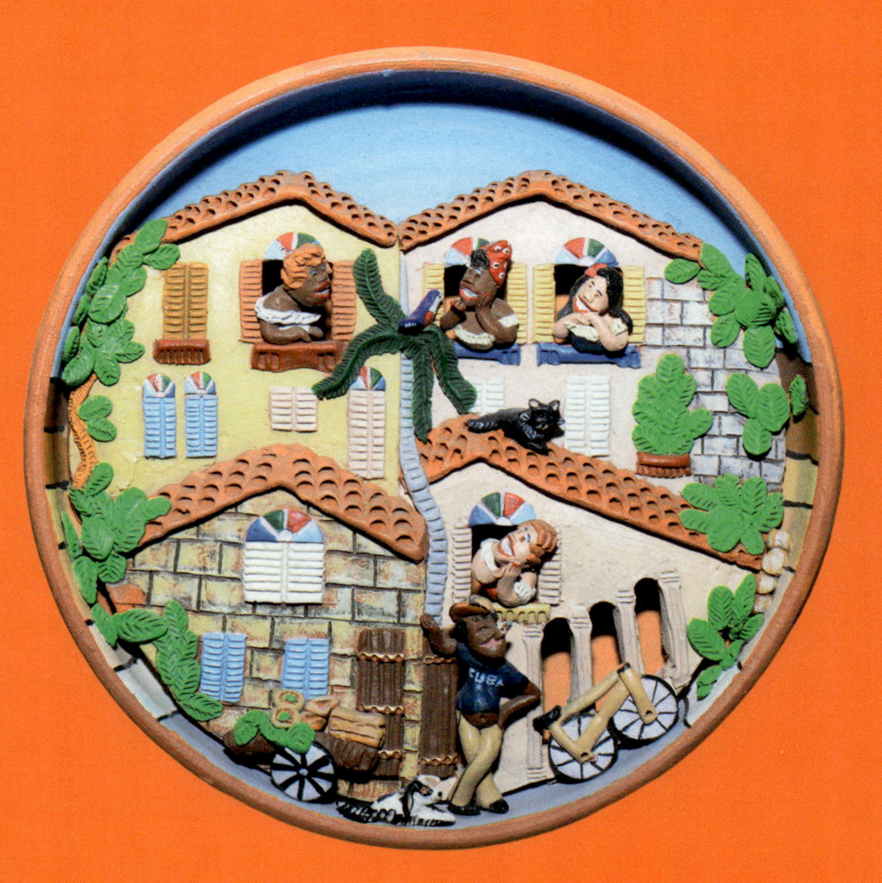
CUBA